CROWDED HOUSE

private universe

Kerry Doole and Chris Twomey

OMNIBUS PRESS
LONDON · NEW YORK · SYDNEY

Edited by Chris Charlesworth
Book designed by Lisa Pettibone
Picture research by Nikki Russell & Kerry Doole

ISBN: 0.7119. 6653.2
Order No: OP 48023

Exclusive Distributors:
Book Sales Limited,
8/9 Frith Street,
London W1V 5TZ, UK.

Music Sales Corporation,
257 Park Avenue South,
New York, NY 10010, USA.

Music Sales Pty Limited,
120 Rothschild Avenue, Rosebery,
NSW 2018, Australia.

To the Music Trade only:
Music Sales Limited,
8/9 Frith Street,
London W1V 5TZ, UK.

Photo credits:

Piers Allardyce/SIN: 74,75; Tammie Arroyo/Retna: 40,49; Colin Bell/Retna: 102; Kent Blechynden/Performing Pictures:126,136/7, 138,139,146; Garry Brandon/Performing Pictures: back cover,61, 63,73,76b, 91t&br,95, 98tl&b,99bl&r,107,111,134; Larry Busacca /Retna: 66; Chris Carroll/Retna: 58; Lorna Cort Archives: 22,23,30, 105b; Kerry Doole: 3,4,5,84,85; Patrick Ford/Redferns:128,131; Steve Gillett: 44,46,47,77,114; Martyn Goodacre/SIN:108,113,117, 118; Steve Granitz/Retna: 45; Martin Hoffman/Retna:96; Jana/SIN: 93; Ray Johnson/Retna:129; Glenn Jowitt/Performing Pictures: 121b; Graham Kennedy/SIN: 76t; London Features International: back cover,31,39,41,52,54,60,88 101,104,127; Ross Marino/Retna: 34; Wayne Martin/Performing Pictures:119t,121t; Anna Meuer/ SIN: 80; Tim Mosenfelder/Retna: 94; Philip Morris/SIN: 6,10,15; Katia Natola/SIN: 92; Greg Noakes/Retna: 57; Brian Rasic/Rex Features: 79; Rex Features: 37; Honey Salvadori/Retna: 51; Roger Sargent/Rex Features:22,124; Kevin Statham/SIN:65,69;Jim Steele: 105t; Barbara Steinwehe/Redferns:119b,120,132; Lorinda Sullivan /Retna: 68,71; Chris Traill: 25,28,90,91bl,98tr,99t,100.

contents

introduction

THE SOUND OF CROWDED HOUSE is the sound of Neil Finn's cascading, dream like melodies, an aching verse topped with a mellifluous chorus that shimmers and dissolves in the air like a blazing, multi-coloured firework. To their many fans the sound is inimitable, sacred like the sound of Te Awamutu, the perfect synthesis of guitars and voices, and where it came from is the subject of this book.

Its genesis was a small rural town in New Zealand and it's been heard as far afield as Auckland, London, Paris, New York, Toronto, Los Angeles, Sydney and all points in-between. It almost took Crowded House to the top of the American charts, but in the end they stalled at number two and for reasons explained herein never came close again. It attracted a truly massive crowd to a Fleadh in London's Finsbury Park where one reviewer was sufficiently moved to opine that it was the most beautiful noise in the world. Bruce Springsteen certainly agreed: he rang up their record company and castigated the head honcho for not selling enough of it.

It has helped to give pop a good name again, insofar as the sound of Crowded House has been recognised for its quality not just by their fans but by peers both young and old. It is difficult to find a musician of stature who does not appreciate Neil Finn's songwriting, his chord structures, his hook lines and the vocal harmonies he layers on top. This probably explains why the sound of Crowded House won both critics' and readers' polls in magazines across the globe. Many of their rivals have sold more records, but few enjoy the same respect. Researching this book, it became clear to us that those fortunate enough to have discovered Crowded House and taken them to heart tend to care about them much more deeply than fans of other artists.

If the sound was all they had to offer, then maybe the oft quoted tagline that this is what The Beatles might have sounded like if they'd stayed together would be accurate. Fortunately there was more to it: the Crowded House live experience. In concert they exuded a crowd pleasing charm that won over the most sceptical of critics. They mastered the tricky feat of bringing intimacy and spontaneity to concerts in arenas and larger halls. They were 'unplugged' before the term was invented and their 'no two shows the same' guarantee helped keep fans coming back for more time and time again.

All of which would seem to imply that the story of Crowded House is a fairy tale wherein a supremely gifted musician formed a band and achieved the pinnacle of his dreams simply by exercising his innate talent. Not so. The contrast between the surface and reality is often echoed within Neil Finn's songs: behind the irresistible hooklines are sophisticated and often darkly disturbing lyrics. Madness, death, infidelity and the perils of fame are all themes that Neil tackled head-on, with courage and grace.

And the image of carefree camaraderie that Crowded House projected live and in their videos was calculated to mask the often turbulent dynamics within the group. They never functioned as a democracy. Neil was always the boss, as bassist Nick Seymour — fired at one point, then reinstated — and drummer Paul Hester — always knew. Then there's the sibling rivalry between Neil and his elder brother Tim, whose band Split Enz launched Neil's career in the first place, and whose presence often hovered over Crowded House like a wise but occasionally eccentric old uncle. Tim's entry into the band for the 'Woodface' era was short lived but creatively fruitful. These matters form the private universe that this book attempts to explore.

With global success, peer respect and critical acclaim in his pocket, Neil Finn seemed, from his Down Under home, to be a man on top of the world. But a continuing creative restlessness kept gnawing at his Catholic soul, and in 1996 he shocked both the pop world and his bandmates by closing the shutters on Crowded House.

His decision broke the hearts of the band's fans, but they proved forgiving enough to keep Crowded House's 'Recurring Dream' collection on international charts for what seemed an eternity.

And the group excited with a bang, not a whimper. Their final concert was also their biggest, and the famed landmarks of Sydney Opera House and Harbour Bridge provided a fittingly impressive backdrop to the swansong of one of pop's greatest treasures.

Throughout their rollercoaster career, the triumphs and the failures, the smooth sailing and the leaky boats, the sound held true to Neil Finn's original vision—melodic pop that appeals in equal measure to the heart, the soul and the brain.

It is a sound that will never go away.

Kerry Doole and Chris Twomey, August 1995

ACKNOWLEDGEMENTS

Kerry Doole would like to thank everybody who provided information and agreed to interviews for this book. Extra thanks go out to Mike Chunn, Johnny Waller, Nandita Ray, Peter Vitols, Lisa Elliott, Mitchell Froom, Gary Stamler, Hale Milgrim, Denise Donlon at MuchMusic for generous access to her files, EMI Music Canada, Mary, Mary-Lou and Dave at *Impact*, Murray Cammick and, above all, The Doole Family for support and a great clippings service.

For reasons of their own, Crowded House and manager Grant Thomas declined to assist with this project. The author appreciates their earlier cordial professional relationship.

Chris Twomey would like to thank Tony Wadsworth, Malcolm Hill, David Field, Carrie Spacey-Foote, Mitch Clarke, Lorna Cort and Brian Jardine.

Some of the material quoted from The Sidney Morning Herald and The Sun Herald comes from articles written by Peter Holmes and is reproduced with his kind permission.

1

te awamutu

"And the sound of Te Awamutu had a truly sacred ring" NEIL FINN, 1986

That may have been so to the young American girl obsessed with Split Enz, the one with 'a blind date with destiny' who trekked all the way to New Zealand to be closer to her musical heroes and whose encounter with Neil Finn inspired the song 'Mean To Me' which appeared on Crowded House's début album. To Neil Finn and older brother Tim, however, Te Awamutu wasn't just some exotically named town on the other side of the world. To them, it was simply home; a place in which to grow up, and a place they were inevitably destined to leave behind.

Although the brothers Finn retain fond memories of this quiet rural town, there can be few more unlikely spawning grounds for internationally famous rock stars. Back in the Fifties, the decade in which Tim and Neil were born, it was the kind of community that gave New Zealand its economic backbone, but it was also an innately conservative cultural backwater that discouraged anything as potentially unwholesome or morally unsound as artistic endeavour, especially in the realm of pop music. Ambition, self-confidence and creative energy were all too often seen as character flaws in such an environment, and those exhibiting such tendencies were likely to attract flak for being 'up themselves' or 'arty wankers'. Escape to the city and, commonly, abroad was mandatory, and such was the case for the Finn boys when they came of age.

Towns like Te Awamutu functioned primarily as service centres for the agriculture-related indus-tries that gave New Zealand one of the highest standards of living in the world during the Sixties and Seventies. In that golden age, Britain was the country's primary export market, eagerly accept-ing New Zealand lamb, butter, cheese and other fruits of this fertile land. Britain's entry into the European Economic Community in the Seventies would gradually diminish this reliance on New Zealand's produce, but when the Finn lads were growing up, New Zealanders genuinely believed, with good cause, that they were living in God's Own Country.

A welfare state the envy of other nations was firmly in place, and unemployment was practically non-existent. Ties to Britain weren't just economic, for the majority of the then two million population was of British stock. New Zealanders were strong believers in the monarchy, and would happily rise from their seats to sing the national anthem before any movie screening or sporting event.

Until recently, a continual refrain of visitors to New Zealand was that it reminded them of Britain a couple of decades earlier. Since the Eighties, however, a new sense of national identity has emerged — one based on the realisation that economic reality and geographic location dictate that New Zealanders link themselves to the Asian and Pacific region, and not to a decaying Empiric power in another hemisphere on the opposite side of the globe. Thirty years ago, the suggestion that New Zealand should become a republic, free of all ties to the British crown, would have been looked on as treason. Now, it seems set to become policy.

New Zealand's political and social policies

were, by the standards of the day, often quite progressive – this was the first Western country to give women the vote – but pressures to conform to certain social or moral norms were strong.

Artists of any type were treated with suspicion, rather than acclaim, a situation that forced them to emigrate to more receptive environs. Jane Campion's acclaimed 1990 cinematic portrait of writer Janet Frame, *An Angel At My Table*, is an incisive indictment of the social climate prevailing in Fifties era New Zealand. Her inability to conform saw the young Frame institutionalised, and it took a trip to Europe to give her the self-confidence to follow her muse. In one telling scene, Janet's father comes to collect her from the house of writer Frank Sargeson, who cheerily bids her farewell while brandishing a bottle of wine. Horrified at this eccentric artist type, dad drives off in great haste.

New Zealand's small population and geographic isolation meant that technological advances were slow to take root. When television did arrive, it was confined to one state-owned channel broadcasting for just a few hours each evening. Radio had a strong reach, however, and the NZBC (New Zealand Broadcasting Corporation) managed to produce some stimulating programmes as well as the inevitable (and important) farming shows and weather reports. There was no local film industry in this era (that didn't develop until the mid Seventies), but the country did, against the odds, spawn talented writers, poets, artists and musicians.

Physically beautiful, economically prosperous, socially repressed, culturally isolated, this was the New Zealand in which Tim and Neil Finn were raised, and Te Awamutu was the epitome of all this.

With a present day population of 8,000, Te Awamutu is situated in the Waikato region of the North Island, some 100 miles south of Auckland. Lying 70 miles north of the famed Rotorua area, home of geysers, boiling mud pools and other manifestations of a highly active geology, its name is Maori and translates as 'end of the navigable river'. Here, however, the earth is stable and fertile. Dairy cattle, sheep farming and horticulture have been the staples of the district's

economy, and they've been joined in more recent years by such activities as angora goat raising, deer farming, carnation growing, and scientific calf rearing for export to developing countries. Thoroughbred race horses are also raised and trained in the region.

Every New Zealand town seems to sport a title of some kind. Te Awamutu has been designated Rose Town, for it boasts picturesque Rose Gardens – some 2000 bushes representing 80 varieties of thorned beauties. Around 50,000 rose devotees from all over the world visit the gardens annually.

The Te Awamutu region was at the heart of the so-called 'land wars' between the native Maori and British settlers in the 1860s. During this turbulent era, the site of the current Rose Gardens was occupied by one General Cameron and 1,000 colonial troops out to quell the militant Maori. A century later, New Zealand prided itself on its race relations, but the gap between the two remained wide. "The sadness in some NZ towns is a lingering, festering kind of sadness, a residue of the Maori Wars, the thing that never healed properly," Tim Finn has been quoted as saying, but it's unlikely his compatriots would agree with such a dramatic interpretation.

Finn told American music magazine *BAM* in 1987 that he never realised when he was young that New Zealand was far from being an integrated society. "But just the fact there are a lot of Maoris around means their culture is in your face, as opposed to Australia, where whites can conveniently forget that Aborigines exist because you just don't see them. I didn't think about racial unrest or prejudice until I was older. I grew up with Maori friends, but it was still separate cultures."

———

DIRECTLY ACROSS the street from the Te Awamutu Rose Gardens are the offices of Finn & Co, Chartered Accountants, at 250 Arawata Street. Dick Finn, father of Tim and Neil and sisters Judy and Carolyn, grew up on a family farm in nearby Te Rore, but moved to Te Awamutu to work in accounting and eventually start his own business.

• Finn & Partners, Te Awamutu

Mary Finn, his wife, was born in Ireland as Mary Mullane, daughter of farmhand Tim Mullane. Her family emigrated to New Zealand when Mary was just two. Their strong Catholic roots meant her courtship with Protestant Dick Finn caused some concern in the family's ranks, and they insisted that Dick take three months of intensive Catholic instruction

• Finn family home, Teasdale Street

prior to the marriage. There was mutual suspicion between Protestants, the predominant religious faith in New Zealand, and Catholics but there has never been any serious social unrest as a result.

Half a mile to the south of the Finn & Co. office, on the other side of the town's main drag, Alexandra Street, sit two buildings of major significance to the brothers Finn. The first is Dick and Mary Finn's original family home at 78 Teasdale Street, though a change in the town's method of numbering streets later saw it elevated to 588 Teasdale. Observant Crowded House fans will already know that, as 78 Teasdale Street, it is immortalised in the video for 'Don't Dream It's Over'. Set slightly back from the street, it is a pleasant wooden single-story bungalow which once boasted a swimming pool, a luxurious accessory for the town in the Sixties. The building is now an old folks home, the Te Ata Rest Home.

Just a few short blocks away, at 140 Wallace Terrace, is a second address of major significance to the Finn family. Wharenoho is now also a rest home for some of the town's more elderly residents, but in the Fifties it functioned as a maternity hospital where the younger generation of Finns – in birth order, Carolyn, Brian (as Tim was then known), Judy, and, finally, Neil – were all born.

Brian Timothy Finn showed up here on June 25, 1952. Nearly six years later, on May 27, 1958, Neil Mullane Finn joined the party.

Another few blocks away, back from Alexandra Street, is St Patrick's School. Established and run by the Sisters Of St. Joseph since 1921, this is the Catholic primary school to which Dick and Mary Finn sent all their children. Its large grassy playgrounds and asphalt basketball court testify to the continued importance of sport in the New Zealand school curriculum. As would have been the case in the late Fifties and early Sixties,

• Wharenoho Rest Home, Te Awamutu, where Tim and Neil Finn were born.

the school population comprises both white and Maori children.

Norma Stewart, the longest-serving member on staff, is a sweet-natured middle-aged teacher who was instructing young charges back in 1963, and she clearly recalls Neil Finn at age five. "He

3

was a very nice young boy," she reminisces, using a phrase that's virtually a mantra amongst all Te Awamutu residents with a memory of the lad. "He was a serious young fellow, but he would also get into mischief. I remember one day he was drawing and he went through the paper and marked the table. They were new tables, and he was very upset!"

Norma saw no signs of creative genius at this early age. "At that age, every child loves to sing and dance, and Neil was no different. He worked very hard, and he was quite bright. When I hear his name now, it does give me a little thrill. He's definitely the most famous pupil of mine."

The highlight of the early childhoods of both Finn boys seems to have been the parties their parents threw. Anecdotes abound on the fun they had. Toronto journalist Katherine Nimetz recalls one interview with Tim Finn. "He started telling me stories about growing up in New Zealand. The most delightful one was about how the priests used to come around to their house They had a piano in their parlour, and they'd all be making music. Their aunts would come over, and the priests would come and flirt with their mum and the aunts. The young kids would crawl around the furniture, thinking this was all so risqué!"

The Finn parties were well-known in the town as fun gatherings. Dick Finn was a keen jazz fan, with a passion for the big band sound, so music was a key party component. Mike Chunn described these gatherings in *Stranger Than Fiction: The Life And Times Of Split Enz*, his definitive biography of that band. "In contrast to other more sedate soirees around Te Awamutu, parties at Teasdale Street would jump to a hefty dose of Dick's jazz music... As the beer and spirits flowed, the voices would grow louder; [family friend] Colin O'Brien would sit himself at the piano, place his gin on the lid and roll his cigarette to the corner of his mouth. His fists would pump out rollicking swing numbers and his hearty voice would sing joy into everyone's

ears. Young Brian (Tim) would look around the room at the smiles, kneecaps and legs, and would be pulled up to dance with one guest or another." Mike Chunn was one of Tim's closest friends during their teenage years and would became the first bass player in Split Enz.

In such a home environment, Tim Finn, and then younger brother Neil, soon linked music with fun, so it's no surprise they were eager young players and performers. By age 10, Tim was taking piano lessons from local music teacher Sister Mary Raymond. "She taught me a couple of jazz chords, and really encouraged my love for music. You never forget people like that." Tim soon graduated to playing the organ at church and family favourites of the day on the piano. The five year old Neil was clearly impressed with big brother's prowess, and, encouraged by his family, soon trod the boards himself. At that age, Neil won his school's talent quest with his version of schmaltzy pop hit 'You Are My Sunshine'. This professional début earned him one dollar!

Neil credits one relative in particular for his confidence on stage. "My eccentric Uncle George used to trot me out at four years old," he told British music magazine *Mojo*. "All the grown ups thought it was great fun, so he helped me conquer stage fright. I still squirmed with fear and trepidation, but most people never get beyond that fear of performance."

Tim and Neil also performed regularly when the Finn family took their annual summer holidays at Mount Maunganui, a nearby beach resort. New Zealand family vacations are not always the most relaxing for parents who often have to contend with quarrelling siblings, but a mutual love of music helped the Finn boys co-exist more harmoniously than most. These occasions often saw Tim and Neil joining in with twin priests and family friends Father(s) Durning, both fine singers who enjoyed younger accompaniment.

• St Patrick's School, Te Awamutu

The firm bond between Tim and Neil Finn was demonstrated in another childhood incident to which both brothers referred in later years. Some of the Te Awamutu toughs were apparently bullying Tim when baby brother ran them off, brandishing a tennis racquet! Tim recalled that event on the live version of 'Take A Walk' on Split Enz album 'The Living Enz'. "I remember it as though it was yesterday, you supporting me when I was getting beaten up by the local boys. That was a good day, Neil!"

As the saying goes, 'the family that plays together stays together'. The Finns continued their family singalongs whenever they gathered together in the decades ahead. When the brothers rehearsed their 'Woodface' songs in Melbourne in 1991, they broke for a fun session featuring mother Mary on piano and dad Dick on lead vocals.

Back in the mid-Sixties, sisters Judy and Carolyn Finn were tolerant of their brothers music-making and were themselves giving in to the appeal of Sixties rock'n'roll. In 1965 Tim went along with his eldest sister Carolyn to a concert by The Dave Clark Five at Hamilton, the nearest city to Te Awamutu. Young girls were screaming hysterically, something a young boy couldn't fail to notice, and this eternal reason for boys to start rock'n'roll bands began to take root.

The Dave Clark Five were prominent, albeit pedestrian, representatives of the British Pop Invasion. In June 1964, The Beatles visited New Zealand for the first and only time, causing unprecedented hysteria everywhere they went and especially at their concerts in Wellington, Auckland, Dunedin and Christchurch. The Rolling Stones toured New Zealand twice, in February of 1965 and March 1966, with similar results. Both groups – and the behaviour of their audiences – scandalised the straight-laced locals, effectively demonstrating the truth of Bob Dylan's 'Times They Are A-Changing' lyric 'Your sons and your daughters are beyond your command'. They also stimulated likely lads with musical aspirations.

After this initial onslaught, New Zealand was all too often visited primarily by washed-up acts, most of them British. The logic behind these tours seemed to rely on the spurious assumption that news of their decline had yet to reach this farthest-flung colony, and it was not too difficult to maintain an illusion of stardom as far as New Zealand's less imaginative concert goers were concerned.

Another landmark in Tim's musical education came in 1965 when Dick Finn suggested piano lessons with local jazz player Chuck Fowler. According to Mike Chunn, "The experience completely liberated the 13-year-old, as he learned chords and picked out melodies by ear. 'Lara's Theme' from the film *Dr Zhivago* was one; when Neil heard it for the first time he resolved it'd be the first thing he learned on the piano when he was big enough to reach the keys."

Shortly after these musical revelations, Tim Finn's life underwent a major change. On January 30, 1966, Dick and Mary Finn drove their eldest son up to Auckland, where he was enrolled in Sacred Heart College, a Catholic boys school favoured by the Finns because it offered the kind of religion-rooted education they wanted for their sons. Tim had thrilled them in November 1965 by becoming one of only two out of 100 applicants to win a boarding scholarship to Sacred Heart.

Seven-year-old Neil Finn watched his brother's departure from Te Awamutu with curiosity, knowing that one day he'd follow in Tim's footsteps to Sacred Heart. They were to prove large ones to fill.

• **Sacred Heart College, Auckland**

2

the sacred years

The move from sleepy Te Awamutu to New Zealand's largest city must have been a daunting experience for 13-year-old Tim Finn. The Brothers he'd encounter at Sacred Heart were more concerned with instilling discipline than fostering personal and creative freedom, but despite this his days there would propel Tim Finn further along musical paths, and offer him his first experience of performing pop songs before a captive audience.

His status as a boarder meant Sacred Heart became home, not just a daytime address for Tim. "It is a school of two halves, the day boys and the boarders," says Simon Lynch, now a successful musician and producer of home-grown soul bands Ardijah and D-Faction who was a peer of Neil Finn there a few years later. "The day boys were considered more fortunate, with a life on the outside, while the boarders were confined within the walls of what could seem like a prison to a 12 or 13 year old."

Mike Chunn verifies the prison analogy in *Stranger Than Fiction*: "Permission to leave the grounds was restricted to the odd 'free' Sunday; the sense of confinement was very real with the school gate a symbol of freedom that boys would glance at longingly, imagining they were out there somewhere eating proper food and wearing civilian clothes."

Not that regular secular secondary schools of the day were much more liberated. Uniforms and corporal punishment were mandatory, single-sex schools the norm, and petty cruelties inflicted in the name of discipline were all too common.

If Sacred Heart was tantamount to a prison, at least it was a picturesque one. Situated on West Tamaki Drive in the eastern Auckland suburb of Glen Innes, it faces north, and beyond its sprawling green playing fields can be glimpsed the Rangitoto Channel, just east of the entrance to Auckland's renowned Waitemata Harbour. The school's well-tended gardens and pretty Norfolk pines add an extra touch of tranquillity to this area of religious contemplation.

Virtually from day one, Tim Finn excelled on all levels, especially rugby football, the national religion of New Zealand. Rugby was practised almost universally by adolescents with hormones and energy to burn, and Tim was to prove more adept than most. In 1969, he captained the college's 2A rugby team of sixth form 17-year-olds, leading it to a local championship. "A sound, not brilliant half-back... always an inspiration to the team," it says of Tim in the school magazine. In their final year, 1970, both Tim and best friend Mike Chunn reached the pinnacle of sporting success at Sacred Heart, the rugby 1st XV. Tim also shone at cricket and athletics.

Tim and Mike also excelled academically at Sacred Heart. In their School Certificate exams – equivalent to British GCSEs – at the end of 1968, Mike edged Tim 342 marks to 335, out of a possible 400, both fine scores.

On the cultural side, Tim was involved in the school's drama activities, experience he'd later put to good use on stage. In his final year at Sacred Heart College, he took the lead in the school production of Gilbert and Sullivan's *Trial By Jury* and a key role in Shakespeare's *King Lear*.

Tim Finn and Mike Chunn's real love, however, was music, and as in all their other endeavours they left a distinct impression in this field. As precocious 15-year-old fourth-formers, they requested permission to give a class concert in the assembly hall, and with the aid of friends on bongos and guitar, they performed five pop hits of the day – Procol Harum's 'Homburg', The Beatles' 'Ticket To Ride' and 'With A Little Help From My Friends', The Bee Gees' ballad 'To Love Somebody' and Simon and Garfunkel's 'Homeward Bound'. Mike Chunn cites this event as a landmark occasion in Tim's young life.

"On the 28 September 1967 Tim and I walked onto a stage together for the first time... Tim hid behind my piano in fright but did his duty at the microphone and stunned the class. He sang like a bird and froze the lot of them. We were ecstatic and the response was good. Tim had felt his voice fill the assembly hall and it was a peak moment." Buoyed by the triumph, the group then recorded seven songs on the school's tape recorder.

In 1968, Tim, Mike and friends took a shot at winning the annual Walter Kirby Music Prize, one of the school's most-coveted trophies. Their version of Paul McCartney's Beatle ballad 'Yesterday' with a band that included Mike's younger brother Geoff Chunn on drums didn't quite do the trick, but the following year, switching to the Bee Gees' 'Words', they emerged triumphant. This passionate weepy gave Tim Finn an opportunity to fully flex his vocal muscle.

The following year, a combo featuring Mike, Tim and Geoff Chunn (now on guitar) actually spent an hour at a professional recording studio in Auckland, putting down three songs – a cover of The Beatles' 'Got To Get You Into My Life' and two originals, 'Take It Green' and 'Near Hosts'.

One Sacred Heart teacher, Brother Ivan Genneway, held major sway over music-obsessed pupils like Tim Finn and Mike Chunn. As Mike explains, "Brother Ivan was enigmatic and influential; had we been aware of the term at the time, he would have been 'cool'. He was a beatnik in disguise and we would hear him at nights, off in the distance, playing Dave Brubeck on the assembly hall piano. He played guitar, too, and would bring Bob Dylan records to music class."

Brother Ivan's *piece de resistance*, however, was to have the entire school sing John Lennon's psychedelic Beatle masterpiece 'Strawberry Fields Forever' at one school assembly. "He was holding a torch for us all and a few of us took the opportunity to follow the beam," said Chunn.

That spotlight often fell on the Fab Four. Mike Chunn vividly recalls the impact each new Beatles album had on the impressionable teenage boys at Sacred Heart. "The arrival of *Abbey Road* into the school grounds in 1969 found virtually every resident in Leonard House (a dorm for older students) seated around the common-room record player. There would have been 30 of us waiting in anticipation that Friday afternoon. The needle was put on at the start of side one; it was taken off at the end of side two – and not one boy spoke for the entire duration of that record."

In 1970, Tim Finn and Mike Chunn combined to win the Walter Kirby Prize again, this time teaming for a flute, guitar and vocals rendition of 'So Long Frank Lloyd Wright', a song from Simon and Garfunkel's million selling 'Bridge Over Troubled Water' album. The audience that evening included a proud Dick, Mary and Neil Finn.

Tim bade farewell to Sacred Heart in December 1970 in a blaze of scholastic glory, winning the Brother Stephen Prize for English Literature, the Old Boy's Essay Prize and the English Prize. Clearly he was destined to excel in whichever field he chose to pursue. Tim's recollections of Sacred Heart life are rosy. "I revelled in it. I was able to succeed there and formed great friendships," he said in 1983. "The brothers for us were symbols to rebel against; we completely persecuted a couple. They were romantic, idealistic days."

Neil Finn, when the time came, would be unlikely to utter any such rose-tinted sentiments about his alma mater.

◆

BACK IN 1967, while Tim was excelling at Sacred Heart, he'd sent his younger brother a copy of the tape that he, Mike Chunn and friends had recorded. Neil was highly impressed. Even at the tender age of nine, the performance bug had nipped Neil and in the school holidays he'd join big brother at social gatherings whenever possible. Chunn recalls Neil was taking piano lessons then. "He also had an acoustic guitar that Tim had brought home from school. He found the guitar easier to master, picking out chords to accompany himself. The first song he shaped up was The Monkees' 'Daydream Believer'."

Like his brother, The Beatles and other popular acts of the day were occupying a major part of Neil Finn's world view. He had begun to buy records, the first of which was Donovan's 'Hurdy Gurdy Man'. The psychedelic folk of the British troubadour made quite an impression on the lad, and he even composed some music to the poem – basically hippie mush – on the record's cover.

In the summer of 1970, Neil was confident enough to enter a talent quest at the beach resort of Mount Maunganui, the Finn family's preferred summer holiday destination. In this, the Woodstock era, Neil offered a rendition of Arlo Guthrie's drug-running anthem, 'Comin' Into Los Angeles'. He didn't win! Two years later, Neil exacted revenge for this setback at the Mount Maunganui Talent Quest via a safer song choice for the contest – Carole King's schmaltzy 'You've Got A Friend'. It marked Neil's first large showbiz pay-day, $100. An extravagant sum for that era.

In February 1971, it was Neil's turn to trek to Sacred Heart College. Tim's distinction in all fields made him a hard act for Neil to follow, and once there Neil wasted no time in establishing a Finn family dynasty for the Walter Kirby Music Prize, scooping it up at the end of his first year.

"Neil, then aged 13, played in the group category with my older cousins, The McHardys," recalls Sacred Heart peer Simon Lynch. The age gap of three years between Neil and new guitar-playing friend Bernard McHardy would normally have been a chasm, but the younger Finn's precocious talent made any such barriers redundant. "They won the award with a stirring rendition of [James Taylor's] 'Carolina In My Mind', complete with a cappella intro," says Lynch. "They brought the house down. Even then, Neil was showing signs of greatness."

His musical aspirations were nicely bolstered at Sacred Heart. According to Lynch, "Despite a

fairly disorganised music department, the College offered a surprisingly thriving musical environment. That was created partly by the legacy of the recently departed Tim Finn and Chunn brothers Mike and Geoff, who would later join them both in Split Enz.

"Neil spent as much time as he could in the tiny concrete music rooms, where there was always jamming on pianos and acoustic guitars. Only Brother Ivan Genneway encouraged this condemned form of avoiding study period and chapel."

"At that time, 1971-72, our age group was listening to lots of different music,' adds Simon Lynch. "'Led Zeppelin IV', Joe Cocker... I remember a few of us, Neil included, listening to Elton John's 'Honky Chateau'. Neil was really into that album, and, of course, The Beatles."

Although they would later grow heartily sick of all the Beatles references and comparisons, especially when Crowded House gained world acceptance, both Tim and Neil Finn unquestionably doted on the Fab Four in their teen years, and Beatles songs always comprised a large part of both their repertoires. In an interview with *Mojo* in 1994, Neil also cited James Taylor, Crosby Stills & Nash, and David Bowie. "I loved 'Hunky Dory', and I still love the sound of that record. There was a real mystery to it and he was also slightly gender-challenging. I found that deeply mysterious, because I hadn't experienced anything like that in Te Awamutu."

Another Elton John album, 'Tumbleweed Connection', was a special Neil Finn favourite at Sacred Heart. It was Neil's rendition of 'Burn Down The Mission' – an unlikely choice at a Catholic school – that caught the ear of sixth former Bernard McHardy and led to their musical friendship and subsequent Kirby Prize triumph.

Music was Neil Finn's major, but not sole pursuit at Sacred Heart, as Lynch recalls. "Neil was pretty cool. He was completely into music, he played rugby, and ran around with an energetic bunch of hell raisers. I'm almost certain a Sunday drinking excursion to Devonport (over on Auckland's North Shore) nearly brought about an early departure from the school, and a few good lashes with the cane."

In fact, Neil was no stranger to the cane and

the resulting multi-coloured welts on his rear end. He ended his first year with another notable achievement – third out of the entire third form in most canings! There was a fierce rivalry for that dubious and painful honour, and Neil boosted his tally with a series of pillow-fighting escapades.

According to Mike Chunn, "One night, as a member of a horde of pillow-bearing mutineers, Neil took on the other lads in his dormitory for a spot of pillow fighting. They were sent scurrying by the brother on duty. A second time they lashed out, only to be ordered back to bed. Then, for a third time, in a true display of foolhardiness, they charged off with pillows aloft only to be met by the Master Of Discipline, 'Dog'. The whole dormitory was herded into the gymnasium where interrogations commenced. Finn was deemed to be guilty and Dog looked him in the eye and declared: 'Finn! You are a water rat undermining the foundations of the school!'"

Once the novelty of rebellious mischief-making wore off, Neil Finn quickly tired of boarding school life. After just one year and a term, he wanted out. Mike Chunn cites the setback of not making the school rugby team as a turning point. Simon Lynch, however, offers a more plausible reason. "Much of Neil's decision to leave Sacred Heart College had to do with the pressure of trying to live up to Tim Finn's legacy. Tim had been athletics champion, in the First XV for rugby, First XI cricket, an academic and a multi-talented musician. Neil returned to Te Awamutu to follow his own direction."

In a 1994 interview with *Mojo*, Neil suggested that a major reason for his inability to accept boarding school life was the influence of his brother who was filling him with late Sixties propaganda. "He'd just gone to university and was in the demo marches. He was telling me to paint obscenities on the chapel wall. I ran afoul of the whole system and left to go to Te Awamutu College."

On May 5, 1972, after just over a year at Sacred Heart, Neil left for home where he enrolled at Te Awamutu College later in the month. His home town must have seemed even more claustrophobic after his stint in Auckland, but it retained a comfortable feel for the younger Finn brother. "It was a fantastic place to grow

up," he told American magazine *Musician* in 1987. "I had a blissfully happy childhood there."

Judging from the brief mention he receives in the Te Awamutu College magazines of his time there, Neil kept a comparatively low profile. Keith Bain is now the college's Physical Education teacher, with a physique to match but back in 1972, he was Head Boy at the school, and he candidly confesses he has no recollection of Neil Finn. That presumably indicates Neil never ran too afoul of the disciplinarians in his midst.

"Neil wanted to write his own timetable, one that included lots of music," says Judith Finlayson, now a science and agriculture teacher at the college, who was a peer of Neil's sister Judy at school. "They didn't go for it, and I think he was quite discouraged at that. I remember him playing a Bee Gees song at school assembly."

Compared with the comparatively thriving music scene he had encountered at Sacred Heart, Te Awamutu must have depressed eager teenager Neil Finn. There is no mention of him in the Music Department news in the school magazine, probably because the department then comprised one Mrs Martin, a piano, and a deadly dull repertoire.

"Music is now one of our greatest attributes," insists current music teacher George Brooks. "Neil would have a field day if he was a pupil here now. There are lots more chances to perform."

One musical momento of Neil's stint at Te Awamutu College would surface in 1983 in 'Kia Kaha', a song on the Split Enz album 'See Ya Round'. This Maori phrase translates as 'Forever Strong' which is the school motto of Te Awamutu College. Current principal Keith Miller notes that fact with pride, aware that the motto has now reached an international audience.

According to Mike Chunn, the song reflects on schooldays when Neil and his mates would hang out in a house adjacent to the school, and its lyrical yearning for a return to youthful innocence contains echoes of Bob Dylan's prayer-like song 'Forever Young'.

Neil compensated for the lack of musical opportunity by enrolling in drama classes at the local Little Theatre. May Rhodes, now Co-ordinator of the town's Information Centre, was also involved. "We used to get lots of bright kids in," she recalls. "For someone to go and act at that age, it shows a certain self-confidence. And on Friday nights Neil used to work at Martin's Refrigeration downtown. That was the big shopping day in town [throughout New Zealand then], and I remember he used to play the piano outside the store."

Another witness to Neil's burgeoning talent is Ray Spence, a local electrician who serves as President of the Te Awamutu Light Operatic Society (TALOS) . Back in 1976, his group put on *Henry Tudor's Flying Circus*, a Monty Pythonesque look at the legendary monarch. "It was written by two local women, and Neil composed a song for it. Yes, I could tell he was talented," he says. Such experience might even have helped Neil once he joined brother Tim in the highly theatrical Split Enz. Ray Spence would like to think so. "Performers have to start somewhere. Amateur societies exist for that reason."

Another outlet for Neil's talents in this post-Sacred Heart, pre-Split Enz era was the All'n Some Folk Club whose driving force was Felicity Saxby and their friendship raised eyebrows in this conservative community, as Felicity, then a mother of four, cheerfully admits. Described in Mike Chunn's book as a "warm, encouraging woman with hippie tendencies of which Neil approved," she wasn't overly appreciated by many of the townsfolk, mainly because of her proabortion stance, amongst other things.

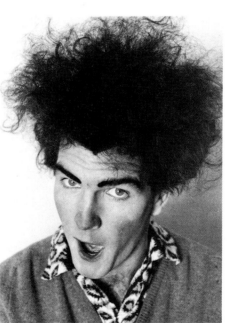
• Tim Finn, Split Enz, 1978

"Yes, I'm considered a bit weird here," she says. "The age difference was something people wondered about. Of course, I was old enough to be Neil's mum, but we were just real peer music friends. I always went around with a bunch of kids anyway. I had four of my own. I collected them!

"When I first met Neil, he'd have been about 15," she reminisces. "He was sitting at the piano in the Little Theatre which our folk club shared. We started talking, and shortly after that he began playing music with my eldest daughter, Frith. I played with her a lot too, and we all got on well together. I remember the song the two of them played the most was The Beatles' 'Blackbird'. Neil would be in and out of our house, we'd go to his house, and we rang each other up quite a lot.

"When Frith went away to teacher's training college, I sort of picked up with Neil where she left off, although I was nowhere near as competent a player as she was. He was a keyboard man when I first met him, and then we both played guitar, and I played autoharp."

The duo's repertoire included traditional English and Scottish folk songs, Saxby's originals, and contemporary hits from singer songwriters like James Taylor and Elton John. Neil had also begun writing original melodies to accompany some of the traditional material.

In one pre-Christmas shopping season, the couple got a gig in a pottery shop. "We just sat down in a corner, surrounded by pots! We basically went through our entire repertoire, as well as learning new things," recalls Felicity. "I don't think Neil had done as much performing as I had. I didn't have as much music in me as Neil, so we were very complementary. He taught me a heap about music and playing and I taught him a bit about production and performance – singing the words and getting the timing right. We got on really well together."

Singing early Seventies pop-folk covers in a ceramics store in rural New Zealand town is definitely not a traditional route to pop stardom, but in Te Awamutu, opportunities for conventional performance were highly limited. "Neil's success wasn't a surprise, but I don't know if I completely sensed the talent," says Felicity. "I just thought he was a very fine, nice, natural person who had no kinds of affectation. He was in fact sort of shy, but he was dedicated to getting on with it. He was a totally committed musician even then."

As well as playing Te Awamutu streets and shops, Neil sharpened his performance skills with folk club gigs at nearby Tokanui Psychiatric Hospital and Waikeria Prison, captive spectators in crowded houses. Clearly, the authorities at these institutions were only too pleased to welcome such harmless activities inside their walls. "We were always doing things like that," says Saxby. "We were just very keen on performing and entertaining people. There was a whole collection of slightly older people at the Hamilton Folk Club, and we'd join forces."

Neil's other important musical collaborator in this period was Hamilton singer/songwriter Rod Murdoch. "I met Neil when he was about 15 and I'd have been 25. We played and wrote songs together for about two years. I was working at the university in Hamilton, and Neil would go to my place where we'd write songs all weekend. It was a very equal partnership. Looking back, I think I learnt more from him than he from me. We'd jam together for hours, often with the tape recorder running, and we co-wrote a lot of stuff."

Like Saxby, Murdoch sensed Neil's talent and dedication. "He was a tremendous amount of fun to work with, and it was quite challenging sometimes. At one stage, he took a couple of lines from a song of mine, 'Late In Rome', and made a whole song out of it. He made it much more interesting than mine, changing the key and meter. That's when I realised he was doing some pretty special things."

Rod could understand the creative frustrations of someone growing up in Te Awamutu, a place he terms 'a desert'. "Hamilton didn't seem a large improvement, but at least Neil and I could invent something for ourselves there."

They would play their original material at folk clubs – Murdoch was a founding member of Hamilton's Kon Tiki Folk Club – and other gatherings, but would throw in some recognisable cover songs at their Waikeria and Tokanui performances. "We had a lot of fun at those," recalls Rod. "We'd clown together a lot. Neil would start off something and I'd follow it up. There was plenty of musical spontaneity... you can change a lot of things if you know what you're changing." This, of course, would become a characteristic of Crowded House shows.

By April 1977 the days of these dynamic duos were numbered, as was Neil Finn's time in New Zealand. Rod Murdoch, like Neil, was now living in Auckland, and Neil said farewell in fitting fashion. "He came around the day before he left and we wrote another piece of music!"

"We were all going to the Easter Folk festival in Hamilton," explains Felicity Saxby. "Then he flew out on Good Friday to join Split Enz in London!"

3

split enz
1972-77

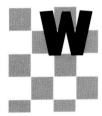

While Neil was woodshedding in Te Awamutu, Tim Finn had formed his first band and tasted the kind of success that was hitherto a fantasy for young musicians from New Zealand. They may have made a ripple rather than a tidal wave internationally, but Split Enz truly revolutionised the Kiwi music scene. They would have also have an equally profound impact on Neil Finn, transforming him from music-obsessed teenager in small-town New Zealand to an accomplished singer/songwriter with an international reputation.

This wasn't just a case of 'pop star's first band'. Neil Finn and Crowded House owe an incalculable debt to Split Enz. Without them, there'd be no Crowded House. The periodic, oft-spontaneous reunions of Split Enz keep the legacy and the legend alive, as do the ongoing collaborations between Tim and Neil Finn.

If you'd suggested to Tim Finn and his comrades in those heady days of 1972 that they'd spawn such a legacy, you'd likely have been accused of consuming too much of the LSD making the rounds. But maybe not. Tim Finn has never lacked a healthy ego, but he was aware of the crushingly heavy odds against a New Zealand band in the early Seventies even succeeding in their own country, let alone foreign turf.

Split Enz would need every ounce of stubborn self-confidence they could muster. In the Seventies, the 'cultural cringe' – a national inferiority complex in certain areas, including music – reigned supreme in New Zealand. Kiwis, with

every justification, prided themselves on many things – the physical beauty of their country, their sporting prowess, independent spirit, economic prosperity and compassionate welfare state – but when it came to culture, national pride was non-existent. There was no local film industry at all and home-grown theatre, television and radio programming, music, literature and art were constantly crippled by a deep-rooted belief that nothing indigenous could compare in quality to the imported counterpart. "Not bad for something local," was the familiar refrain.

Tim Finn realised this. As he told US magazine *Musician* in 1991, "There's so much apathy and indifference in New Zealand. Everything was 'copy, copy, copy' and 'if it's local, it must be bad'. To survive you had to have this huge amount of self-belief."

Martin Phillipps, leader of The Chills, next to the Finns the most internationally-acclaimed New Zealand singer/songwriter, sums up this attitude perfectly. "What possible reason would there be for our music being inferior to overseas stuff, especially Australian? The only difference is that most New Zealanders have been persuaded that what we do here can never be as good as that done elsewhere."

It was a stigma that blighted New Zealand pop music for three decades. Sure, some local artists made it onto the charts and became popular domestic concert performers, but they generally fell into a safe, suitable for the family, category. Overseas performers, no matter how faded their career, would be treated like royalty, with local stars eternally relegated to opening status at their shows.

The English weekly music papers arrived in

New Zealand three months late, but were still devoured eagerly by NZ music fans. The idea they could ever form a band that'd play in a hallowed venue like London's Marquee Club was quite unthinkable. The especially ambitious and talented might make the trek across the Tasman Sea to Australia, but once there they would be treated as second-class citizens by Australians, who tended to suffer from the same inferiority complex themselves, albeit not quite so desperately as their Kiwi cousins.

In hindsight, many New Zealand bands of the late Sixties and early Seventies were every bit as talented as their best-selling counterparts in North America and Britain. Bands like The Underdogs, La De Das, Larry's Rebels, The Avengers, Human Instinct and Fourmyula were victims of geography, not artistic ability. The patriotic NZ rock fan was even driven to mild spasms of excitement by the mid Seventies British semi-star status of home-grown bassists Gary Thain and Charlie Tumahai, respectively members of Uriah Heep and Be-Bop Deluxe, and pub-rocker Max Merritt.

Split Enz would change all that, but it wasn't easy. The odds against them were increased by their determination to take the path least travelled, by insisting on performing all-original material, in daringly theatrical, extroverted fashion. Their image seemed at times to have been drawn from a travelling circus, with costumes of bizarre design, hairstyles that defied gravity and more than a touch of theatrical make-up. In New Zealand, that meant questions were asked not just about your sanity but about your sexuality too.

Split Enz began life as Split Ends and their roots date back to the Sacred Heart musical pursuits of Tim Finn and Mike and Geoff Chunn. In 1971 Tim and Mike enrolled at Auckland University, Tim reading for a Bachelor of Arts degree, and Mike studying Engineering. They soon encountered Rob Gillies, Geoffrey Crombie and Phil Judd, all of them free-spirited students taking the Elam Fine Arts course at Auckland University, who introduced the newly freed Sacred Heart alumni to a new world of underground music and comics, surrealist art, pot and acid.

Of all the fascinating characters in the Split Enz saga, Phil Judd was always the most enigmatic. A precociously gifted artist and musician, his talents were often hindered by a shyness misconstrued as aloofness. "Phil was incapable of the social, gregarious behaviour that came so easily to people like Tim," says Mike Chunn. In this small circle of creative students, however, Judd shone, and he'd have a huge effect on Tim Finn.

In this heady era, hair and beards grew, minds expanded, faiths were rejected. Mike Chunn explains in *Stranger Than Fiction* that he and Tim had by now completely discarded the Catholic faith. "The endless repetitive mix of discipline and fear had ensured we weren't going to stick it out," he says. "For Dick and Mary [Finn] this shift was uncomfortable." Neil Finn would make a similar transition shortly after, pegging himself as a lapsed Catholic from age 15.

Musical tastes also changed radically. The Beatles, Bee Gees and Elton John took a back seat to the progressive rock of the day – Family, Jethro Tull and the mighty Led Zeppelin. The university mates would jam together from time to time, and in early 1972 one spontaneous grouping cleaned up, financially at least, in Te Awamutu. With Tim on piano, Mike on bass, Rob Gillies on flute, Geoff Chunn on drums and bongo-playing friend Ben Miller, they entered a talent contest at the Te Rapa racecourse. Playing an original song they'd recorded back in 1969, a hippie-influenced ode called 'Take It Green', the quintet won $500.

In Auckland, drastic change continued apace. Phil Judd was becoming recognised as an immensely talented painter, but he dropped out of arts school, sensing his lack of social skills was a hindrance. Encouraged by Phil's example, Tim followed suit. In the early Seventies, dropping out was considered cool, so this was no big sacrifice. The acid-fuelled musical experimentation heated up. At the Auckland Students Arts Festival in August 1972, Tim Finn and Phil Judd, in a combo dubbed Mellodrone, performed a 20-minute progressive rock epic that featured Tim on piano, Phil on drums and Rob Gillies on flugelhorn. Various friends onstage stood motionless, knitted, or walked around, all adding to the overall weirdness. The germ of Split Ends(z) was incubating.

13

Phil and Tim shared a house and the creative sparks kept flying. Determined now to start a proper band of their own, they recruited a brilliant young violinist called Miles Golding. Mike Chunn joined in mid-November, after Phil, Tim and Miles had cunningly asked to use his bedroom as a rehearsal space and blown him away with their new songs.

Mike Howard, a flautist friend of Miles, also joined, and the first line-up of the band was complete. Tim Finn came up with their name, Split Ends, reportedly culled from a page of his scribbles. With a top heavy line-up and eclectic range of instruments, it is not surprising that their line-up would fluctuate frequently over the next five years.

Geoff Chunn was playing a Sunday blues night at downtown Auckland pub, the Wynyard Tavern, and he gave them an opening spot. In *Stranger Than Fiction*, Mike Chunn recalls that... "Tim and Phil were buzzing at the chance to play and we rehearsed in a frenzy until the day came. At 7.30pm on Sunday 10 December 1972, Split Ends gave its first performance to 30 people in the Wynyard Tavern... We sung, strummed, blew, and bowed our hearts out, and in a flash it was over."

The gig-hungry band immediately headed to another downtown Auckland club, Levis Saloon, where, again through Geoff, they had a spot on folk night. If there'd been an opening on polka night somewhere, they'd have snapped that up too. At Levis, they ran through the same mini-set of three songs – 'Wise Men', 'Split Ends' and 'For You' – to a response warm enough to see them asked back. This time, the crowd included Tim Finn's three siblings, Judy, Carolyn and Neil. It was a momentous event for 14-year-old Neil Finn, as he described later. "I first saw Split Ends in 1972 at Levis Saloon. Back then I was still a pimply schoolboy but that performance and those first songs made a lasting impression on me. I went back to Te Awamutu and wrote Split Ends on my pencil case."

From there, things moved rapidly. Levis booker Barry Coburn was very impressed. A former florist in his late twenties, he had a penchant for country and western fashion (he is now a noted artist manager/music publisher in Nashville) and ears open for new musical talent.

He was delighted to discover a local band that played original material, and began acting as their manager.

Coburn set his sights much higher than Sunday nights for hippie folkies, and was booking New Zealand's first major outdoor music event, the Great Ngaruawahia Music Festival. Designed to duplicate the American rock festivals of the Woodstock era, it would feature acts as eclectic as former Fairport Convention singer Sandy Denny and heavy metal pioneers Black Sabbath. He offered Split Ends a coveted Saturday night slot.

Festival time. Ngaruawahia, Jan. 1973. What they'd hoped would be their first big break just about destroyed the band's spirits. Tense and nervous, Split Ends hit the stage at 8pm, only to find the beer-guzzling crowd of 18,000 restless to hear Kiwi rock heroes The La De Das, not this totally unknown bunch of weird-sounding psychedelic folkies. The band struggled through half their planned set before obnoxious MC Adrian Rawlins ordered them off lest the crowd began throwing something more dangerous than abuse.

Spectator Neil Finn was very disappointed, Tim quickly shrugged it off, but the sensitive Phil Judd was crushed. "His natural psychology was towards the euphoric moment," says Mike Chunn. "The setback left him with a crisis of faith."

Despite this mini-disaster, Barry Coburn remained a firm believer. Split Ends' spirits revived after recording their first single – 'For You' coupled with 'Split Ends' – to be released locally on Vertigo/Polygram, a one-off deal arranged by the well-connected Coburn. He also snared their first tour, opening for Australian hard-rockers Itambu on a New Zealand university tour. Such gigs were just about the only way a local band performing original material could reach an audience, even if that crowd often comprised students seeing how much cheap cider and draught beer they could guzzle before puking over the dance floor. In the event, Split Ends went over well. Tim Finn was becoming increasingly comfortable in his flamboyant frontman role, which contrasted nicely with the intense silent stare that Phil Judd was mastering.

The enterprising Barry Coburn then arranged another tour. "I was managing them and also promoting a tour by John Mayall. What else was I to do?" he recalls. The odd musical pairing of Split Ends and veteran British bluesman Mayall worked, and the band made new fans and press allies. "Rather than being isolated as some art band, I almost made Split Enz mainstream by giving them exposure in concert situations," analyses Coburn.

In April 1973, the line-up changed radically. Violinist Miles Golding left for London and classical music studies, flautist Mike Howard was

• **Phil Judd, Split Enz, 1978**

edged out, Geoff Chunn came in as drummer and Wally Wilkinson as guitarist. The high of the tour's success was punctured by the single flopping on release, and the group sought new means of exposure.

Split Ends refused to join the then-expanding pub circuit, insisting on an ambitious stage show for an audience intent on listening. It was a daring approach in early Seventies New Zealand, but it reflected their confident belief they had something new to offer. Equally audacious was their bid for maximum television exposure. New Zealand still had only one TV channel (TV One) and a talent show of dubious distinction, *New Faces* , had a huge audience. The enterprising Split Ends decided to take the plunge, recording a track for the heats, and these studio sessions saw a giant step in the evolution of the Enz sound.

"They confirmed the Split Ends ethos," says Chunn. "We were never to stand still... With The Beatles still fresh in our minds, Phil and Brian arranged string quartets and wrote brass parts; we threw in percussion, bagpipes, banjos, gongs, and sound effects. Life in the studio was magic and in contrast to the fragile live shows, Phil, particularly, was in his element."

Split Ends won their August *New Faces* heat, and Phil and Tim wrote a brand new number, 'Sweet Talking Spoon Song', for the final in October 1973. That they placed seventh out of eight hopefuls should have been no surprise. Clearly a cut above, talent-wise, they were nonetheless far too bizarre for such a middle-of-

the-road show. Even appearing, however, was somehow deliciously subversive. The legend was building.

Phil Judd and Tim Finn were again bitterly disappointed, though, and they pledged that Split Ends would become solely a recording act for the next year. It was yet another unconventional move for a new band, but they would calm down and relent before the year was out. In November, a new EMI single, '129' backed with 'Sweet Talking Spoon Song', flopped, and the future of the band was still fragile. When Tim went home for a family Christmas, however, he declared to Dick and Neil Finn that the group was his passion, his quest. This wasn't a fun pastime, this was his life, he told them, and such was the passion in his voice that parental objections were futile. Neil was in awe of his brother's commitment.

◆

IN EARLY 1974, Split Ends signed two year management contracts with Barry Coburn, inserting a clause that read: "If, in the last six months of the period we have individually earned less than $50 per week, options could not be taken up." It wasn't that Split Ends were overtly pessimistic, as New Zealand's bands had been brought up to be, just that they needed room to manoeuvre if things weren't going well.

In the event things improved, thanks to Coburn's initiative. As *New Faces* finalists, Split Ends were offered a 30-minute TV special, for which they had to record four new songs. Major national TV exposure like this was a huge boost, and clearly one advantage New Zealand artists had over those from countries where crowded TV schedules wouldn't permit cottage industries taking over. It's difficult to imagine relative unknowns getting such an opportunity in Britain or North America. Equally significant for Split Ends was the news they'd headline the first Radio Hauraki Buck-A-Head concert in May.

Hauraki was New Zealand's very own pirate radio station, a beacon of hope on the sterile local radio scene. Their desire to be seen as supportive of home-grown music gave Coburn an opening. "I went to Radio Hauraki and created the Buck-A-Head concept. It was the only way to get Split Ends exposed further," he explains. The series gave local artists a chance to strut their stuff on a real concert stage, Auckland's beautiful old His Majesty's Theatre, and the ticket price of a dollar ensured a healthy audience.

While all this was going on behind the scenes, the line-up of Split Ends fluctuated yet again. Phil Judd would still be their master conceptualist, writing songs and directing the sound, but he wouldn't play live. "I hate it. It disturbs me," he told new Kiwi rock magazine *Hot Licks*. Old comrade Rob Gillies was recruited on sax and trumpet and Eddie Rayner, Wally Wilkinson's friend from his earlier band, Orb, joined as keyboard player. Eddie, of course, would later play a significant part in the early era of Crowded House. Mike and Geoff Chunn remained as the rhythm section. Beefing up the new line-up's sound was Tim Finn's latest pride and joy, a mellotron, a radical instrument that with the aid of pre-recorded tapes could duplicate a string section. This helped the band recreate the ambitiously baroque sound of their recordings onstage.

Another change saw Split Ends become Split Enz, Tim and Phil favouring the nationalistic "nz" part of the new spelling. About a year later, it was decided they'd use second Christian names as their first, mainly in an attempt to separate performing and private lives. Brian Finn (as he'd been known until now) officially became Tim, Mike Chunn became Jonathan, Paul Wilkinson became Wally. Ever the maverick, Phil Judd remained Phil.

As Split Enz, then, the group kicked off the Hauraki Buck-A-Heads on May 12, 1974. It was an unabashed triumph that saw the 1,200 strong crowd clamour for an encore. Despite the euphoria, the shadow of Phil Judd still loomed large, especially over Tim Finn. In his book, Mike Chunn recalls that at the start of their new song, set highlight 'Stranger Than Fiction', Tim told the audience, "There's a certain somebody who's with us tonight... he's not on stage but still very much a part of the show. His name is Phil Judd and it's his music which is our privilege and joy to be playing."

Chunn felt Tim was being too deferential, downplaying his own compositional contributions. Onstage, however, there was nothing modest about Tim's extravagantly over-the-top persona. By now, the group's trademark theatricality and bizarre image was taking hold. Sound effects – birds, running water, breaking glass, singing monks – were used liberally, stage props included pot plants and stuffed animals, and, to further the impression of asylum inmates on acid, they incorporated a sketch that saw pith-helmeted 'psychiatrist' Geoffrey (Noel) Crombie chase a straitjacketed, bandaged 'patient' (Phil Judd) across the stage in the middle of 'Stranger Than Fiction'.

To complete the effect, the band members chopped their hair severely short, a drastic move in days when long hair was not just mandatory for rock musicians but in a broader sense symbolised the spirit of the era for young people of independent mind. They sported apparel ranging from a burgundy crushed-velvet suit (Wally) to pyjamas (Geoff Chunn), to a harlequin's costume (Tim). Auckland's vintage clothing stores must have been thrilled!

"Those Buck-A-Head shows were regarded as the hippest place to be in Auckland. By then, Split Enz were arguably the only New Zealand act that had been championed in the local press," says Murray Cammick, now publisher of *Rip It Up*, New Zealand's premier music magazine.

The post-gig high was short-lived. To Tim's delight, Judd decided he wanted back in the band, but scepticism reigned elsewhere. Unhappy with the new line-up, Rob Gillies and Geoff Chunn left in July, the latter being replaced by former Orb drummer Emlyn (Paul) Crowther. The next few months saw more Buck-A-Heads, less-successful out of town shows, and the recruitment of another member, Geoffrey, now Noel, Crombie. As well as his stellar spoons-playing, he contributed hand-sewn, originally designed, vividly-coloured stage costumes. Another trademark was thus established.

By year's end Split Enz had clearly estab-

• Split Enz in 1976, left to right: Rob Gillies, Eddie Rayner, Tim Finn, Mike Chunn, Phil Judd, Malcolm Green and Noel Crombie.

lished themselves as the country's most excitingly innovative new band. They were adored by the press, as David Gapes of Radio Hauraki recalls. "We were involved in publishing *Hot Licks* and Split Enz were a real boon. They gave us lots of great copy."

In the January 1975 issue of *Hot Licks*, editor Roger Jarrett called Split Enz... "The cream of the crop... the finest band New Zealand has ever seen." They won Group Of The Year, and Concert Of The Year categories in the magazine's readers poll the next month.

Rave reviews, of course, wouldn't pay the rent, and all of the band were obliged to take day jobs. For Tim Finn these included sorting mail alongside Phil and Noel at the Auckland Post Office, working the sausage line at a local freezing works, actually a slaughterhouse and meat processing plant, and, with Phil and Eddie, working at a confectionery factory, a post involving regular chocolate-scoffing.

On March 13, 1975, Split Enz crossed the Tasman for their first tour of Australia. Musically,

the band's heart was in England, but that was a world, well, 12,000 miles, away. Split Enz were dubious about the unfashionable Australian music scene, but were up for a new challenge. Barry Coburn had set up three weeks of dates in New South Wales and Victoria, plus a couple of TV appearances. Their incredible voyage was beginning.

According to New Zealand music journalist John Dix, Split Enz's overseas début was a rude awakening. "At the Bondi Lifesaver, Sydney's premier rock venue, any expectations were quickly dispelled," he says. "'Jesus, Bruce, a bunch of fuckeen poofters. Get off, ya mugs!' was the reaction of the crowd," according to *Stranded In Paradise*, his excellent history of NZ rock. Australian pub audiences aren't renowned for their musical tolerance, and the band's extravagant image wasn't appreciated.

Some equally disastrous gigs saw the band doubt the wisdom of this visit, but things looked up when they encountered Michael Gudinski, Australian manager of raunchy glam-rock sensations Skyhooks, a booking agent and head of the Mushroom record label. He took a shine to the idiosyncratic Kiwis when he caught an early gig, and quickly signed them to a recording deal with Mushroom, also inking song publishing deals with Tim and Phil.

He also secured them a gig opening for Roxy Music, one of Split Enz's major influences, who were then touring Australasia. "We went over well with the audience, but, more importantly, most of Roxy Music were watching and we really surprised and impressed them," Tim wrote in a letter home, adding that Roxy guitarist Phil Manzanera wanted to produce their album. Younger brother Neil was awe-struck. The low after that high came when Split Enz opened for Skyhooks and ear-splitting rockers AC/DC in Melbourne. The rowdy teenage audience hated them.

Manzanera couldn't commit to a definite production schedule, so Split Enz quickly went into Festival Studios in Sydney in May to record their début album with tour manager and former rocker (The Invaders) Dave Russell as producer. The band weren't thrilled at the final sound of 'Mental Notes', Chunn complaining about confusing overdubbing and some mannered Tim Finn vocals. The starvation subsistence wage of $1.50 a day wasn't helping morale or concentration either.

In June 1975, somewhat illogically in view of the album's late July release, the band toured New Zealand. Siblings of Split Enz provided the opening acts – Geoff Chunn on most dates, Neil Finn and Rod Murdoch on two. The shows sold out, and the press gushed, but a live performance on the cheesy TV variety show *Town Cryer* proved embarrassing. Taken aback by the interviewer's opening question of "Why do you look so stupid?" Tim Finn, according to Mike Chunn, "lost the plot and in front of the whole nation with his pancaked face sweating profusely, he came across as a bit of a tool. As we mimed the single from 'Mental Notes', maybe the rest of us also looked particularly toolish". The next week, Dick Finn was fined at his Rotary club for having produced such a wayward son, a telling comment on the parochial conservatism of life in New Zealand.

Neil Finn, now 16, felt no need to apologise for Tim's behaviour. He was deliriously excited at the chance of opening Split Enz's shows in

Tauranga and Hamilton, and these dates can be seen as the first public collaboration between Tim and Neil, so their fascinating and fruitful working partnership now extends over 20 years. "His admiration for Split Enz nearly bordered on the fanatical," recalls performing partner Rod Murdoch. "Those gigs were great. We just had the usual nerves, but that was never an issue with Neil. And I remember Split Enz paying us the compliment of calling one of our songs great."

The July 12 Hamilton concert also earned Neil his first review. City daily the *Waikato Times* wrote that... "Finn's younger brother Neil from Te Awamutu and Hamilton musician Rod Murdoch contributed three interesting pieces, with Neil Finn sounding reminiscent of his brother." For Neil, there was now no turning back.

When 'Mental Notes' was released locally, it made a huge impression; not just on the charts, where it peaked at No. 7, but in the living rooms of student flats where Enz fans congregated and rejoiced in the fact that their heroes had made a great album, not just one that was 'pretty good for locals'.

After its release Split Enz returned to Australia. Mushroom Records was based in Melbourne, so it made sense for the band to base themselves there. Regular gigging, three to five nights a week, saw Split Enz's following grow steadily, if unspectacularly, and they opened on a variety of artists, including Leo Sayer, Santana and, more appropriately, Frank Zappa. Line-up changes continued, guitarist Wally Wilkinson being axed in November, necessitating increased guitar contributions from Phil Judd. His replacement through the revolving door was horn player Rob Gillies. Phil again dropped hints about leaving, the band's hoped for UK record deal with Island fell through, and 1976 was ushered in to the strains of internal confusion.

This didn't stop them undertaking another tour of New Zealand. Dubbed the *Enz Of The Earth* tour, it featured a solo Neil Finn as opening act. The critics were again impressed. Prophetically, Christchurch's *The Press* said: "I'd like to get it on record now that Neil Finn is a singer of great potential. He sang and performed (on mandolin, guitar and piano) his own material along with two or three Lennon/McCartney numbers. The standard of both lyrics and tunes was astounding. Neil's writing and use of voice is already quite sophisticated and sensitive."

Hot Licks' Jarrett raved about Split Enz's show – "The finest here since Roxy Music last year" – but by the time the review appeared on April 5, 1976, band and entourage – 11 in all – were winging their way to London where Phil Manzanera was waiting to produce their next album.

"London was the City of Dreams, literally," says Mike Chunn. "For more than a decade we'd relished the music emanating from that place; we had looked at photographs of The Beatles, The Kinks, Abbey Road, Carnaby Street, and the peacock revolution of youth, and imagined ourselves being there, being part of it, and yet believing it might never be."

London didn't exactly roll out the red carpet for the green new arrivals, but the first few weeks were promising. With fancy digs on Chelsea's King's Road, the members of Split Enz found themselves at the epicentre of London's most fashion conscious square mile. Particularly memorable was the day when Tim Finn and Noel Crombie strolled into infamous punk boutique Sex, drawing quizzical looks from shop owner Malcolm McLaren and soon to be punk icon Johnny Rotten. With their geometric hair-styles and arty dress, the Kiwi upstarts looked as bizarre as he did, and he was not best pleased to be upstaged by New Zealanders of all people.

Split Enz quickly entered Island's Basing Street Studios in Notting Hill Gate with Phil Manzanera. Unhappy with the sound of 'Mental Notes', the plan was to re-record the album, add a few new tracks and release the result as their début in the Northern Hemisphere. They still had no UK record deal or booking agent, but were confident enough to proceed anyway. An interested Chrysalis Records arranged an audition, an opening slot at a Gentle Giant gig in Southampton. The lads passed with flying colours, and Split Enz signed on the dotted line with Chrysalis, on June 8, 1976.

• **Split Enz in 1977, top row: Neil Finn, Eddie Rayner and Tim Finn; centre: Nigel Griggs, Rob Gillies and Malcolm Green; bottom: Noel Crombie.**

ON THE OTHER SIDE of the world, things were changing for Neil Finn. Tiring of school life, he opted out of starting university in early 1976, and instead found a job at Te Awamutu's record store. The Split Enz tour heightened his restlessness, and Tim wrote encouraging him to move up to Auckland and chase his musical dreams. "Get into it, man, and show those Aucklanders what a Finn is capable of," he wrote from London.

Neil didn't need much urging. In Auckland, he hooked up with Mark Hough, a friend and fan of Phil Judd. As Buster Stiggs, Hough would later front early New Zealand punk band The Suburban Reptiles. Neil and Mark began sharing a flat, Neil wrote music to Mark's lyrics and the duo grabbed ex-Enz drummer Geoff Chunn and a keyboard player and put four new songs down on tape.

The results drew praise from London. "If the band thing doesn't work take solace in the fact that Split Enz believes in you," responded Tim. That would have cheered Neil, who spent his days working as a hospital orderly.

On August 9, 1976, the Split Enz album was released as 'Mental Notes' in the UK, but sporting the apt title of 'Second Thoughts' for Australasia. Considering the British music press' usual antipathy to Australasian acts, initial reviews were encouraging. "One of the few bands of any originality to have emerged over the last year," wrote *Melody Maker*. "Compulsively droll humour and exacting musicianship," praised *NME*.

The ensuing period of inactivity saw another casualty, drummer Emlyn Crowther. After a round of auditions, Split Enz found themselves with their first non-New Zealand member, Englishman Malcolm Green, who in the past had played on an occasional basis with Love Affair and The Honeycombs. Split Enz, however, was his first serious band.

The new line-up took off in October on a 26-date British tour supporting Jack The Lad. a Lindisfarne spin-off folk rock outfit. This earned some press attention, but their arrival in the UK coincided with the explosive rise of punk rock and Jack The Lad were unlikely to attract the attention of a hawkish rock press now well disposed towards the newly arrived punks. Although not totally out of step with the mood of the time – their hairstyles and dress saw to that – Split Enz were concerned with theatrics and musical experimentation while all that mattered to the punks were short bursts of violent guitar noise. Split Enz were too young and new to be looked upon with disdain like the dinosaurs of old, but the new wave which followed punk – their natural home – had yet to take hold. Caught somewhere between two stools, Split Enz were both before their time yet after it too, a uniquely unfortunate position compounded by their nationality.

• **Noel Crombie and Tim Finn in Split Enz, 1977**

Astutely analysing the great divide, Tim told *NME* that "for those who want an alternative to the punks, here we are and intend to stay. Split Enz is a very close, cohesive family and we've worked very hard to get this far." Still, punk princess Siouxsie and assorted Clash and Sex Pistols members checked out Split Enz's headlining London show in December 1976, so it wasn't all-out war between the factions.

During this period, the band recorded a new single with Manzanera entitled 'Another Great Divide'. As with most earlier Enz singles, it stiffed, but showed Tim Finn's improvement as a singer. "Gone were the twittery mannerisms and inflections," analysed Mike Chunn. "His rococo vocals were in need of a natural death, so they went, never to surface on record again."

At the end of 1976, Split Enz headed back Down Under. Their British incursion had been expensive, so it was time to bolster the coffers with an Australasian tour. They certainly hadn't 'conquered' Britain, but the attention they'd attracted there helped ensure full houses in both Australia and New Zealand.

Split Enz visited the US for the first time in February of the following year. Chrysalis showed real faith in the band in bankrolling a six-week trip. Club dates were interspersed with promotional activities including record store appearances, interviews, and even a serious of Split Enz look-alike contests which the band were obliged to judge. In the South, things turned sour. In a classic *Spinal Tap* scenario, a look-alike contest in Atlanta drew just one genuine contestant, forcing Chrysalis reps to talk the club's staff into joining in. One set during their four-night stand there between February 23-26 saw Split Enz play to an audience of two.

The enigmatic Phil Judd, in one of his sporadic downer phases fuelled by too much brandy, snapped. Mike Chunn recalls Judd storming offstage in mid-set on the last night, blaming his histrionics on an out-of-tune guitar. When the usually-deferential Tim Finn queried the excuse, Judd punched him in the face.

Clearly something had to give. Judd handed in his notice the next day in Atlanta, coincidentally the same US city where 17 years later another abrupt departure was to shake the foundations of Crowded House. Call it the Confederate curse. Judd played out the rest of the American tour, but in effect his exit strengthened the band. Everyone else remained confident that Tim Finn could handle the songwriting chores, and they soldiered on.

March and April 1977 proved watershed months in the lives of both Split Enz and Neil Finn. After the US tour, Tim Finn and Eddie Rayner stayed on at Tim's uncle's house in Baltimore to write new, post-Judd material. The rest flew to London, save for Chunn, who headed back to New Zealand charged with finding a new guitarist for Split Enz.

He arrived just in time to catch the first public performance of After Hours at the University of Auckland's Maidment Theatre. This new combo comprised Neil Finn, Geoff Chunn, Mark Hough and bassist Alan Brown. Mike praised their 'intricate arrangements and melodic mastery'. "Neil's voice sounded far more mature than his 17 years," he said. Family ties obviously make Chunn biased, but After Hours went over well enough to score an invitation to return there a few weeks later.

Guitarist Alistair Riddell, ex-Orb and glamrockers Spacewaltz, turned Mike Chunn down when he approached him to join Split Enz. Back in London, the band advertised in *Melody Maker*, the orthodox method for finding musicians. In a rare example of candour, their ad read: 'Guitarist wanted for band with an increasingly complex history, shaky record deal and a new batch of songs'.

Chunn flew back to England to find the group excited about Tim's new material. The guitarist problem remained, though, and the band wasn't looking forward to auditioning wannabe Pom guitar heroes. "I couldn't stand the thought of weeks upon weeks of auditions of longhaired British guitarists," Mike laughingly recalls. Then he had a flash of inspiration. Recruit Neil Finn.

"Guys, we need someone who knows what Split Enz is all about," he told his sceptical bandmates. "They may not be the greatest guitar player in the world but that's not what we want. We want a natural member... someone who can fit in instantly and commit fully. That person, you fools, is Neil Finn."

At the After Hours show, Chunn had recognised Neil's emerging talent as a singer/songwriter, and this, more than guitar prowess, had impressed him. The others saw the logic, and Tim rang Mary Finn in Te Awamutu, asking her to track Neil down and have him call London.

Offered the gig of his dreams, Neil coolly replied, "I'll have to think about it. I'll call you back." His hesitation was partially based on the fact he'd never really played electric guitar before.

Neil, of course, accepted, so no auditions were held. Never one to break a commitment, he played with After Hours on Thursday April 7, recorded five tracks with them (reportedly a potential-packed demo), and flew to London that night.

He was just 18, and his life was changing irrevocably.

4

neil and split enz

Unsurprisingly, the 'bye Phil, hello Neil' transition of Split Enz was greeted with trepidation and cynicism in some quarters. Sceptics were inclined to inquire how a teenage novice could replace founding member/ musical visionary Judd? There were also charges of nepotism, as Mike Chunn readily concedes. "Yes, he was there because he was Tim's kid brother, just like my kid brother [Geoff] was in there earlier." Obviously, though, a band with so much at stake would only take such a chance if they were convinced the kid had talent.

Back in New Zealand, many observers still viewed Split Enz as Phil Judd's band. For all his frequent criticism of Judd's attitude and behaviour, Mike Chunn agrees that Phil was ultimately the foundation stone of the whole thing. "The Judd era set the stage with a musical excellence that Tim felt he had to match," said Chunn. "People like Neil Finn still highly rate Phil and all he stood for."

Author John Dix typified the sentiment. "Like a lot of industry people at the time, I thought Split Enz was Phil Judd. My initial reaction [to Neil joining] was that this was just nepotism. They proved me wrong, and I'm glad they did. When Phil Judd left, we thought it'd be the end of Split Enz. For them to come up with Neil... good call, boys!"

The enigmatic presence of Phil Judd would feature again in the Split Enz saga, but for now Tim Finn was firmly at the helm. Just as his vocal style had become less mannered, more direct, so his songwriting had become more focused. This would be the key to escaping the ghetto of 'cult favourites' in which the band was then imprisoned.

As Tim told *Rip It Up*'s Alastair Dougal in 1977, "The new songs are much rockier. We've always told people that our roots are in The Beatles, The Kinks, The Move and so on, but I think that's becoming more obvious now."

Once Neil arrived in London yet another line-up change occurred with the departure of another original member, Mike Chunn, who decided he'd had enough. "Family commitments and the private hell of agoraphobia," were his reasons for quitting. English bassist Nigel Griggs, a friend of Mal Green then playing in a cover band in France, took his place. Griggs had previously played with art-rocker Steve Hillage and a flamenco-rock band in America. The fact that Split Enz now sported an English rhythm section demonstrated just how far they'd come from their origins as adventurous New Zealand students less than five years earlier.

Neil's immediate priority was to buy his first electric guitar, and he chose a Yamaha. It was then straight into rehearsals and a recording studio, as Split Enz had begun working with former Beatles engineer Geoff Emerick on a new album for Chrysalis. Emerick's CV definitely inspired the Fab Four-adoring Finn brothers.

Neil later confessed, "I was really nervous because I hadn't really played electric guitar before I joined Split Enz. I was out of the sound mix for the first six months. Nobody ever heard me, which was just as well! I jumped around a lot to make up for it. I was probably quite an entertaining little prat to watch!" His baptism by fire would prove to be a valuable learning experience.

On April 27, 1977, Neil Finn performed as a member of Split Enz for the first time at a gig in St Albans. The full line-up now comprised Tim and Neil Finn, keyboardist Eddie Rayner, horn player Rob Gillies, percussionist Noel Crombie, drummer Malcolm Green and bassist Nigel Griggs. A seven-piece band was quite a contrast to the fashionable punk minimalism of the day, but the British dates confirmed that the band had a devoted, if small, following. Some were even devoted enough to follow them from gig to gig, Deadhead or Kiss army style. Dubbed Frenz of the Enz, they had begun imitating their bizarre costumes and hairstyles as well.

Between the Frenz and young New Zealanders and Australians living in London, Split Enz could now fill out a concert-sized venue, London's Victoria Palace. Things were moving, but the band and Emerick failed to gell as they had hoped. A reported fondness for liquid lunches was cited as one reason, and he left the project before the album was mixed.

In July, the band headed back to New Zealand to rehearse for another tour, during which Tim and Neil Finn wrote the first joint composition, 'Best Friend'. The new Split Enz album, 'Dizrythmia', was released in August, and the tour was a triumphant sell-out.

Around this time, Tim and comrades decided to lessen the emphasis on their visual, theatrical side. "That has taken more and more second place with us," he told *Rip It Up*. "We're far more interested in the music, so I think we'll tone that whole aspect down a little. It's a tricky dilemma, because people expect that of us now."

Response to the new material, live and on record, was very positive in both Australia and New Zealand. 'Dizrythmia' spent 12 weeks on the NZ charts, peaking at No. 3. With 'My Mistake', they scored their first ever charting single – No. 21 in New Zealand and No. 12 in Australia. There was no chart action in the UK, but the album scored some favourable press. In October, a full hour on television, on the BBC's *Sight And Sound*, definitely aided the cause. One impressed viewer was Paul McCartney, whom the Finns got to meet through the Emerick connection.

Yet another line-up change followed an extensive British and Dutch tour. Almost unbe-lievably, this one saw the return of Phil Judd. The new material he'd been writing impressed Tim and Eddie, who brought him back in over the objections of Noel Crombie. To make room, Rob Gillies got the heave-ho, in rather poorly-handled fashion, according to Mike Chunn. Internal communication was never one of Split Enz's strengths.

By now Chrysalis were fretting over their lack of chart success. Looking at the books, they saw red to the tune of a reported £150,000, and dumped the Enz. The band had also fired manager John Hopkins, with whom they'd worked since 1975, so they were now without a UK label or manager. They signed on the dole and Phil Judd quit again, this time for good. Back in Auckland, Judd hooked up with The Suburban Reptiles, producing their great Kiwi punk single, 'Saturday Night Stay At Home'. He and Mark Hough (aka Buster Stiggs) then formed The Swingers, a new wave styled trio that were to make noises in Australasia.

Tim and Neil Finn ignored British rejection by throwing themselves fever-ishly into songwriting, generally separately. There was a new energy and aggression in this material, and help with funding arrived in two forms. Split

• Split Enz in 1978 with Tim and Neil

Enz were finally recognised as worthy cultural ambassadors and they received a $5,000 bail-out from the Queen Elizabeth II Arts Council back home. The other source of income was Michael Gudinski, head of their Australian label Mushroom and still a believer. Split Enz had been recording with 18-year-old studio wizard David Tickle, and Tim was especially happy with rockin' new tune 'I See Red'. Gudinski pledged to fund another album, but wanted a more experienced producer.

American Mallory Earl, who'd worked with Jimi Hendrix and Steely Dan, was hired but after rehearsals at rural Welsh studio Rockfield and some recording sessions at the Manor Studios in

December 1978, the relationship with Earl soured. The album they recorded together, 'Frenzy', was shopped around the British labels, and Split Enz headed back Down Under for summer dates. 1978 had been a frustrating year business-wise, but the pre-'Frenzy' sessions had renewed their musical enthusiasm.

A January headlining gig at NZ festival Nambassa in front of 45,000 fans was a triumph, considering all their gear was destroyed (suspected theft and arson) two days earlier. New single, the driving 'I See Red', caught fire in Australia, reaching No. 2, and its inclusion on new pressings of 'Frenzy' helped make it Split Enz's best-selling album to date Down Under. Still, total sales there of 40,000 didn't make it a blockbuster.

Now basing themselves Down Under, at least temporarily, Split Enz were restless to record again. After yet more touring, they booked a Melbourne studio in August and one of Neil Finn's songs, 'Things', was chosen as a new single. An edgy guitar rocker, it marked a return to form - it stiffed!

Tim and Neil then set up house in Sydney suburb Rose Bay with respective partners Liz Malam, a former dancer in London and Tim's girl-friend since 1976, and Sharon Johnson, whom Neil had recently met in Auckland. As was now the pattern, the brothers were writing songs separately, with Tim actively encouraging Neil's work. Tim was finding a lighter tone to comple-ment the oft darker colours on his songwriting palette, while his fresh-faced younger brother confirmed he was as deft with a hook as Ali in his prime. These Sydney songs finally kicked Split Enz's career into overdrive.

One tune, in particular, with its paranoid-sounding refrain of "I don't know why sometimes I get frightened" may have echoed earlier Split Enz material lyrically, but Neil's catchy chorus on 'I Got You' screamed out potential hit. David Tickle, flown in during mid-October to capture the new material, sensed this, and astutely kept this and the other numbers direct and to the point. The songs went over well on Split Enz's year end Australian tour, and for once the band was thrilled at the final recorded sound. They kissed the Seventies adieu in fine spirits.

MUSHROOM RECORDS released both new album, 'True Colours', and single 'I Got You' simultane-ously in Australia on January 21, 1980. Both the sound and look of the album grabbed attention immediately. With Phil Judd out of the picture, Noel Crombie remained as resident graphic artist/fashion designer. His modernistic cover art and graphics and novel idea of having the album cover available in different colour combinations proved winners, as did his video clip for 'I Got You'.

In this pre-MTV era, music videos were a fledgling form, but the genre was off to a strong start in Australasia. By today's slick standards, the 'I Got You video is amateurish and cheap-looking. Back then, however, it heightened the buzz around the single and the album.

Musically, 'True Colours' hailed from another planet compared to the adventurous art-rock of early Split Enz. In *The New Trouser Press Record Guide*, critic Jon Young sums it up well. "They had become a bubbly pop band with sweet vocals, crackerjack melodies and hardly any strangeness. Fortunately, the material is genuinely first-rate."

Helped by extensive touring, 'I Got You' and 'True Colours' raced to the very top of charts in both New Zealand and Australia. In NZ, the album spent eight weeks at No. 1, selling over 30,000 copies over a chart run of 76 weeks! In Australia, it was No. 1 for an astonishing 10 weeks, and Split Enz took great pleasure in the fact that it kept Pink Floyd's 'The Wall' out of top spot, likely the only chart it didn't conquer.

"We're very proud of that," boasted Tim at the time. "It's good to keep the heavyweights out every now and then. It almost became normal – number one again? Album sales in Australia closed in on 200,000, a huge tally for a market of 16 million. 'I Got You' fared equally well, topping both charts. As a sign of genuine Enz-mania, reis-sues of 'Mental Notes' and 'Frenzy' both made the NZ charts in March 1980.

The pop-friendly nature of 'True Colours' won them teenage fans, and the girls were soon singling out Neil Finn as prime lust object. Neil was still shacked up in Melbourne, sharing a house with Sharon, Noel Crombie and Swinger

• Neil and Tim Finn, Split Enz c. 1980

Buster Stiggs. Tim remained in Sydney, but all involved knew they'd soon have to travel north of the Equator again.

New star status at home was fine, but they couldn't allow the years of struggle in London to be wasted entirely. Michael Gudinski's friendship with A&M head Jerry Moss helped nail down Split Enz's record deal with A&M Records in May 1980, by which time the band was being managed by another Gudinski associate, Nathan Brenner. A&M pledged a big push on 'True Colours' when it was released in August, and even pressed laser-etched graphics right onto the vinyl, allegedly a first for any album.

In mid 1980 it was still common for bands to release an album a year and Split Enz were back in Melbourne during the summer recording 11 songs for the next album with David Tickle. This was followed by American press and promotion and British dates to support 'True Colours'. Both Finns stressed Split Enz was a much different band than in the Chrysalis era. "The past is irrelevant now," claimed Neil at the time. "Split Enz is now just simpler and more effective." Tim

sounded almost apologetic about their previous visual excess. "How can you sing out a love song when you look like a parrot?" he asked in self-mockery. To David Fricke of *Rolling Stone*, he moaned, "I hate the word weirdo, I hate zany, I hate wacky." That past, however, has often returned to haunt them, with cynical English critics ever quick to dish out the ridicule.

Things in Britain were looking up, as 'I Got You' scored airplay and charted. Mike Chunn singles out September 27, 1980 as 'a crowning achievement' of Split Enz's career. That's when 'I Got You' entered the Top 20 (at 19), they were on *Top Of The Pops* (estimated audience, 11 million), and they performed a sold-out show at the Hammersmith Odeon.

'I Got You' peaked at No. 10, but by then Split Enz were in the US, where the single had reached No. 40 on the all-important *Billboard* chart. When it stalled there, tempers flared. In Chunn's account, Nathan Brenner angrily accused A&M of dropping the ball by not pushing it enough. He wanted Mushroom to dish out extra money for independent promotion that would help get the song playlisted on more pop radio stations. This scenario is standard music business practise in the US, but one that often has shady, corrupt connotations. "You pay an independent promoter and they basically control stations," Neil told *Rip It Up* in 1987. "They have good relations with the stations, maybe as a result of shoving coke up radio programmers' noses." This practise was later to have a strong effect on Crowded House's career as well, but at the time Brenner's outburst just served to alienate A&M.

Things fared better north of the US border where Canadian music fans have a tradition of embracing British and Australasian bands before they catch on in America. Acts ranging from Genesis to Supertramp through to Midnight Oil can testify to that, and 'True Colours' found a very happy home there. Their first-ever dates in Canada, in October 1980, coincided with 'I Got You' reaching the Top 10 and the album closing in on platinum (100,000) sales. The national press couldn't find enough superlatives to describe 'True Colours'. "If XTC is the Pink Floyd of the new wave, Split Enz is its Beatles," gushed the *Edmonton Journal*.

Toronto actress/singer Anya Varda remembers their visit there well. "I was working at [chic bar] The Fiesta then, and the band ended up there after the show. I remember I was sitting in the corner by myself. I got up at one stage, and when I came back I saw Neil sitting in my chair. I said, 'OK, you've got two choices. You're either moving or I'm sitting in your lap. Which would you prefer?' I ended up on his lap, and we just sort of dated after that." Their paths would cross later on Split Enz and Crowded House visits to Toronto.

While the rest of the world was focusing on 'True Colours', Split Enz had another album ready to roll, and their new single 'One Step Ahead' was already out and selling strongly in Australasia.

In January 1981, Tim Finn took time out to marry long-time girlfriend Liz Malam in Hamilton, now hometown to Dick and Mary Finn. Next came another Split Enz line-up change. After an unprecedented period of internal stability, drummer Mal Green was edged out, amidst some acrimony. Writer John Dix reports that... "He'd been booted out at the behest of Tim Finn, who had decided the band needed to pursue a different

musical direction. Green departed Australia mumbling nasty words to the media." Percussionist Noel Crombie was deemed capable of filling his seat. The personnel was now down to five.

Neil Finn was monopolising Split Enz singles now. 'One Step Ahead' was his song, as was follow-up 'History Never Repeats', another Top Ten hit in both New Zealand and Australia. Coincidentally, top slot was then taken by Phil Judd's band The Swingers,' whose 'Counting The Beat', a gloriously infectious rocker, has become a Kiwi pop classic.

It is difficult not to assume that Tim Finn must have envied the contributions of his younger brother, especially as Tim was the senior partner in Split Enz. Neil had brought Split Enz the commercial success Tim had toiled so hard for so long to achieve. In public, at least, he was being diplomatic about it. In a joint interview with Toronto music TV show *The New Music* around this time, he berated Neil in joking fashion. "I didn't know you'd write all the bloody hits though, did I? I wouldn't have let the bastard in if I'd known that!" he said.

Split Enz's triumphs of 1980 were recognised at Australian music industry awards the ARIAs in March, with 'I Got You' predictably grabbing Best Single honours. On April 1 the much-anticipated new Split Enz album, 'Waiata', appeared. The title is a Maori word which translates "celebratory song". The nationalistic Australians, however, insisted on 'Corroboree', an equivalent Aboriginal phrase. "There is a celebratory aspect to Split Enz because we have survived through thick and thin and there is that ecstasy of being a young band whenever we play together," was Tim's explanation.

'Waiata' went straight to No. 1 in New Zealand, accompanied by the now standard successful tour. On US dates, however, Nathan Brenner kept alienating A&M with constant complaints, as well as his own charges. Mike Chunn describes a water pistol fight that turned ugly, with the usually placid Eddie Rayner punching his manager out. 'Waiata' stalled at a disappointing No. 50 on *Billboard*, while during the Britain tour that followed concert attendances of 2,500 to 3,000 per night weren't matched by any chart success at all.

Better treatment awaited in Canada, where 'Waiata' reached gold status with sales of over 50,000. "Special guest" status on a Tom Petty tour saw them play large venues of 10,000 and upwards, and drew 3,000 to their own shows there.

Their Toronto stop was again memorable. "We fell in love with it, a very classy, stylish city," Tim told Canadian magazine *Music Express*. The Finns had every reason to enjoy Toronto. This visit coincided with Anya Varda's birthday party at the Fiesta, and saw some other fascinating encounters. Toronto music journalist Angela Baldassarre had just interviewed Ralf Hutter and Florian Schneider from pioneering German synth-rockers Kraftwerk and she brought them along to the party. "When I introduced Neil and Tim to Florian, they seemed genuinely impressed, even awed," recalls Angela. "Florian, though, had never heard of Split Enz, and asked me what kind of music they played right in front of them. Neil and Tim were visibly mortified!" Champagne with Angela and Florian back at the luxurious King Edward Hotel later cheered Neil.

En route back to Australia, Neil made a detour to Wellington to accept a special award from the Minister Of Broadcasting for Split Enz's contributions to New Zealand music. Those *New Faces* judges who'd slapped them down eight years earlier must have been red-faced.

Tim's joy was tempered by personal problems. His marriage had quickly disintegrated and Chunn later painted a rather lurid picture of a philandering Tim Finn on that North American tour. "For the first time in his life he was anybody's, drowning his shaky foundations under a sea of flesh," he wrote. Officially, he was 'in a state of acute clinical anxiety bordering on a nervous breakdown'. Neil helped him through the crisis, but Tim was to suffer other such bleak periods in the years ahead. In 1995, he courageously appeared in an Australian TV documentary *Brainstorm*, explaining his states of depression.

Tim was still willing to step back on the treadmill. Songwriting proved fine therapy, and Split Enz began looking ahead to their next album. They recruited Hugh Padgham, who'd worked with The Police and Genesis, to produce and pledged a less bubbly pop sound. Entering a Sydney studio in November 1981, they found everything clicked. Excitement and creative spontaneity prevailed, all members were fully integrated into the process, and the result was an album viewed by many as Split Enz's – certainly Tim Finn's – finest achievement.

Neil Finn did contribute and Eddie Rayner brought in his now customary instrumental track ('Pioneer'), but a trio of Tim's songs gave 'Time And Tide' its heart and soul. He has never been afraid to use aspects of his own life or his emotional state as raw material for songs, and these semi-autobiographical numbers were simultaneously cathartic and honest.

A catchy groove propelled 'Dirty Creature', which can be interpreted as Tim railing against his internal demons, but even more explicit are the lyrics of 'Haul Away', simply a story of Tim Finn's extraordinary life voyage framed in the style of a sea-shanty. It was an audacious experiment that worked beautifully. A similar sensibility launched the third triumph, the jaunty 'Six Months In A Leaky Boat', which, with its lilting refrain, can easily be viewed as a metaphor for the challenges that Split Enz had faced and overcome.

Tim's former songwriting hero Phil Judd was to tell him it was the best song he'd ever written and Tim conceded that 'the lyrics on this album are far more revealing than any past albums'.

The release date for 'Time And Tide' was set for April 13, 1982, with 'Dirty Creature' appearing as the first single a month earlier. A more significant date for Neil Finn was February 13, the day he married Sharon Johnson in Melbourne suburb Glen Iris. A gruellingly hot day took its toll on mom Mary Finn – the whole clan had flown over from New Zealand – with Mike Chunn reporting, "She almost collapsed from heat exhaustion but the sing-song hooley back at Neil's house allayed her distressed physical condition." Another near-casualty was the happy groom – bubbly and beer on an empty stomach necessitated a cessation of frivolities while he rested for while.

On its release, 'Time And Tide' went straight to No. 1 in New Zealand, while 'Dirty Creature' was a smash hit in Australasia and Canada. International reviews of the album were generally positive, so Split Enz left for North America at the start of May, 1982, with high hopes. The scenario, however, could have been predicted. Without a

• Tim Finn 'Split Enz
Sweetwaters Festival, 1980

charting single in the US, they could draw well only in Los Angeles with 4,000 attending their Palladium show and in New York where Duran Duran opened for them.

Canada was a whole different kettle of salmon. With 'Time & Tide' already staring at platinum, an 18 city, 19 date cross-country tour was booked, May 12 to June 6. This was in arenas – 8,000 showed in Edmonton – and large concert halls and confirmed Split Enz were in the top league of rock acts there. Canadian radio was more open than its American counterpart, A&M Canada was totally committed to the band, the press were unanimously supportive – a perfect marriage.

Split Enz's show at Massey Hall, Toronto, featured a band at the peak of its creative powers. The stage set reflected the nautical theme of many of the new songs, the earlier hits were interspersed seamlessly with the new material, Tim's showmanship and Neil's musicality neatly complemented each other, and the crowd was both attentive and enthusiastic. A surprise club gig at the Horseshoe Tavern the next night saw British guitar hero Mick Ronson sit in, playing a soaring solo on Tim's vocal tour-de-force, 'I Hope I Never'. Tim and Neil echoed their early years of Te Awamutu parties and Sacred Heart performances by offering encore renditions of calypso classic 'Jamaica Farewell' and Bee Gees hit 'To Love Somebody'.

The band's triumphs in the Great White North were recorded in a cover story in the fifth anniversary issue of New Zealand music magazine *Rip It Up*. In a rare interview, the usually publicity-shy Eddie Rayner interestingly admitted that 'Time And Tide' marked "the first time I've really got something out of our lyrics, and Tim is certainly

feeling prouder of them now".

The screaming teen portion of their audience was causing Rayner a little concern. "We do see all the young girls getting hysterical and a few of them fainting. Perhaps we appear as father figures to them. I feel that old, but Neil does look very young and cute. Unfortunately it does put off older people who I'd feel more comfortable with." A similar situation was to recur with Crowded House five years later.

In the midst of this Canadian tour, fate in the form of the Falklands War intruded on Split Enz's career in bizarre fashion. 'Six Months In A Leaky Boat' was receiving promising airplay in Britain, especially on London's Capital Radio, but when boats on both sides starting going down in the South Atlantic, the title of the song was deemed to be temporarily inappropriate, and the song was pulled. A publicist worth their salt would have whipped up a storm of publicity around the ban, but instead single and album sank without so much as a splash. 'Six Months' fared better elsewhere, hitting the Top 10 in Australasia and Canada.

The end of 1982 marked the 10th anniversary of Split Enz, however, so a couple of major New Zealand dates were arranged to celebrate this milestone. A compilation album, 'Enz Of An Era', was released in time for the Christmas selling season, and it quickly racked up a healthy 30,000 sales, hitting the top of the charts.

On January 30, 1983 came Sweetwaters, the big outdoor festival they'd played before. Some 35,000 attended and there were hints that it might produce a reunion of former Split Enz band members, but it wasn't to be. A disappointed John Dix called the concert "a bit of a fizzer... The only guests to appear were Mike Chunn, Paul Crowther and Rob Gillies. Despite rumours akin to the Second Coming, Phil Judd did not perform." One peak moment occurred during 'Haul Away', when a spotlight caught proud parents Dick and Mary Finn watching from the side of the stage. It had been quite a decade for them as well.

Naturally, it was an emotional concert for Mike Chunn, too. "For a few brief minutes I was able to share the musical vision that 10 years before I had imagined might happen," he said.

IN HINDSIGHT, the 10th Anniversary Concert was the climax of the chequered career of Split Enz. They'd survived through all manner of hardships and put downs, they'd even put New Zealand on the map as far as rock fans were concerned, but despite their Australasian success, fatigue and frustration had begun to sink in. Success in Britain and the US seemed an impossible dream and as they packed their guitars, drums and less conventional instruments away after the Sweetwater show, they were all contemplating a good long break for Split Enz. Tim Finn was already accumulating material he didn't see as fitting the band format.

He had told *Rip It Up* in May: "I'd like to be idle for a couple of years, just to see what it's like," but also pledged that... "I'm pretty determined that Split Enz carry on for at least another 10 years." Neither scenario was to transpire.

Once back in Melbourne, the members of Split Enz agreed to take a six months break. That meant outside recording activities for some. Neil Finn recorded some tracks for Karen Ansell, a project that brought him into contact with Nicholas Seymour, then bassist in her band Bang. Noel Crombie released a single, a cover of the novelty song 'My Voice Keeps Changing On Me', and Eddie Rayner worked with veteran Australian rocker Russell Morris.

More significant was Tim's solo excursion, appropriately entitled 'Escapade'. There are differing accounts of the effect this move had on the band. John Dix wrote that... "Some of the Enz members certainly weren't happy. Schedules had been rearranged as a result of the solo project. There were mutterings. Rumours abounded of divisions within the band, but no-one was saying anything publicly."

Tim got the green light from Mushroom to make a solo record in February 1983 and he had some 35 songs from which to choose. One, 'Fraction Too Much Friction', dated back to 1979 but had never quite fitted into the Split Enz sound. It was to be the album's smash hit.

In March, Tim and Neil flew to New Zealand for the wedding of their sister Judy. With Sharon Finn now expecting the couple's first child, it was an eventful year for the Finn family. While in the country, Tim and Neil announced plans to set up an Enz Records label, under the umbrella of Polygram Records. They envisaged this assisting promising local bands, but it was not to have much impact.

To Mike Chunn, this step was just another sign of internal problems. "With solo albums, pet production projects, forming labels to sign Kiwi bands, and taking time off to retrieve some domestic normalcy, the Split Enz united sense of purpose was now well and truly weakened."

Tim's growing self-confidence was boosted further when 'Escapade' was released in June 1983. Thanks to 'Friction', the album soared to the top of both New Zealand and Australian charts, selling over 175,000 copies. Combined with the success of 'Time & Tide' and the Oz Top Five status of two covers of his songs (by Jimmy and The Boys and Jo Kennedy) the year before, Tim Finn was now on a roll.

'Escapade' certainly sounded different to any Split Enz album. Top session musicians and former Beach Boys/Joe Walsh drummer Ricky Fataar's co-production resulted in a slick pop-rock album that sounds more Los Angeles than Antipodean. Interestingly, 'Fraction Too Much Friction' and 'Escapade' both became huge hits in Holland, for some reason, establishing Tim as a real pop presence in that market. That'd pay dividends later for Crowded House.

Split Enz reconvened in July 1983. By then, band relationships were strained. Neil had been writing prolifically, but Tim's new songs for the band were unimpressive. More dangerously, Tim was now infatuated with the drumming of Ricky Fataar and invited him into the studio. Unsurprisingly, drummer Noel Crombie felt threatened, and Tim's suggestion that they use a drum machine didn't help matters either. In Mike Chunn's account, Neil Finn and Eddie Rayner went along with the idea, Nigel Griggs and Noel Crombie did not. Eventually, it would feature an unhappy hybrid of contributions from Fataar, Crombie and the machines.

This dilemma typified the lack of spark and unity in the studio, and even Tim recognised his songwriting contributions were below par. In the newsletter of Frenz Of The Enz, the now formidable Split Enz fan club, he tellingly reported, "The songs are shaping up well (Neil's anyway)". The fact that Tim was absent for much of the final mixing further indicated his heart was in something else – promoting his solo album, just released in America.

Anxieties on Neil Finn's part were at least temporarily dispelled on September 24, 1983, with the birth in Melbourne of his son Liam Mullane Finn. The birth had already inspired a new song for the album, the tender 'Our Day'.

In mid-November 1983, the new Split Enz album was released, bearing the curiously revealing title of 'Conflicting Emotions'. Coming after the triumph of 'Time & Tide', this was a disappointingly uneven record, though it sported a couple of gems in 'Strait Old Line' and 'Message To My Girl', its first two singles. 'Strait Old Line' fared just moderately well, and the album peaked on the NZ charts at No. 3. Compared to the previous three albums, however, it had to be rated a commercial disappointment.

Before the inevitable tour, Split Enz found a new drummer, one better suited to their more groove-oriented sound, and Noel Crombie returned to his former role as percussionist. Helping in the search was band friend Rob Hirst of Midnight Oil, one of the country's best rock drummers. He suggested Paul Hester. Paul had been drumming with promising funk-influenced band Deckchairs Overboard, who had released a mini-album and a couple of singles by this stage. They evolved from Melbourne outfit Cheks, Hester's first band of note. "Pop inclined with strong harmonies with a willingness to experiment beyond the normal rock structures" is how Deckchairs Overboard were described in *The Who's Who Of Australian Rock*. Such a tag might well have been appropriate for a later band to feature Paul Hester.

Hester was living in Sydney, so taking the job meant relocation to Melbourne. In all, around ten drummers were auditioned. One hopeful came offering coke, but was quickly shown the door. No typical rock'n'roll vices for these lads. According to Mike Chunn, Hester passed the test with his performance on 'Dirty Creature'. His sharp sense of humour also helped his case, and Tim Finn discovered with pleasure Paul's love of housework when the two began sharing a house in Melbourne.

Neil and Tim Finn soon learned Paul had a musical childhood similar to their Te Awamutu upbringing. Hester's free-spirited mother liked to play drums and would drag the pyjama-clad lad from his bed to pound the skins to entertain drunken party guests.

Paul Hester's début as a member of Split Enz came at a show in the Victoria country town of Ballarat. It attracted plenty of media attention, but not all favourable as it was hampered by nerves and muddy sound. The presentation of special discs celebrating career-sales of over a million records in Australia cheered the band though. The highlight of their January 1984 New Zealand tour was a show in Te Awamutu, held as part of the town's centenary celebration. This would always be seen as their hometown by Tim and Neil Finn, and they paid it tribute by performing 'Kia Kaha', based on Neil's schooldays there.

Prophetically, Neil told *Rip It Up* then that... "This is a crunch year for the band... We've been going for a long time and we need new challenges... I wonder if it would be good for me to do something else, to start something with my own stamp." The writing was on the wall now, in broad brush strokes.

• **Split Enz in 1984, left to right: Eddie Rayner, Neil Finn, Noel Crombie, Nigel Griggs, Paul Hester and Tim Finn.**

The album's second single, Neil's touching paean to Sharon, 'Message To My Girl', was released in January to moderate success. With gentle, uplifting verses that accelerate towards a melodic, sweeping chorus, it anticipates the sound of Crowded House and is a very far cry indeed from the quirky material that Split Enz had recorded for much of their career. The news from abroad wasn't good, though. A&M didn't see any commercial potential, and declined to release 'Conflicting Emotions' in the UK and the US (although Canada and Holland did release it), so touring there would have been pointless. Split Enz was now essentially an Australasian phenomenon only. More Australian dates kicked off in February, after which Tim headed to Sydney to begin work on another project that was to both change his life and hasten the end of Split Enz.

DUSAN MAKAVEJEV was a Yugoslavian film director, best known for the raunchy *Montenegro*. He was to set to shoot a new film, *The Coca Cola Kid,*, in Sydney, and it would star British actress Greta Scacchi and American Eric Roberts (*Star 80*, *Runaway Train*). Tim Finn was approached to compose the film's music as well as take a cameo role, and news that the gorgeous Scacchi would star set his pulse racing.

Pop star, actress and director met for an introductory dinner, and Tim impressed Scacchi and Makavejev with his conversational agility. Greta had initial reservations, however, later telling Mike Chunn that... "Tim had this terrible habit of staring at me. Gazing. At the end of the night I thought – no way. But the next night was different."

Finn could hardly be blamed for staring, transfixed, at this young beauty. Besides, he'd recently seen her in the film *Heat And Dust,* in which she'd excelled in the role of a free-spirited but unfaithful young wife of a Government official in India during the days of The Raj, so he already knew how she looked naked. Their affair soon sizzled, and the relationship was to dominate Tim's personal life for the rest of the Eighties. The romance was the only good thing to come out of *The Coca Cola Kid*. The movie ended up a failed attempt at a satire of the corporate world, and

• Actress Greta Scacchi

Greta was later to condemn it in the strongest terms, slagging off Eric Roberts as the most obnoxious actor with whom she'd ever worked.

This new passion placed Split Enz further down Tim's priority list. Still revelling in his new solo success, particularly after having been at times overshadowed by Neil's hits, a flood of industry awards further fed his ego. Then, on June 16, 1984, he told his comrades he was leaving Split Enz. Although this was no great bombshell to the band, who'd seen it coming for months, the news did make the front page of several New Zealand newspapers, coverage usually reserved for stories about local sporting heroes.

The other members of Split Enz had sufficient confidence in Neil's songwriting to want to forge ahead, and began thinking about a new album. According to John Dix: "Tim had become a pain in the arse. Now that he'd finally made the move, the others could all get back to being a close-knit group again."

Initially agreeable, Neil began having second thoughts after rehearsal sessions without Tim offered no musical breakthrough. The idea of a clean break and fresh start became gradually more appealing to Neil and three weeks after Tim's announcement, he told the others he would leave as well.

Clearly, this closed the curtain on Split Enz. The musical contributions of the remaining members had been valuable, but a Split Enz without the Finns would have been akin to a Ringo-led Beatles. On July 25, 1984, a press conference in Melbourne's Hilton Hotel made it official. As is standard at these affairs, a brave face was displayed. "It's as amicable a split as it can possibly be," said Neil. "There were a few tensions but nothing beyond those of a normal group."

As evidence, they decided to make one last album (without Tim) and head out on a final Australasian tour (with Tim), fittingly calling it the Enz With A Bang tour. The last record, 'See Ya

Round', was a mixture of older, never recorded songs (including 'Kia Kaha'), and new tunes, one of which, 'I Walk Away', was widely interpreted as Neil's farewell to Tim and Split Enz.

This was chosen as the LP's first single, and released in October to moderate success. 'See Ya Round', an Australasian colloquialism for "goodbye", followed in early November. Despite all the publicity surrounding the band's demise (or perhaps because of it), the farewell album didn't fare too well in Australia, making little chart noise. It reached No. 5 on the NZ charts, but only had a short chart run. Clearly, Split Enz's commercial punch was rapidly weakening.

Behind the scenes, however, legal punches were flying. The soured relationship between manager Nathan Brenner and record label head Michael Gudinski was now heading to the courts. The two had clashed back in 1980 over money for US radio promotion of 'I Got You', and the personal enmity between them now bubbled over. "Had Split Enz not folded, their support structure may well have suffocated them to death anyway," said Mike Chunn.

The band's parting with Brenner wasn't amicable. After this final tour, the manager claimed both his 15% of gross tour income as manager, plus a 15% share of net revenue as tour promoter, a figure deemed excessive by the group.

Split Enz's many friends flocked to their final Australian shows, and Tim and Neil were in good spirits – having Greta and Sharon along helped. A party after the final Melbourne show saw an emotional Neil Finn knock back the tequilas and vodkas in style. Not known for his capacity to drink alcohol, this took its toll, and it was in this advanced state of inebriation that he was approached by itinerant local bassist Nick Seymour, asking to be considered for a spot in Neil's band to be. Neil agreed, and Nick gratefully drove him home.

During their farewell New Zealand tour, the local press eagerly waxed philosophical about Split Enz's contribution to the local music scene. *Rip It Up*'s George Kay declared: "Few people would deny their time was up. The institution was in danger of losing its dignity." He called their Dunedin show... "Too pat, but there were moments of magic and they belonged mostly to Neil Finn, whose writing keeps improving. And don't forget we owe them. In the Seventies, when music was a music degree, Split Enz worked with the world's best and so helped destroy the Kiwi inferiority complex as regards the great Overseas myth. They made the grade and encouraged other bands to take their goods to supposedly superior markets. That's got to be appreciated."

Writer John Dix detected tension on these dates. "There were just little things you could feel, like Tim at soundcheck just staring offstage. In Wellington, he was staying at a different hotel. This is meant to be the final tour, all buddy buddy. From what I saw, that showed some problems they didn't want to address. On the other hand, Eddie Rayner, always the one to tell it like it is, told me he had a good time and wasn't aware of any problems. Maybe I read it wrong, but I wasn't the only one."

Four sold-out nights in Auckland's Logan Campbell Centre during the first week of December brought the final era of Split Enz to a close. In the audience for the final show, virtually by accident, was someone who would become a key player in the Crowded House story. Los Angeles entertainment lawyer Gary Stamler, arriving in Auckland on holiday that day, went along on a whim. In his view, "Neil was very much the front guy driving the band. Tim seemed to be walking through it."

Split Enz's last encore was 'Hard Act To Follow'. Neil Finn and Paul Hester were about to try.

5

the mullanes

Split Enz would resurface in various guises over the next decade, but now Neil Finn and Paul Hester had fresh dreams.

Neil's burning desire was to build a band from the ground floor up, with him as the principal architect. This reflected his perfectionism, rather than a gargantuan ego. He could clearly sense he was coming into his own as a songwriter and wanted a group format built around his writing and singing skills. If that meant at least a temporary demotion in status from the level Split Enz had achieved, so be it. Neil actually found that exciting.

"After 12 years I felt like starting a new band," he explained to MuchMusic VJ Erica Ehm in August, 1986. "Just starting a band is different for me. I never had to organise a rehearsal before. I was becoming a bit cocky, but now I carry a guitar all by myself! This is a real effort to redefine ourselves. With Split Enz, I inherited a whole set of values, but now I'm starting afresh. I'm unlearning everything."

Neil told *Rip It Up* that... "For a long time I'd been thinking about the fact I'd been in Split Enz since I was 19, and I've never played in another band barring two gigs as After Hours. I guess I'd formed my own reasons for wanting to call it a day. We're still very ambitious, particularly me as far as another band goes. There'll be plenty more heard from us." Prophetic words.

Finn and Hester's search for a bass player didn't take long. Nick Seymour, who'd confronted a tipsy Neil Finn backstage after Split Enz's final Melbourne gig, was first and last in line. Neil knew

Nick as a visible figure on the Melbourne scene, and in 1983 he'd produced a single for Bang, a band featuring Nick. Fronted by keyboardist/singer Karen Ansell, Bang, according to *The Who's Who Of Australian Rock*, played Grace Jones and Nile Rodgers-styled funk. Other Melbourne groups Nick played with in the early Seventies included The Romantics, The Glory Boys, Plays With Marionettes and Horla.

Seymour had much in common with Neil Finn. Both had older brothers who were very prominent Austral(as)ian singers. Mark Seymour was lead vocalist in Hunters & Collectors, a tough, musically adventurous Oz rock band that had begun to develop an international cult following. Like Neil, Nick grew up in a professional middle-class family in a rural area, Benalla, Victoria. His father Frank was a school principal, and the Seymour family was a highly musical one. Nick, Mark, sisters Hilary and Helen and their mother Paula comprised The Seymour Family Singers, an ensemble that performed Irish folk songs in country towns around their home state of Victoria. "We'd sing at weddings, things like that," Nick once explained. "We made the front cover of the *Victoria Times* and once entertained the Governor-General."

Art and music were the young Seymour's twin passions, and he indulged both simultaneously. He studied at art school for five years, specialising in printmaking. "I was turned off painting there," he explains. "Unfortunately I went to a school that was a bit more hobby-oriented, but I graduated from a school that was more serious a couple of years later." Throughout his studies, Nick kept improving his proficiency on bass. When he began playing with various Melbourne punk bands, teachers warned he couldn't be both a rocker and an artist. "I was always told I'd have to make a choice, but I was always happy to do both," he recalled. Nick's revenge on the doubters came when Crowded House's subsequent success aided his profile as an artist. "This has boosted my art career. I'm being offered exhibition space in some of the better galleries now. I might have struggled for years for these offers otherwise."

The design of Crowded House album covers, stage costumes and sets have, of course, now given Nick Seymour's work an international exposure the envy of his art-school peers. His employment as art designer and set decorator for Australian movies *Annie's Coming Out* and *The Leonski Incident* shows his talent has been widely recognised.

After that party pitch to a drunken Finn, Nick tried out with Neil and Paul the following week. "We were impressed with his enthusiasm and his style of bass playing," recalls Neil. "He was very much from a funk background, and I thought that'd be a good contrast. The tension created by different backgrounds can be really good." Not that Nick was given the final nod immediately. During the final Split Enz shows in Auckland at the start of December, Paul and Neil also auditioned former Suburban Reptiles/Swingers bassist 'Bones' (Dwayne) Hillman, but Nick won. In a curious twist of fate, Bones later joined Midnight Oil, the band whose drummer Rob Hirst, had recommended Hester for the Split Enz gig.

Seymour quickly fitted in, but he attracted some flak from Neil with a comment he made about Split Enz to Australian music journalist Lesley Sly. She has written for many major rock publications, including *Rolling Stone*, [and authored an analysis of the Australian music scene, *The Power And The Passion: A Guide To The Australian Music Industry*], and she interviewed Crowded House very early in their career..

"I didn't know how they were going to look or sound, so I asked if they were going to do anything theatrical like Split Enz," she says. "Nick said they would be [theatrical], but that it wouldn't be pretentious like Split Enz. Neil said, 'pretentious?!' He reacted really violently to it. Nick said, 'I didn't mean it in an offensive way.'

Neil says, 'Pretentious is pretty offensive in my book. What dictionary do you use?' or words to that effect. It was in good humour, but Neil was being very protective about Split Enz. He realises it gave him such a good start, growing up in a sheltered environment with his brother and friends."

Sydney guitarist Craig Hooper brought their initial complement up to four, the ideal figure as far as Neil was concerned. He was determined to avoid the top-heavy situation that had occurred from time to time with Split Enz. Hooper's resume included stints in major Australian bands The Reels, Do-Re-Mi, and The Church, but he wasn't destined to last.

The group's original moniker, The Mullanes, would be another casualty. Mullane was Neil Finn's middle name, and mother Mary's maiden name. Sentimental attachment aside, everyone soon realised it was a naff name for a pop band. Aside from conjuring up images of a bunch of Irish folkies, it could easily be twisted into negative incarnations, as Neil soon realised. "Nobody could say or spell it properly," he once said. "We'd get Mundanes, Dullanes, The Malaise. Any name that could be twisted like that had to go!"

As The Mullanes, however, they recorded a demo tape they hoped would land them an international record deal. The tape was shopped around in London, New York and Los Angeles. Amazingly, Neil's fledgling group were cold-

• **Nick, Paul and Neil, in uniform, 1987**

shouldered by every major Australian record label. Despite an impressive track record that included writing most of Split Enz's later hits, Neil Finn's commercial potential was ignored.

To Lesley Sly, this was a gross oversight. "Here's someone whose past includes writing big hit singles venturing out and no record company in Australia has enough faith," she said. "It wasn't that they put up offers that weren't acceptable, it was just that there weren't any. I think that's extraordinary! A bit like the people who passed on the Beatles."

Neil Finn maintains scoring a deal out of LA or London was his priority all along. "We wanted to get the album out everywhere at once," he said in 1986. "A lot of Australian bands have suffered over the years because of delayed releases. They should be going into the studio to record their next album, creatively, but they're stuck with touring an old album for six months. That can really destroy a band's flow." Such words proved prophetic.

Neil and Paul did much of the foreign sell job themselves, but managed to have fun along the way. A brief stay in London, during which they stayed with Melbourne pop peers Do-Re-Mi, also chasing foreign fame, proved fruitless, but enjoyable. "I showed Neil the finer points of drinking tea in the mother country," joked Paul Hester. Their stay also coincided with a Tim Finn solo show in London, and Neil naturally joined him onstage for a few songs. New York saw no bites, so it was on to Los Angeles, the cut-throat hub of the entertainment industry.

It was here in balmy California that Gary Stamler and Tom Whalley, two young Americans, got the ball rolling for The Mullanes. Whalley was an A&R man who had just left his job at Warner Bros to join Capitol who offered him a freer rein to sign fresh talent. His legal adviser was Gary Stamler, who had raved about Neil Finn back in January 1985, basing his opinion on Split Enz's final show in Auckland.

When Neil Finn, Paul Hester and Lars Sorenson (former Enz tour manager now acting as The Mullanes manager) reached LA, Whalley got a call. "They just phoned up labels naively thinking that's the way you get signed," recalls Stamler with a droll chuckle.

Whalley listened to their demo tape, and found himself in trouble. "The last thing I wanted to happen in my first week at Capitol was to fall in love with something. I wanted to get settled first," he recalled. "I kept playing it and loved it even more, but I sat on it for a while and played it for some people at the label. I got mixed reactions, so I told Neil I wanted to hear some more songs if possible. He sent another batch I just loved."

Whalley suggested they contact Stamler. "There's a friend of mine who told me in January you were the greatest thing he'd seen and I should sign you without listening to the tape," is how Gary summed up that conversation. Stamler met Neil and Paul, listened to the tapes, and made a good impression on the duo. "I found out later Paul was all excited because I represented Ringo Starr, his idol. Paul told me Neil was excited because I thought he was better than Tim!"

Gary Stamler still has that first tape, entitled simply "Finn/Hester". One song, 'That's What I Call Love', made it onto the Crowded House début, while 'Walking On The Spot' surfaced nearly a decade later on 'Together Alone'. The other two tracks were 'Walking On The Pier' and Paul's 'Girlfriend'. "That tape is worlds apart in style and approach from the first album. They were a very spirited and aggressive group then," says Gary. A third demo tape included 'Don't Dream It's Over', with the same lyrics and arrangement as the final version. Both Whalley and Stamler sensed its potential, but were less keen on the three Paul Hester songs on that tape.

Encouraged by Whalley and Stamler's enthusiasm and sensing a deal was imminent, The Mullanes decided to roadtest their line-up and Neil's new material in time-honoured Australian rock fashion, the pub tour. "We wanted to go out on the road and see if we were really a band or a figment of our imagination," Neil later explained to MTV. "We found out three-quarters of us was a band. The fourth was an individual, so we sacked him!," he adds with a touch of glee. Post-tour, Hooper rejoined Sydney rockers The Reels.

The June 1985 Mullanes tour down the Australian east coast saw the band put on the kind of fun performances that would become synonymous with Crowded House. A typical set consisted of a few Split Enz favourites, a rockin' cover of Led Zeppelin's 'Dancing Days', and some of the songs destined to appear on the début album. Strangely, though, the audiences were apathetic.

Tom Whalley and Gary Stamler made the long trip down under to catch some shows and hammer out a possible deal. "We were really horrified at the lack of interest and vibe," explains Stamler. "Given Split Enz, we thought this'd be a major thing, but the audiences were disinterested. This gave Tom some pause. And one major Australian publisher told Tom not to sign them under any circumstances because they were terrible!"

Whalley stuck with his instincts and pursued the deal. Signing an Austral(as)ian act directly to Capitol in LA, however, wasn't easy. "It was almost unprecedented at that point," says Stamler. "Only one other deal was structured like that, an Australian group called Dear Enemy [a Melbourne band who released just one album, 'Ransom Note', in 1984], and it hadn't worked out. [Capitol exec] Don Grierson kept pointing back at that, but we forced it through."

Signed in June 1985, the deal only included Nick Seymour at the last minute. "The original draft I have only listed Neil and Paul," says Gary Stamler. "They felt Nick would feel bad if he wasn't on there, so he only became an official part of the band on signing day."

Now all Whalley needed was a producer, but finding one didn't prove easy. According to Mitchell Froom, who eventually took the job... "Almost every highly-regarded producer in Los Angeles passed on it. They were getting kind of desperate." Whalley concurs. "The people I thought could make a great record with them didn't hear it, or they didn't have the time, or whatever excuse they gave me. I went through a lot of people."

Mitchell Froom was a young musician/composer from San Francisco just beginning a career in record production. A classically trained keyboardist (pipe organ and piano), he played with various Bay Area rock bands in his teens, but never quite found his niche. "All the stuff I was involved with 'till my late twenties was really miserable. I couldn't figure out how to put together all the things I'd learnt," he told New Zealand magazine *Rip It Up*. Ace producer and songwriter T-Bone Burnett (Elvis Costello, Bob Dylan) recognised Froom's talent as an organ player, and utilised it on albums by the likes of Peter Case, Marshall Crenshaw, Costello and the BoDeans.

Mitchell's own production career began with Boston roots rockers the Del Fuegos. His work caught the ear of Tom Whalley, and the glowing testimonial from that band and their manager further piqued Whalley's interest. So Froom found himself with the Mullanes tape, one that would change his life. "I just couldn't believe it," he says. "I thought, 'Here I am, a guy at the bottom end of the production scale and I get a tape like this. If I get famous, I'm going to get the most incredible tapes in the world!' Later on, of course, I rarely got demo tapes of that quality."

Froom's quick and insightful response to the music he heard won over Neil Finn, now based semi-permanently in LA. "As a songwriter, I appreciated the fact he was looking at the structure of the songs, tightening up any loose ends," said Neil. "He had definite ideas about the songs right from the start, and they were very impressive. We worked together for a few days before we even decided who we were going to use, but I was instinctively convinced Mitchell was the right guy."

As well as his dry sense of humour, Froom's deep knowledge of American roots music endeared himself to the band. "Meeting him, he'd explain things based on some of the influences he showed us. That was really worthwhile," explains Paul Hester. Such influences included the likes of Hank Williams and Booker T and The MGs, figures largely unfamiliar to Crowded House.

The newly consummated marriage between Mitchell and Crowded House was to be long and fruitful. A slight hitch was that former Enz producer David Tickle had been lined up for the project before Froom came along. Tickle was then offered the engineering role, but, says Gary Stamler... "His ego wouldn't allow it, and he backed out." A happy Tom Whalley was so confident he'd found the right producer he only visited their rehearsals and pre-production sessions once in three weeks.

This period saw Nick, Neil and Paul sharing

living quarters that were, as every Crowded House fan now knows, the inspiration for their new name, though an earlier "crowded house" was the Santa Monica townhouse of Gary Stamler. Prior to recording the first album, the lads stayed here, in a room above the kitchen. That experience was to be immortalised in the song 'World Where You Live' – "high above the kitchen and we're strangers here" – a number reportedly written by Neil Finn in that room. "It's about disorientation and living with your attorney," he said. "I wouldn't recommend it."

The 'Crowded House' that is now a music biz legend is in the Hollywood Hills and was rented by the trio while they recorded their first album together. Paul Hester laughingly termed it… "a pretty domestic set-up. It's enough getting to know each other in a band, but now we're living in this house together. Seeing Nick in the mornings, you have second thoughts!"

Hester was designated cook and bottle-washer – "There's nothing he likes more than a good tidy," laughs Neil – while Nick Seymour was designated social magnet. "We had a whole collection of people traipsing through the house," Neil told an Australian DJ. "I'd come back from the studio at midnight and find seven pyjama-clad types out by our Japanese garden with their gin bottles. Pretty wild stuff!"

Paul describes the mayhem with a hearty laugh. "Nick would be directing it like a mad movie. He's such a social animal. He just drags people in, while Neil and I wouldn't tend to do that as much. Nick forced us to be in these situations with these weird people. Four or five times out of ten, they'd backfire completely. It'd be like 'The Friend Who Wouldn't Leave'."

Tales of guests surfing down the stairs on card-board boxes and trays become a regular interview anecdote for Crowded House. Neil seems to have

been very tolerant of his comrade's gregariousness. "Nick will take a place on," he said. "He'll go out and find what's good and bad about it. He forced us to grasp certain aspects of LA, and it's good to meet real people there. It's very easy to just see the superficial elements."

According to Mitchell Froom, Capitol wanted Neil to record under his own name, but he was dedicated to the concept of a group. "We wanted a name with more pizazz," says Finn. "It had got to the point of going to the library to look for names. I came across 'Crowded House' one day, and as we thought about it, the implications seemed right."

Ironically, if you now go into certain public libraries looking for information on the band and punch up 'Crowded House' on the computerised index, you'll find some amusing derivations. Alongside *Rolling Stone* articles in the Boston Public Library's file, you'll find *Congressional Quarterly*'s piece headed "Crowded fields develop in three House races" – a reference to American election contests. *Crain's N.Y. Business*' entry on Crowded House refers to a shortage of hotel space in the Big Apple!

Other names considered by The Mullanes reportedly included Largest Living Things, Barbara Stanwyck's Chest and Krakatoa Chorus. "My recollection is that 'Crowded House' was the original name for the album," says Stamler. "But the clock was ticking, so out of desperation it was chosen as the name. No-one was very happy about it; it sounded awkward and weird."

Although Neil Finn was no stranger to The City Of Angels, having passed through many times with Split Enz, Hester and Seymour were LA virgins who took to the city like a kangaroo to boxing. That quintessential American sport, basketball, became a shared passion, they got used to the real-life

Hollywood soundtrack of helicopters and gunshots, and even got a kick out of the LA freeways. "We'd go to work each day by driving across this 10 lane highway, navigating out the back window... 'Yes, no, go now'," says Paul. "That's an exhilarating way to start the day, dicing with death."

Work each day meant the journey to Sunset Sound Factory, the LA studio Mitchell Froom continues to favour. Once ensconced there, producer and band found initially positive vibes strengthening. After David Tickle quit, finding a compatible engineer proved more difficult, but this turned out to be more blessing than curse. Neil estimates they went through six. "It was a saga we could have done without, but it actually helped us be more careful with the entire album as it went down," he told LA magazine *Music Connection*.

The two weeks plus pre-production paid off, for it enabled the band to lay down their rhythm tracks quickly. According to Neil, "That way you've got something solid to start with. We started off thinking we'd use quite a few different people to get a good amalgam of influences, but we ended up stripping it all down. We got rid of some of the backing vocals and guitars already there, and a lot of the decisions were based on what was the most *us*."

This was a band in the process of finding themselves, and Froom's temperament proved perfect. "We didn't know what we were doing then," says the producer now with refreshing candour. "We just worked on stuff. I've never been any kind of guru with the band. It's more about sitting around and everybody throwing out ideas to see what works. That generally happens with every record I work on. It's about not having an ego about the music, but rather following whatever sounds the best."

That meant sometimes radical changes to the songs Neil brought to the table: 'Something So Strong', for instance, which dated back to Split Enz days, but was never recorded. "That song was a ballad, and we turned it into a more up-tempo, pop/r&b kind of groove," explains Froom. His suggested changes earned him a songwriting credit, a nice bonus given the song's eventual success.

Neil agrees with Froom's 'we learned on the job' assessment. "Working with Mitchell, we all learnt together. If we'd had a producer who was immediately giving us a real stamp of his own, then we wouldn't have learnt a lot from our first album. If we'd had a hit with someone else, we wouldn't have known how we did it."

The phrase 'LA album' is often synonymous with slickly over-produced work created largely by the city's skilled but often soulless session players. Crowded House avoided that trap, even though some of Mitchell's muso mates were employed.

"One guy made what he thought was the ultimate compliment to us about one of the songs – 'Oh, this sounds really LA'. He wondered why our faces dropped," laughs Neil. "One of the good things about LA is having access to great musicianship, but I think we used it in a reasonably earthy way. We didn't slick anything out too much."

Another song to be revised was 'Now We're Getting Somewhere'. The original version had a Seymour-written bass riff in one verse, but Froom suggested the verse of another song with a similar swing feel would work better. As further insult, Hester and Seymour were excluded from the recording of that song. "We were trying to get an old-fashioned shuffle feel for it, and the three of us couldn't really do it with enough down-home conviction," says Neil. "Because we were in LA, the source, we got in [drummer] Jim Keltner, who used to play with everybody in the Seventies, and [bassist] Jerry Scheff, who used to play with Elvis Presley."

These shuffle demons decreed the song 'a three beer shuffle'. Sure enough, they downed three beers and did three takes, the last one the keeper. Froom knew the duo slowed up a bit after three takes!

They put on a brave face, but Gary Stamler recalls this incident as devastating to Nick Seymour and Paul Hester. "When Mitchell replaced them on that track, they were very down. Paul was on a thin thread throughout that recording process – Neil had come close to sacking him a couple of times. When they were brought back into the proceedings, it was to record 'Don't Dream It's Over'. Because they'd seen their own demise the day before, they added a much more melancholy feel to it."

Other album guests included the Heart Attack Horns, who added some punch to 'Mean To Me' which was chosen for the all important track one side one. "They're pretty well-known around town, but tend to do the more dirty stuff," explains Neil. "Not like The Phoenix Horns, who do the very crisp, clean brass stabs on Phil Collins records. They were great. Came in with no music, worked it out by ear, but were just very loose and had a great time."

Having fun in the studio is one thing, commercial imperatives are another. Tom Whalley was making sure band and producer were aware of them, and they discussed potential singles as the recording was going on. 'We discussed 'Something So Strong', 'World Where You Live', 'Mean To Me' and 'Don't Dream It's Over'," says Whalley. "We were obviously looking for an up tempo record to start as the single, because ballads take longer and radio doesn't play ballads from new acts, all that sort of stuff."

The whole scenario became pressure-packed as the end of recording neared. "We were so exhausted at that time," confides Mitchell Froom.

"Very few people know this, but that whole record was mixed slow," explains Froom. "It was recorded faster than it was mixed! I can hear that a lot in Neil's voice sometimes. It sounds funny on some songs, but it probably really helped 'Don't Dream It's Over'. It relaxed it a bit more. We really were just flying by the seat of our pants, but when you're just learning to do something, it's often the best." That slow speed, plus the depressed mood of Paul and Nick gave the song a different feel than the demo version. "We probably backed into a hit song by accident," reflects Stamler.

It was now time to hand the finished product over to the label. Initial reaction in the Capitol Tower wasn't totally positive, and even Crowded House's key supporter there, Tom Whalley, had a few misgivings about the sound of the record. "Yes, there was a time when the record was complete when I thought there were things Mitchell did to it that were surprising to me," he said. "It was different from what I heard on the demos and what I expected. Mitchell put a touch in there which was more 'American' than I expected. But the more I listened to it the more I realised how well-produced the record was."

6

now we're getting somewhere

So just what did an eagerly anticipatory Capitol Records receive? With the benefit of hindsight, Crowded House delivered one of the strongest début albums of the Eighties. It heralded the arrival of a fresh, exciting talent into a stale, oft sterile music scene, but was not a complete musical triumph. It contained some classic pop songs, but should not be viewed as a classic in itself.

Even Mitchell Froom now admits he has a hard time listening to the record that kick-started his production career. "Aesthetically, I have a lot of problems with it. That first record has so many studio effects, so much reverb. I can hardly hear the music in there, but that's what some people like about that record!"

Considering the magnitude of Neil Finn's songwriting talent, the album could have been even better. Some potentially strong numbers are sabotaged by annoying arrangements or fussy production. Slightly strained vocals and overwrought production mar 'Love You 'Til The Day I Die', the archaic keyboard sounds on 'Hole In The River' irritate, and last track, 'That's What I Call Love', is a mediocre pop/funk romp that should have remained buried in the Crowded House basement.

These glitches aside, the album served notice that the compositional skills first glimpsed in Neil Finn's songs for Split Enz were now entering full bloom. Within the three minute pop song, he was prepared to tackle such diverse themes as suicide ('Hole In The River'), the redemptive power of love

('Something So Strong'), and the need for personal change ('I Walk Away', often viewed as his farewell ode to Split Enz and reprised from the final Split Enz album 'See Ya Round').

'Crowded House' also represented the sound of a band still forging its own identity. The delightful melodicism of Neil's big-hearted vocals was readily apparent and the soaring vocal harmonies that would become a band trademark were already present. The empathy between bassist Nick Seymour and drummer Paul Hester was still developing and their contributions weren't always well-served. As manager Gary Stamler observed, "This was very much a Neil Finn solo record. Basically, Nick and Paul were told what to play."

There was no lack of available material from which to select. Tom Whalley reports that... "Neil had 30 songs to choose from. We could have done a double album." Given the strength of 'Can't Carry On', later recorded in Melbourne by Neil and Eddie Rayner, and added as a bonus track to later pressings, it seems likely the album could have been near-flawless with a more judicious song selection.

Such weaknesses are easy to forgive in a work that offered such shining pop gems as 'Don't Dream It's Over', 'Something So Strong', 'World Where You Live' and 'Now We're Getting Somewhere'. Although 'Don't Dream It's Over' and 'Something So Strong' became major hits and American radio staples (they've each clocked over a million plays there) they're great songs regardless. Unusually, they became hits because their quality simply could not be ignored – an occurrence unfortunately all too rare in America.

Here, everything worked. Neil's warmly sincere vocals were to the fore, the harmonies were in place, the instrumentation clean, the hooks irresistible, and the lyrics simultaneously intelligent and accessible. How could these songs, this album, possibly fail? Quite easily, it began to seem.

When Capitol Records released 'Crowded House' in July 1986, any misgivings they had about the album's production were kept hidden. "When the record was delivered, there was a lot of excitement in the company," recalls Tom Whalley. "Although, because it was not a typical record, I'm not sure people quite knew what to do with it at first."

Gary Stamler assumed the management of Crowded House in July 1986, just as the début album was about to be released. Sydney-based New Zealander Grant Thomas, who had worked with Neil and Paul Hester on the final Split Enz tour in 1984, was hired to work the first album in Australasia. As time went by Thomas would seek greater involvement and in time he became their co-manager.

Based in LA, Stamler had the closest relationship with the band's American label, Capitol, while Thomas would have greater contact with the band. Initially, Stamler found some resistance towards Crowded House at the Capitol Tower. "They had a feeling there was no single, and were very confused about how to promote and market the band," he says. "Below the top level, however, we quickly had a fair complement of people who felt strongly about the band but were somewhat paralysed with the implementation of how the record would reach the marketplace." Stamler praises then Capitol President Don Zimmerman for being particularly supportive.

Heinz Henn, then Director of International at EMI, who responsible for marketing and promoting US signed artists in Europe, supports claims that the label failed to support Crowded House. "I should say most of the American company was not initially into it, except the A&R department," he says. "Outside of that, there wasn't a lot of immediate belief in the artist."

They didn't launch it in a flurry of hype, but Capitol were hopeful that the good reputation Split Enz still enjoyed within music industry and rock critic circles would give the album a head start on the other new releases fighting for radio airplay and media attention. Early reviews were generally positive. US music trade bible *Billboard* picked it as 'New And Noteworthy', cautioning that "The advertising and packaging campaign does the trio a disservice by suggesting they're Stray Cat clones," a reference to Nick Seymour's surreal cover portrait which inadvertently confused some punters with its pseudo-rockabilly feel. But *Billboard* added: "Crowded House is an outstanding band with its own sound bred of pop and charged with vigour." To *Newsweek* "Crowded House delivers dreamy, enjoyable pop – a refreshing album." *Spin* and *Musician* magazines weighed in with raves too.

• Neil Finn

Some major publications were late in taking notice. *Rolling Stone* was slow off the mark, not reviewing it until February, 1987. Awarding it three stars, critic Chris Willman termed the album, "A rootsy and infectious batch of songs. Rarely has any modern music sounded so cheerful and so creepy as some of the offcenter love songs that pop out of the red head of Neil Finn.

Almost all of the album is brash and overtly saleable. It's hard to follow radioland's not finding room for Crowded House among its many mansions." Of course, by the time this appeared, radio had done just that.

Rolling Stone was to hail it as 'A Top Album Of 1987', raving that... "It was as packed with infectious hooks, bubbly pop'n roll arrangements and offbeat messages of love as anything since the heyday of Split Enz."

Crowded House appeared on many 'Best Of 86' lists, but Neil Finn responded sarcastically. "Critic's polls and the prizes we got for making them are fantastic," he joked to Canadian magazine *Music Express*. "We're set up in houses, boats and cars. These critics send us money, did you know that?"

The album didn't make Robert Christgau's Best Of list. The influential *Village Voice* critic and self-appointed Dean of American rock criticism wrote the album off as "an overrated record by a New Zealander from El Lay". In his *Record Guide –The 'Eighties*, he wrote: "Hooks you can buy anywhere these days, and for directness you might as well apply straight to Bruce Hornsby. Beyond the occasional hint of guitar anarchy, this is product for sure." It scored a C on his subjective ratings system.

From his Split Enz experiences, Neil Finn was quite cognisant of the obstacles ahead. "It is frustrating to see that the American industry is a hard place for new things to happen," he told LA music magazine *BAM*. "The kids in America are denied a lot of great music through the way the corporate structure is set up. But it's a challenge too in some degree if you can break through that with a good album; it's a measure of your worth I guess."

One hurdle that Crowded House faced was the structure of radio in North America. It comprises highly regimented formats referred to in acronyms or euphemisms – AOR is Album Oriented Radio, CHR is Contemporary Hit Radio, Urban is black music. Then there's Rock, Modern Rock, Classic Rock, Country, Jazz, Adult Contemporary (AC), Top 40, a seemingly endless list of pointless pigeon-holes into which music is routinely categorised by self-styled arbiters of taste, many of whom have vested interests in the success of certain records. To release a record

which doesn't fit into one of these pigeon-holes just confuses everyone – insofar as it demands greater critical perception than the arbiters are capable of – and is likely to be quietly ignored.

Rather than increase opportunities for a new artist with a new record, this segregation severely limits opportunities, especially for bands with eclectic ambitions. It has often led to a ridiculous situation whereby an act generally regarded as 'rock' will be ignored if they record a song out of genre. Crowded House would later come up against precisely this problem.

The days of disc jockeys playing a new song because they like it are long gone. Programming consultants eyeing demographics and advertising revenue rule the roost, and risk-taking is discouraged. Far better to playlist the new Billy Joel or Bryan Adams single than take a chance on an obscure new band from Australasia.

Radio play remained essential if 'Crowded House' was to avoid a quick dive into the bargain bins. This, after all, was a pop band. They couldn't claim credibility through being ignored by radio the way a death metal group could. One way or format or another, American radio had to be cracked, no doubt about it. As Stamler explained, "This was a radio promotion-based era. You either got a song on the radio and it sold or you didn't know what to do."

Tom Whalley knew the minefield ahead. "Our fear was that we'd go out in a normal way and try to get it on radio, and if we didn't catch a hit that the record would be over. We were trying to avoid that at all costs."

Capitol's first strategy was to service AOR stations with up-tempo pop-rocker 'World Where You Live' in May, simultaneously releasing a three-track EP so anyone hearing the lead track on the radio had something to purchase. The song fell on deaf ears at AOR, which meant Weapon No. 2 had to be brought out from the Crowded House armoury. Conventional wisdom – not the most accurate phrase when considering the workings of the American music biz – decreed another up tempo track should be released, but Whalley and his Capitol comrades bucked the norm.

"Everybody kept pointing to 'Don't Dream It's Over'," said Whalley. "We finally said, 'Instead of playing this game – trying to figure out what up tempo song is the best one to lead with – let's go with what we believe is a hit record'." To manager Stamler, 'Don't Dream It's Over' was seen by some as a retro throwback in production style and instrumentation. There were even comments that having a B3 [organ] on it meant it wasn't modern enough to get played. This was, after all, the heyday of the programmed synthesiser-heavy sound.

On August 27, 1986, 'Don't Dream It's Over' was released in the US. It would be a critical, career-making single for Crowded House, and it must have seemed like do-or-die time for Whalley. His first signing to Capitol was in very real danger of stiffing. Initial response was lukewarm and there were other factors which seemed to be conspiring against it. The first was that the fiercely competitive Christmas season, the time when superstars released new product, was looming. Secondly, this was also the year when major US record labels stopped using independent record promoters.

Traditionally, these promoters were paid, often exorbitantly, by the record companies to 'plug' or promote singles to radio, a situation at the heart of the payola or 'pay to play' scandals that have often plagued the US record industry. An NBC-TV expose and Senate committee investigation fuelled the controversy, and the labels officially severed ties with the so-called 'indie' record promoters, at least temporarily.

To Crowded House's enterprising new manager Gary Stamler, however, this offered a window of opportunity which he threw wide open, arguably saving the début album, maybe even the band. "I watched that first TV news report on independent promotion and it got my mind spinning," he said. "These promoters were now out of work and in desperate need of a calling card. It was an excellent opportunity."

The resulting scenario was a cloak and dagger affair full of subterfuge and intrigue. Stamler made a desperate, last-ditch attempt to, in his words, "blow on very very dim embers. By the fall of 1986 it was pretty clear the record company had pulled the plug on the record. Back in July, things had got so bad between the band and the label that they wouldn't pay for anyone other than Neil alone to come out to more promotion conferences."

Stamler and Tom Whalley struggled to keep things together. "It had got so bad we were trying to close a publishing deal to give us some seed money to keep things going," recalls Gary. "The publisher withdrew the offer, saying the record was dead and that the label actually told them not to offer Neil money! Things couldn't have got worse."

With nothing to lose, Stamler approached Capitol's Head of Promotion with a daring idea. "I offered my services outside the label to muster an effort in this vacuum with independent promotion. I thought we could enlist these people at a fraction of their earlier cost to help push 'Don't Dream It's Over'."

Sure enough, Stamler snagged these guys at a modest fee, and his Capitol ally kept the deal quiet. "He prided himself on the fact that no-one else at the label thought any independent was working the record." The executive's job would have been in jeopardy, as EMI's head Bhaskar Menon had emphatically ordered his staff not to have any dealings with the indies.

The Capitol promotions head was so paranoid he told Stamler to use payphones when contacting the indies from the ski resort at which he was holidaying, so... 'It didn't look like I had more money than the small amount I was paying them. He was that nervous about things falling apart!"

To further stack the odds in favour of the single, Stamler was pushing it in the traditionally quiet post-Christmas period, but his gamble paid off as stations began playing the single and the in-the-dark Capitol began to get excited. The label's in-house radio promotions department had been working the record themselves and, as Stamler explains: "I didn't feel a need to rain on anyone's parade. I felt it was better to let the label take pride in thinking they were part of something that just happened organically. The secret remained with me and the band and a couple of people at the label only for the longest time."

After a slow start, there was a stirring of interest from some regional stations (including Adult Contemporary or soft pop broadcasters) hopes raised. Helping the band now was the goodwill generated by their own extensive and novel promotion. Rather than place their fate totally in the hands of the label, indie promoters, and radio, Crowded House had pressed their case by getting in the faces of key music industry types, literally.

A conventional North American tour is a huge undertaking financially, and the slow start to the album would likely have dissuaded Capitol Records from offering enough tour support. Instead, the band travelled to key North American cities to perform for/schmooze with the music business. A stripped down, semi-acoustic set at an album launch party in Melbourne had been incredibly well-received, and the seeds were sown. "It really came about off the cuff," explained Neil. "You don't usually play at those things, but now we intend to do it as much as possible. It's a good way to communicate the real character of the band. Meeting press and record retailers, you just talk about what you do. The best way of communicating yourself is to play, and that's much more satisfying for us too."

Clearly, the cost factor applied too, as Neil acknowledged. "It was a way Capitol Records thought they could get us over here before financially we could afford to tour properly. This is a way of introducing ourselves without roadies!"

A slightly different explanation is offered by Heinz Henn. "It was my [London] office that came up with that original idea, and it really happened by accident," he claims. "In Nashville in August 1986, we had an international conference of product and marketing managers from all over the world. We had Neil come in at night, it was after midnight. All unplanned, but we put about six tables together in the middle of the hotel. We put a chair on top, and Neil got out his guitar and played Beatles songs for hours. He had the whole place singing along – one of those magical moments. Out of this little surprise came the idea of taking that principle to introduce the band to different territories. We asked Neil if he could do that with the band, and he said, 'absolutely'."

• Crowded House, Town & Country Club, London, 1988

A gruelling, month-long, 25-city publicity tour of Europe further honed Crowded House's performance and chat skills. "We had them play radio and TV stations, record stores, even the canteen at the record label," recalls Henn. "We schlepped them everywhere. The first gig we ever did with Crowded House in London was at Tower Records in Piccadilly Circus. Everyone does that now, but they were the first band ever to play there."

The strategy definitely boosted enthusiasm within the label. Veteran British record executive Malcolm Hill, Head Of Promotions at Parlophone Records, was responsible for Capitol artists there. In 1986 he was involved in marketing and promoting Crowded House, and recalls a Henn-organised showcase in Kensington. "Tim Finn [then living in London with Greta Scacchi] turned up and played a couple of numbers with them at the end. That's when everybody said, 'They are great. Let's get going.' Seeing them live turned us all on."

• Crowded House at one of their many in-store appearances

A mid-October showcase at a crowded (private) house in Auckland suburb Orakei had the Kiwi critics gushing. "What a night, what great music," said Paul Ellis in *The Auckland Star*. This wasn't actually their début New Zealand appearance – that came back in April 1986 when they played a Greenpeace benefit, the Rainbow Warrior Music Festival (named after the anti-nuclear protest ship sunk by French agents in Auckland harbour) alongside Neil Young, Bonnie Raitt, Graham Nash and Jackson Browne.

In November '86, Neil, Paul and Nick flew back to North America for their novel promotional tour. Capitol chose unconventional settings for their private Crowded House parties to further arouse interest, and these included a seafood restaurant in Seattle, a Japanese garden in LA, an Indian restaurant in New York City, and English-style pub The Duke Of Gloucester in Toronto.

In each locale the trio would set up with a minimum of fuss and equipment – stand-up drum kit, practice monitors and little else. The reaction at each party was equally enthusiastic, for the intimate environment proved perfect for show-casing both the quality of Crowded House's songs and their entertaining performance style.

As Paul Hester observed, "You can really tell the value of a song if you can play it on just guitar. The guts of it comes across. Neil writes those kinds of songs, very strong on the basics. And I've been playing with brushes at these parties, and I haven't done that since I was a kid and my mum showed me how. We get excited about playing these songs differently. All too often in a band, that doesn't happen."

This 'busk 'n schmooze' tour helped a media and industry buzz develop, but simultaneously public awareness of Crowded House was growing. The newly-honed performance style worked perfectly for the TV and radio stations and record stores at which they played.

The rest is now pop lore. Early in 1987, the airplay trickle became a stream, and the crucial major city stations playlisted it with dramatic results. New York's Z100, a key Top 40 station added it in December, and others soon followed. 'Don't Dream It's Over' was finally becoming a chart smash.

Back home in Melbourne for the holiday season, Crowded House saw in the New Year by performing live on national television. It was a short period of relaxation before the real fireworks began.

On January 17, 1987, the name Crowded House first appeared on the *Billboard* charts, the all-important arbiter of American success. 'Don't Dream It's Over' entered the Top 100 Singles chart that week at No. 85. Other artists with singles debuting that week included Janet Jackson, Lionel Richie, actor Bruce Willis (his cover of r& b classic 'Respect Yourself'!) and Huey Lewis. The top five artists that week were Gregory Abbott, Robbie Nevil, Duran Duran, The Bangles, Billy Vera & The Beaters.

The next week it moved from 85 to 68, with the much-prized 'bullet' denoting significant gains in sales and airplay. On it leapfrogged - 59, 52, 44. On the February 21 chart, it officially became a Top 40 hit, placing at 38. Fuelling the drive was MTV, by now playing the 'Don't Dream' video in medium rotation.

Chief beneficiary of all this exposure was the 'Crowded House' album. On February 7, virtually seven months after its American release, it débuted on the *Billboard* Top 200 at No. 180. A huge jump to No. 120 the following week confirmed that, yes, band and label had a hit album on their hands too.

By March 7, MTV had upped the video to high rotation, 'Don't Dream It's Over' was at No. 23 and the recipient of the *Billboard* Power Pick/Sales tag, and the album was nudging the Top 50.

Genuine hopes of a Number One single were now realistic, and the band did everything in its power to ensure that happened. That meant appearing on every American television talk show that would have them, and Capitol Records were able to snag some much-coveted slots. Crowded House made their début appearance on the highly-rated *The Tonight Show With Joan Rivers* on February 17 and the brassy comedienne took an immediate shine to these cute, funny boys from Down Under. Introduced as 'One of the hottest new groups out of Australia', the band launched into a fine rendition of 'Don't Dream It's Over,' marred only by Neil's bad hair day – his rooster-like quiff doing little for his image.

Chatting with Joan after the song, they related, yet again, the story behind their name, then Paul Hester took over proceedings. He described some of the 20 jobs he'd held in a year, prior to Crowded House, including 'a trolleyologist at Safeway (collecting carts) and working on a chook farm'. A mystified Rivers was then told that a chook was a chicken! Other very temporary jobs held by the impish drummer included making fillings at a dental factory, working in a timber yard, and taking a small role in Australian film *The Coca-Cola Kid* (as a session drummer). Clearly Hester was taking to his new job as Crowded House court jester like a shark to a surfer.

Spontaneity was indeed the law by which Crowded House lived. Whether it be in performance or interview, they relished the unexpected. Improvisation, verbal and musical, was proving a key to their charm.

• **Neil Finn, Town & Country Club,London, July 1988**

A March 23 showcase date at New York's prestigious Bottom Line club, for instance, saw the band rock out on Buddy Holly's hit, 'Not Fade Away', enlivened by Paul Hester's ad-lib line, 'Your President's a peckerhead'. A *Rolling Stone* review noted that "Their early Fab Four style banter was strained, but both the patter and playing warmed up." Crowd participation here included a surfer boy singing 'I Got You' and young fan Natalie singing on Split Enz classic 'Six Months In A Leaky Boat'.

On the other coast, during two sold-out shows at the Roxy Theatre in Hollywood, it was a medley of 'Twist And Shout' and 'I Got You' that brought the crowd to its feet, and helped earn a rave *Billboard* review. Having his bag and passport stolen there, though, didn't endear Los Angeles to Paul Hester this time.

Crowded House also proved skilful improvisers when a potential major setback arose. With the single still rising up the charts, it was essential to hit the road in North America with a real tour. A new artist rising even faster at the time

• Paul Hester at the Town & Country Club, London

was singer/pianist Bruce Hornsby, with his smash hit, 'The Way It Is'.

A support slot on a Hornsby tour early in the New Year provided good exposure, but trouble lurked. Crowded House played MTV's Spring Break in Florida, a weekend of mayhem and music popular with students celebrating the end of term. To get a visa and replacement passport, Paul Hester had to fly on to Toronto, site of their next gig, early. Ironically, Neil and Nick's flight north was delayed, so they didn't reach Toronto until an hour before their Massey Hall concert opening for Bruce.

The delay meant that Hester had been forced to go alone to an interview set up with MuchMusic (Canada's equivalent to MTV) earlier in the day. Carrying the torch admirably, he soon had VJ Erica Ehm in stitches. With typical flippancy, when asked about Crowded House's slow ascent to success, he introduced a conspiracy theory that Michael Jackson and Bon Jovi had united to keep them down! "I think they got together and said 'let's hold this thing back for

another couple of months!' But if the record had happened straight away, it'd have been lots simpler for everyone. We could have made another one by now."

With his comrades still not in town, Paul jokingly threatened to go it alone. "This is my big break. I've had a word with Bruce Hornsby, and he's lent me his piano!" Neil and Nick thwarted his plans by arriving in the nick of time.

At the 2,500 capacity Massey Hall concert that night, Crowded House spontaneity flourished again. Australian fan Peter Vitols recalls that "They had no time for a soundcheck, so the sound was all over the place. But they blew everyone away, especially when they went into 'Don't Dream It's Over'. Nick's bass had unbelievable feedback, so he had to stop playing it. It could have been disastrous, but Neil continued acoustically. Hester jumped out from the drums, lay down in front of Neil, and began mimicking the section of the 'Don't Dream' video, in which pages of an imaginary book are turned. Neil finished the song, Nick's bass was fixed, and they did the electric version of the hit. The crowd thought this was amazing."

Crowded House soon faced another serious problem. Bruce Hornsby came down with laryngitis and cancelled his next two weeks of dates, effectively stranding the band. Given the expense of touring in North America, it was imperative that they piece together a date or two on their own before the Hornsby tour resumed.

One non-paying gig saw them appear at a benefit for Casey House, a planned AIDS hospice in Toronto, then they snared a show at the city's major club venue, The Diamond. Randy Charlton was responsible for booking acts there then, and he picks up the story. "They came and approached me at the Diamond on a Saturday night – about 11 o'clock. It was chaos. The guys in the band and their agent were sitting in the office with me, when this massive fight broke out outside the door. I jumped over my desk, ran out, and came back five minutes later covered in blood," he recalls. "I sat behind my desk and said 'Where were we?' Neil Finn said 'This looks like our kind of place'. That was their introduction to the club, but they liked it so much the next time around they came and played two nights."

The April 1, 1987 Diamond gig was another triumph. On just days notice, they sold out the 1,000 capacity club, further proof of rising Canadian popularity. It proved an unforgettable night for Toronto singer/songwriter Paul Myers (the brother of *Wayne's World*'s Mike Myers). A major Split Enz fan, his persistent calls for 'I Got You' were rewarded when Neil invited him on stage to sing it. "I'd played it in a band, so I knew it really well, even the right key. I got right into it, even doing the faint echo trick on 'sometimes we shout'. But I knew I couldn't do the high chorus, so I waved Neil in, and we did the two-in-the-mike thing."

Still ecstatic, Myers went backstage later. "I found Neil deep in discussion about John Lennon with someone wearing an XTC 'Drums & Wires' T-shirt. I thought, 'Man! XTC, the Beatles, Crowded House, Split Enz'. It was as if you'd gone to pop heaven and any minute John Lennon would walk in. Neil spotted me and came over. He said, 'That was great', and patted me on the back. He probably does this in every city and meets a million people, but he was very friendly."

That encounter speaks volumes about Neil Finn. Audience participation was now an almost compulsory part of Crowded House's performance repertoire, while the backstage scene demonstrated both patience with his fans and his continuing love affair with pop music history.

In Toronto, the band was approached about playing a music industry gig in Los Angeles the following week. Toronto-based magazine *Music Express* had just been picked up for major distribution in the US via the Musicland retail chain (the country's largest), and were planning an LA launch party. The rapport the magazine's editor, Dianne Collins, had established with the band and American manager Gary Stamler paid off, and Crowded House agreed on short notice. The show/party on Tuesday April 9 was at The Palace, an industry hangout conveniently situated right by the famous Capitol Tower, home of the band's record label.

It went off smoothly, as *Music Express* publisher Keith Sharp recalls. "A lot of record retail people showed. The main room was packed solid and the band went down really well. A public relations company had been hired to get as many stars out as possible, and the celebs were hanging out in their own room." Music and TV celebrities spotted included Pink Floyd's David Gilmour, Jon Anderson of Yes, Steve Van Zandt, actor Lou Diamond Phillips and *Night Court* star Richard Moll.

Neil Finn has always tolerated rather than revelled in this kind of showbiz schmooze, but Sharp remembers that "The following day, he told me he was impressed the industry types would have them. He realised it was good PR."

Now the TV talkshows clamoured to book Crowded House. On April 13, only two months after their debut appearance with Joan Rivers, they were back. The band performed 'Something So Strong', a killer version enhanced by Eddie Rayner's keyboards and a soulful finale. The three lads sprawled out on the studio couch (Eddie was excused – "He's from New Zealand, so he's shy," said Neil) and bantered away with Rivers.

Paul Hester amused her with tales of their recent MTV Spring Break appearance at Daytona Beach, Florida. "We learnt the mating habits of the American college male. Tie cans of beer around your neck, jump out of a lift and go 'aaarr-rgggh!' And the girls go with you!"

Then came a frivolous encounter with Australian superstar guest Dame Edna Everage. As she entered the set regally, two huge stuffed cockatoos on each shoulder of her gown, the three lads bowed down in homage to this international legend. Neil had earlier jokingly admitted that his wife Sharon came along to keep on eye on seductress Edna. To further honour their new famous friend, Crowded House sang, from the sofa, 'Throw Your Arms Around Me', actually written by Nick's brother Mark Seymour, of Oz rock heroes Hunters & Collectors. Visibly touched, Dame Edna hugged them all. Great television!

The next day, the band peddled their wares (and wit) again, this time on major network TV show, *The Today Show With Jane Pauley*. One of those pretty talking heads elevated to celebrity status in America, Pauley tried to be insightful, but failed. "In the parlance of a rock critic I've spoken to, you guys are, in some musical way, important," she announced ponderously.

"Well, I'd like to be as important as you are, Jane," replied Paul, taking the piss superbly.

When she asked the meaning of success, Hester stuck the needle back in. "This is it for me. Here I am talking to you, it's the ultimate!" Nick interjected: "That's exactly what he just said to Joan Rivers!"

They jokingly continued that Jane could interview them in bed, John and Yoko style, when they became mega rockstars. The encounter ended in chaos when Nick insisted they have their photos taken together, something that caused major disruption in this tightly paced show. "This is spontaneous television, folks," a clearly flustered Pauley told the audience.

All the publicity generated helped keep 'Don't Dream It's Over' moving up the charts. The first weeks of April saw it move steadily up the *Billboard* Top 10. On April 25, it reached No. 2, with only George Michael and Aretha Franklin's duet, 'I Knew You Were Waiting' above them.

The moment of reckoning was here. Like compatriot Ed Hillary eyeing the last steps on his conquest of Everest, Neil Finn and friends were within reach of the pop world's pinnacle. The May 2 chart was released. Top spot was grabbed by... Cutting Crew's schmaltzy power ballad '(I Just) Died In Your Arms'. To add insult to injury, 'Don't Dream' had slipped to No. 3, behind Jody Watley's 'Looking For A New Love'.

Neil Finn can recall his exact moment when he heard the news. Along with wife Sharon and son Liam, he'd just survived a flight from hell from Santa Fe, New Mexico. The window Sharon was seated by cracked in mid-flight, causing a passenger evacuation from that area and a rapid descent to a safer altitude. After landing at Albuquerque, he was interrogated by cops who mistook him for an escaped convict. "That's when I just knew we weren't No. 1," Neil told *Rolling Stone*.

It may have been pipped at the post by mediocre British one-hit popsters, but 'Don't Dream It's Over' had enjoyed a long and wonderful ride. As Gary Stamler points out, "As great as the song was, in some ways its success was a fluke." Its ride still wasn't over.

By this stage, Crowded House's home territories of Australia and New Zealand had seen real sales action as well. The one surprise was that it had taken so long. Given the lacklustre reaction to the album up to the end of 1986, Nick Seymour admitted, "We'd given up on Australia. I didn't think we'd have success in our own country, but when we were touring America, we'd get phone calls saying we were No. 1 in New Zealand."

In Australia, the album entered the Top 20 charts at No.18, on January 19, 1987, (The Kent Music Report), and was to peak at No. 4. 'Don't Dream It's Over' entered the charts in January as well, reaching its peak of No. 8 on February 28. Eventually, the album scored quintuple-platinum status there. In New Zealand, 'Don't Dream' began its ascent to the top in March, reaching No. 1 and spending 20 weeks in the charts. Prior to that, the album had been rudely ignored. The first NZ single 'Mean To Me' snagged major airplay only in Te Awamutu, Neil's birthplace, and the album had sold only a meagre 3,000 copies by Christmas. However, it was eventually to spend a healthy 36 weeks on the New Zealand chart, reaching a top position of No. 3. Sales later passed the triple-platinum level (60,000 albums). Local radio, to its eternal shame, only began playing the single after American success.

Rip It Up publisher Murray Cammick explains: "Crowded House may be the darlings of NZ radio now, but they were initially ignored until they had American success. Radio here couldn't think for itself if it tried. Intelligence has never been a mark of quality in those employed by the electronic media here."

Neil Finn was equally scathing. "New Zealand radio is responsible for killing New Zealand music as far as I'm concerned," he fumed to *The New Zealand Herald* in February, 1987. "I don't care particularly about us, but it's a shame more for the bands living here and relying on NZ radio to expose their music."

In Canada, the single peaked at No. 5 on May 18, but long and steady sales saw 'Crowded House' reach the Top 10 and sell past platinum (100,000 copies). Saturation play and personal appearances on national music video channel MuchMusic were major assets.

Unsurprisingly, the United Kingdom proved the most resistant to Crowded House's seductive charms. Pop-rock acts from Australasia still faced real prejudice from the British music press, and Neil Finn wasn't about to devote massive effort to that market. American chart success frequently fails to translate to the more idiosyncratic British version, and 'Don't Dream It's Over' faced a deafening silence when it first reached Brit ears.

In fact, even Crowded House's British label, Parlophone, was rather slow off the mark. Now Head Of Promotion at Parlophone, Malcolm Hill first encountered the band as they were preparing to record their début. He recalls that, "The pick-up from the UK company wasn't that fast, to be honest. Our international division was pushing them very hard to us, but it was a bit of time before everyone understood, 'let's go for it',"

The abject failure of first UK single, 'World Where You Live', released in July 1986, hadn't helped. 'Don't Dream It's Over' was released in the UK in January 1987, but its journey to chartland would be as long and arduous as elsewhere. The song didn't enter the UK Top 50 Singles chart until June 6, but stayed there for eight weeks, a reasonable run by today's standards. Although it peaked at No. 27, extensive airplay gave the perception of a larger hit.

One casualty of the cruel delay in this minor breakthrough was Heinz Henn. He had left EMI [for BMG] in February 1987, and cites the label's lack of support for Crowded House as a key reason. "I was told not to work the artist because it wasn't a priority for the company. There were a lot of other reasons [for leaving], but that was the final straw."

Just as British interest registered for the breakthrough hit, it was time to choose the crucial follow-up single for North America. Goodwill and one smash single do not a career make. Based on hearing the song live, Capitol in LA wanted to change the original choice, 'Something So Strong' to 'World Where You Live'.

At one point, they had supplies of both pressed, but Stamler insisted in the strongest terms on 'Something So Strong'. "On instinct, I called [Capitol President] Don Zimmerman, saying that I'd lie in front of the mailroom if necessary!" He argued that the bright and simple feel of 'Something So Strong' made a positive contrast to the hit ballad. Stamler won, and the song quickly became Crowded House's second US Top 10 single, while 'World Where You Live' flopped on later release.

On its way up, 'Something' met 'Don't Dream' in its descent. In fact, the May 30 Billboard chart saw two consecutive Crowded House entries on the Top 40, 'Something So Strong' in at 33, 'Don't Dream' at 34, a formidable feat for a brand new foreign act.

Crowded House were now MTV darlings (they won Best New Video Artist Award that year), and the high rotation of the 'Something So Strong' clip helped the single reach Top 10 status, finally peaking at No. 7. In Canada, it peaked at No. 15. By mid-1987, then, 'Crowded House' had sold close to 750,000 copies in the US, and eventually reached the coveted platinum (1 million) figure by 1993. This House was open for (big) business.

The tired trio returned to Melbourne in May 1987 for gigs in major Australasian cities – their first back home since cracking it. Predictably enough, they went down a storm, high-pitched female screams confirming their status as pop heartthrobs to some young fans.

In New Zealand for a seven city tour, they received a heroes welcome, from hysterical supporters at least. A sold-out show at Wellington's Town Hall, July 3, saw one young girl carried out of the excited crush of screaming fans to safety backstage. However, Evening Post critic Kathy Stodart was less enthused. "In the end, it was too clean, too pat, with not enough personality. The crowd's reaction to the band was more interesting than the band itself."

Perhaps the band weren't at their best because of near-exhaustion after a year of touring and promotional work around the world. "Even if you're fatigued and sick of touring, playing doesn't seem a pointless exercise if you can keep that small spark of inspiration," said

Neil. "As soon as gigs start to become mundane, you should get off the road."

Despite their road-weariness, Crowded House still found ways to enliven their tour dates. During a national Canadian tour in that frenetic summer of 1987, they developed a good rapport with opening act, melodic pop-rockers Chalk Circle. Their lead singer, Chris Tait, recalls end of tour frolics. "We heard they were going to pull the usual last night prank on the opening band, so we beat them to the punch the night before in Vancouver. We'd double taped keyboard keys and the kick drum pedal. The roadie caught everything we sabotaged, except the keyboard tape. The first song had this godawful drone! On their last song, we ran out with squirt guns, got them, then hung around to sing the chorus. They got us back on the final night in Victoria, when Paul Hester ran across the stage naked during our encore!"

By this time, however, Neil Finn readily admitted feeling the strain. Although bringing its rewards, he was rapidly discovering success came with a price attached. He was caught in the classic trap – itching to begin writing and recording a new batch of songs – it was now close to a year since the release of 'Crowded House' – but unable to do so because of the demands on his time.

Finn was showing signs of stress, often complaining about music business methods. "The worst thing is that the industry continually over-promotes everything. You've got to say no at some point, otherwise it turns into madness, it's bad for the music, you get fried. If I was a fan, I'd be totally sick of the songs by now because they get played too much."

7

in the lowlands

I n August 1987, Neil Finn could finally return to his real love – writing and recording songs. The last 18 months had seen Crowded House establish themselves as important new performers in the pop circus, but Finn was not the happiest trouper.

He hadn't been seduced by fame sufficiently to overlook the sleazy, false sides of the music business – 'the star-making machinery behind the popular song', as Joni Mitchell so eloquently put it. If anything, his sudden ascent simply reinforced Neil's distaste for the star-making process.

The considerable international success of 'Crowded House' had eradicated all his immediate financial worries. On paper at least Neil, who wrote or co-wrote all 10 tracks on the album, was now a wealthy man.

One of his first major investments was both unusual and amusing. Neil and Paul Hester bought six angora goats, producers of highly coveted wool. These were kept at Neil's sister Judy's farm near Cambridge, but weren't proving as frisky as desired. "Goats seem to have strange sexual habits. Ours are probably stranger than normal," Neil laughingly confessed.

Maybe this was an omen, for Neil would never feel comfortable with the wealth his songwriting brought him. Indeed, in 1989, he admitted to Toronto weekly tabloid *NOW* that... "I haven't actually solved the dilemma of becoming successful. The ex-Catholic in me makes me feel guilty about earning money. Oh, maybe I should be giving it all away. I'm not sure I subscribe to the Bono theory of wanting to be the biggest band in the world. I'd like to beat that concept of having to be bigger every time that prevails in this industry and tends to draw people to be safer and safer."

Such misgivings surfaced in 'Mansion In The Slums', a song Neil wrote in the wake of the success of Crowded House's début. Its sentiments explicitly question the value and often fleeting nature of success, and trivialise the fine line between colossal financial rewards and sinking in a welter of debt. As Neil later confessed to *The New Zealand Herald* in August 1988, "There's a lot of truth in that song, but I hope it presents it in a tongue-in-cheek manner. It's a collection of random notes about having success and what is meaningful and not in life."

It may have been tongue-in-cheek, but there was more than a trace of venom in the bite but unlike so many contemporary rock stars who are constantly whining about the price of a fame they allegedly never sought, Finn rarely lapsed into self-pity. In that same interview, he said: "I have my down moments but I'm conscious of not talking too much about it because people could say, 'Oh yeah, Neil Finn's got it really hard'. I don't think anybody should feel sorry for me because anything that's happened which is hard to deal with I've created myself and been well-rewarded for.

"But you do create a monster and become aware you're part of the machinery and totally implicated in the vacuousness of the whole thing. Without wishing to put it too strongly, sometimes I feel like wanting to apologise for the entertainment industry as a whole – apart from our performances," he added with a smile.

Ambivalence towards his new success was the common theme in most of Neil Finn's interviews during 1988. To *Rip It Up*'s Chris Bourke, he reflected: "I don't know if I enjoy success as much as I should. There's a feeling that everyone's expecting you to be incredibly happy about it. But in many cases what it means – in the short term anyway – is that your life becomes completely chaotic. And you can't help feeling it's having an adverse effect on your ability to keep writing good songs."

All these conflicting emotions must have been spinning around Finn's head as he settled down back home in Melbourne to write the material that would comprise the second Crowded House album 'Temple Of Low Men'. Amateur analysts might speculate that the darker mood of this record was a subconscious reaction to the success of 'Crowded House', but Neil would surely scoff at that suggestion.

Rehiring Mitchell Froom as producer was a straightforward decision. The commercial success of the début had forced Capitol to view him in a new light while, in turn, the making of the record had been a valuable learning process for then-novice Froom.

"When it initially didn't do well, the record company would tell me there was no lead track, no single. Then nine months later, it has two Top 10 singles and is suddenly a classic! It was good to get that education early. I've never taken any stock in what these people say. They're invariably wrong!"

Distrust of the 'suits' and 'ponytails' of the record biz was shared equally by Neil Finn and Froom. "The most interesting thing to me is to do a body of work with someone, but only as long as it's alive," says Froom. "I want to hear new songs and new ideas that seem a progression, so it continues to be interesting. After a first record, you often have great ideas for a second. Plus you get over any uneasiness you may have in the beginning. There's more trust, so that side gets easier."

By now, they had an effective pre-production routine established. "We mainly work on the arrangements and decide what's the strongest material," Froom told *Musician* . "That's before we even go into band rehearsal. We usually have a drum machine, and Neil plays guitar and I play keyboard. We come up with ideas and listen to each other."

At rehearsals, Froom essentially joined the band for the weeks of preparation, helping get the grooves on track and writing some keyboard parts. Once in the studio, however, he let the trio find their own working rhythm. The preparation paid off. "By the time we get to the studio, we're pretty relaxed and can just go for a dynamic performance," explains Hester.

All the basic tracks for 'Temple' were, in fact, laid down in just eight days in early 1988. Froom and band had agreed on two recording locales – Sunset Sound Factory in LA, the studio where the first album was recorded, and Platinum Studio in Melbourne. The compromise meant the band didn't have to uproot themselves from family and friends for an overly extended period, but still gave them access to LA's musical expertise.

Not that much was needed. Froom himself again played keyboards, a function that would generally be assumed on tour by Eddie Rayner; the Heart Attack Horns returned; and noted session muso Alex Acuna added percussion flourishes. Another new friend, British guitar virtuoso Richard Thompson added a typically dynamic solo to 'Sister Madly'. At this stage Thompson had just recorded an album with Mitchell Froom, and was being managed by Gary Stamler. Then, of course, there were backing vocals from one Tim Finn, who from this point onwards would enter the Crowded House equation, sometimes on the fringes and other times at its heart. It has never been specified which of the songs during the 'TOLM' sessions Tim actually sang on.

Neil Finn was confident they could produce a stronger record than the début. "We're a better band now," he said as the sessions began. "We play better together after doing all those gigs last year. We've really gelled and learned how to sing together, and we also have similar aesthetics as far as how we want to hear the music sound."

Mitchell Froom had noticed the improvement, and thought they'd moved closer to defining a distinctive style. "On the first record, there was something of a searching for a sound. By the time of the second, I thought they were an incredible band. You could tell who it was the second they started playing."

The result, according to Froom, was a recording experience far more smooth and enjoyable than with 'Crowded House'. "People have the idea that the second record was a misery and the first was joy," he told *Rip It Up* in 1989. "The first was hell and the second a joy. With the first, we were trying to work out what the band should sound like. More electronic? Like Talking Heads? Pet Shop Boys? How should we approach it?"

Neil Finn's musical perfectionism remained, however. *Rolling Stone* reporter Steve Pond was present over Easter 1988 for the final day of mixing at the Hit Factory in New York. He described Froom, manager Gary Stamler and noted mixer Bob Clearmountain all taking pains to ensure Neil was happy to the finish.

• Former Split Enzkeyboard Eddie Rayner joins Crowded House on tour in 1988.

"It's hard on Neil," Froom explained at the time. "He's tortured in the way that he goes back and forth, always thinking he could do better... So we have to feel we haven't left any stones unturned." This attention to detail may have been hard on the nerves of everyone in the studio, but it's one reason Crowded House material wears so well, and why their records often sound better after 20 spins than two.

Although that characteristic is precisely what their fans most cherish about their music – and why rock historians will inevitably treat Crowded House kindly – in the short term this can pose a problem. As Froom points out succinctly: "Basically, as soon as you say, 'It takes a while to get into this album', nine times out of ten that means you have a big flop in America. Nobody's willing to give anything

more than half a listen." That would prove a problem with 'Temple Of Low Men'.

With mixing completed to everyone's satisfaction, 'Temple' was released in North America, Australia and New Zealand in July 1988. The British release followed a month later.

So just how does it stack up against its mega-selling predecessor? The adjectives 'dark' and 'moody' are those most oft employed in describing Crowded House's second album. Neil Finn has often protested this view, and Mitchell Froom has viewed it as... 'Funny, even if it is a bit on the black side.' The début album had its share of disturbing themes – suicide ('Hole In the River') and obsession ('Mean To Me') amongst them. The image portrayed in Crowded House videos and live performances, however, had been of cute, fun-loving, wacky guys from Down Under, which tended to undercut the troubled feel of some of Neil Finn's songs. With 'Temple Of Low Men', the darker shadows and closets of the House came into view.

Various explanations have been given of the album title. "We were in Los Angeles and saw the phrase scrawled on a wall and I liked the sound of it," says Neil. "I looked at some of the songs on the album and it seemed right. Also we saw [sinning American televangelist] Jimmy Swaggart apologising to his congregation on TV and it was a spark – grab that title. It seemed quite current."

The phrase 'Temple Of Low Men' actually appears in the ancient erotic religious text *The Perfumed Garden* in reference to the most private region of the female anatomy. One album title jokingly suggested while work was in progress was 'Mediocre Follow-Up'!

From the 'slightly sleazy overtone' (Neil's phrase) of the album title to Nick Seymour's disturbing cover art (a city in flames) to such song titles as 'Kill Eye', 'Sister Madly', 'Into Temptation' and 'I Feel Possessed', the natural assumption is an album of disturbing images, a bumpy ride for the emotions. Indeed, there's a cauldron of emotional horrors boiled up here – dread, temptation, infidelity, jealousy, revenge, madness. If it was a movie, 'Temple Of Low Men' would probably carry a Parental Guidance warning, but as ever Neil Finn's capacity for gorgeous melodies keeps the bleakness at bay, tempering the darkness with light.

Crowded House supporters in the rock critic fraternity quickly embraced the new album. *Rip It Up*'s Chris Bourke decreed it: "An album of remarkable depth and maturity, touching profound emotions with songs of originality and substance." *Music Express* chimed in with "A more adventurous and ultimately more rewarding record than the début. There must be room for songs this well-crafted and played." *The Globe & Mail*, Canada's national newspaper, called it "A worthy, if somewhat unexpected successor."

Predictably, critics on the British rock weeklies tried, Samson-style, to bring the 'Temple' down with their supposedly witty scorn. Jonh Wilde, in his July *Melody Maker* review was nothing short of vitriolic, pronouncing the album... "Entirely devoid of virtue. It's like getting wet sick tipped in your ear, letting it gurgle about for a bit, before tipping itself out of the other ear for want of something a bit more interesting to do... Finn proves that pretension can be a terrible thing in the hands of stupid men." *Melody Maker* critics often seemed to make a point of expressing distaste for anything of genuine or lasting quality at this time but such reviews wouldn't harm sales of the album since Crowded House fans were unlikely to respect *Melody Maker*'s opinions, or even read the magazine in the first place. Any influence that *MM* might once have wielded was now seriously compromised not just by its dwindling circulation but also by its staff's apparent inability to discover and endorse new acts who were able to sustain lasting careers.

On the plus side, *New Musical Express* gave the album a rave 9 out of 10 rating, much to Neil's surprise. "I was expecting to get slagged as usual," he admitted, though *NME*'s reputation for more discerning criticism has sustained its growth in the now overcrowded UK music magazine market.

True to form, New York's acerbic Robert Christgau slagged the album. In his *Record Guide - The '80s*, he sneers that "The problem's not that philistine tastemakers are quashing Neil Finn's hit début blues, but that Finn has neglected the only thing he has to offer the world: perky hooks. Programmers don't care what he's brooding about because nobody else does. Plenty of popsters have managed to stir up interest in their anxieties. Be thankful there isn't one more." He scored the album a C.

This time around, there was general agreement on the choice of first single, except Neil Finn. "Better Be Home Soon", a beguiling country-flavoured ballad, is one of those songs that connects instantly, a key ingredient of a hit. Label and management agreed on the choice, but Neil later told *Rolling Stone* that... "It really wasn't a clear-cut choice for me at all. I was wary about putting it out first, not because I didn't like the song but because I feel it's not representative of the rest of the record."

This affecting ballad certainly got a good reception back home. It entered the New Zealand charts on July 24, reaching No. 2, the same peak position as in Australia. In Canada, it rose slowly up the charts, eventually becoming a massive hit and reaching the top slot in early October 1988. The popularity of the single lifted the album to Top 20 and platinum status there.

The US reception for 'Temple Of Low Men', however, was decidedly frosty. Reviews for the album were generally positive, but 'Better Be Home Soon' simply didn't happen. Little Top Forty airplay meant minimal sales or chart action and it peaked at a disappointing No. 42 on *Billboard*, which placed the whole album in jeopardy.

Competition in the marketplace that summer was even more intense than usual. Hit albums of the season included George Michael's 'Faith', Def Leppard's 'Hysteria', the *Dirty Dancing* soundtrack, Michael Jackson's 'Bad', Tracy Chapman's self-titled début and even strong competition from Down Under peers, INXS with 'Kick' and Midnight Oil with 'Diesel & Dust'. Not that this accounts for Crowded House's poor performance, but it certainly made the task ahead that much more formidable.

Crowded House's American manager Gary Stamler theorised that Top Forty playlists were now even more regimented, but was mystified at the failure of the first single. "No-one will ever convince me that 'Better Be Home Soon' is not a hit record," he told *Rolling Stone*, with some justification.

Ian James, head of Mushroom Publishing in Melbourne, is responsible for the song catalogue of both Finn brothers, and is an enthusiastic cheerleader for their talent. "'Better Be Home Soon' is, in essence, a country song," he claims. That may help explain the reluctance of American pop radio to submit to its charms. The tune was, in fact, later chosen as the title track on the second album of American country group The McCarters, becoming in the process a moderate hit in the US specialist country charts in 1990. The song was also covered by New Zealand country singer Barbie Davidson on her 1991 album, 'Borderline', which was produced by Neil's former Split Enz comrade Mike Chunn.

With its most immediately accessible song a stiff in both the US and Britain, where it had been released without fanfare in June 1988, 'Temple' was in trouble. As Parlophone UK's Managing Director Tony Wadsworth explains, "Many of the Americans who bought the first album may never have been aware 'Temple' was out. Unless there were singles playing on high rotation on their radio stations, there's no reason they should know."

In Britain, things weren't so much on a slide for Crowded House as still waiting to happen. 'Better Be Home Soon' had flopped in June, and in August 'Sister Madly' followed suit. It did get reviewed in *Melody Maker* whose David Stubbs sneeringly called it... "Antipodean angst from people who have listened to too many John Lennon albums. Crowded House are big in Canada, which sums it up really." Managing to insult three former colonies at once may have seemed clever, but this smug condescension helps explain why Crowded House decided not to expend any excess energy trying to break Britain even though, unbeknownst to them, thousands of potential fans were ready and waiting.

They did make their London début with two shows at the Town & Country Club in July. "We were probably overdue to play there," Neil told *The Auckland Star*. "Up till now people would have been excused for thinking we were a band just making records and videos. But having spent three years in England with Split Enz, I've had the approach that I'm not going to tear my hair out over England until they're ready to listen to us." A *Melody Maker* concert review was lukewarm, praising the stripped-down songs, but accusing others of being "Americanized AOR beasties," the kind of lazy critical assumption they often faced.

Crowded House also made their first Japanese visit, with a six day promotional tour. A Tokyo concert proved that the phenomenon of screaming teenage girls wasn't strictly Western, but Neil was pleased that other Japanese fans... "said our music had serenity." The band had to face a gruelling round of promotional activities. "We did like nine photo sessions a day, plus interviews," complained Paul, but he was quite taken with their hosts – and the food. "It's their politeness, and attention to manners. You can't just go in there, you know, carrying on like a two-bob watch."

"One day they gave us the press schedule and they hadn't even put in a lunch break," recalls Nick Seymour. "When we put our foot down about it, they were quite taken aback. All that team spirit... it's scary."

Crowded House were glad to get back to Australia. "Both Japan and Britain are quite alienating experiences," said Neil. "When you get back to Australia you appreciate the familiarity of home."

In August 1988 the band launched into an extensive Australian tour, playing predominantly big cities, but also venturing off-the-beaten-track to towns most big league bands wouldn't touch, such as Darwin in the Northern Territory and Alice Springs, in the heart of the outback.

After the Alice Springs gig, Nick, Neil, Paul and their respective partners disregarded routine and drove into the desert to chat and drink tea around a campfire until 4 am – a brief period of tranquillity within their manic schedule. "It was probably the best thing we've done together in a long time," said Hester later, implying regret at the way the group's success often obscured their enjoyment of the simple things in life.

Just days earlier in Darwin, the band had been locked in a post-gig screaming match, the result of tension which had been brewing for weeks. With the pressures and ever-increasing expectations being placed on them, it was sometimes easy for them to lose perspective of what they had achieved. Sitting under the stars that night, with nothing other than the occasional scuffle of an animal and the low murmur of their voices to disturb the peace of the vast openness, this was a rare chance to reflect on their changing fortunes. "I grew up in the bush and I can't believe what my life has become in the past two years," said Nick Seymour afterwards. "The astral bodies are amazing out there. Lying on the ground you really do feel a weird force holding you to the Earth."

"And then this train comes by!" laughs Hester, relishing the rude awakening. "Blazing lights, honking its horn. We'd parked right beside the main line from Adelaide to Darwin. Ruined it all. We turned round and drove back to the hotel for the night."

General reaction to the band on this tour was predictably ecstatic. Their home territory may have been slow on the uptake with the début album, but Crowded House were making up for lost time in Australia, and savouring their roles as local pop heroes. In many ways they had it covered: a commercially successful pop act on the one hand, critically-acclaimed, musically credible performers on the other. The reaction they sparked at some of these earlier concerts, however, must have been puzzling.

During a sold-out five night run at the intimate State Theatre in Sydney, for instance, the show was punctuated by ear-splitting screams of over-excited teenage girls, much to the eventual chagrin of Neil. "There's nothing like the frequency of a good scream," he chided good-naturedly on the opening night. "We hate it, it hurts our ears! C'mon everybody let's all scream at once." The crowd obliged with a deafening shrill, as the band blocked their ears.

Another sign of female adoration, the throwing of a bra onstage, led to Neil attempting, unsuccessfully, to burn it. Paul, adopting a mocking tone, reprimanded Neil. "Stop that... it's going to look very nice in tomorrow's *Sydney Morning Herald*," he yelled from behind the drum rostrum.

The amusing irony of teenage girls screaming along to songs dealing with such far from adolescent themes as infidelity, betrayal and death was not lost on Neil Finn. "I like the idea of thumping 12-year-olds with 30-year-old themes," he explained to *Rip It Up*'s Chris Bourke. "Our audience is quite a broad one, but it includes a lot of young people, and it's good to expose them to things other than the teen stuff they're hearing... like the sex trip most bands are on: 'C'mon baby, give me your everything'."

This component of Crowded House's audi-

• Crowded House on stage in 1988

ence often fluctuated. "If we have a single that does well, for the next couple of months the shows will be characterised by young girls filling the first ten rows," Neil later told *Music Express*. "In between singles, it'll be slightly older, less teen-oriented."

During the Australian tour, Crowded House had been watching the US charts with close interest and no little bemusement. They had, not unreasonably, expected big things in the US from their newest creation, considering the rapturous applause of the previous year, but what they were now getting was akin to a Dear John letter from a cruelly dismissive lover.

Despite initial reports that it was selling reasonably well without the backing of a hit single, comparisons with the success of the début were far from flattering. It was eventually to rack up sales of 300,000 in the US, certainly not a total flop, but decidedly disappointing after the near-million sales for 'Crowded House'. Any despondency they might have felt was temporarily relieved by the news that the band was about to secure a major promotional boost, an appearance on the hugely popular TV show *Late Night With David Letterman*. This guaranteed massive exposure, as did an invitation to present and perform at the prestigious annual MTV Awards, one of the biggest events on the music industry's calendar.

These US invitations made cancelling a planned August 31 date in Auckland imperative – which didn't go down well in New Zealand. Disappointed critics accused Neil of deserting his home in favour of chasing the Yankee dollar. "Fuck them! That's not the reason we're not coming," he counter-attacked angrily in *Rip It Up*. "The main reason is that we didn't want to rush through, in one door and out the other. We're incredibly busy, and that's why I didn't want it to feel like a token appearance there. I hate coming in for a day, you see about a dozen people you know quite well and don't get a chance to talk to any of them."

Crowded House arrived in New York at the end of August for a week's worth of intensive US. promotion – kicking off with an unadvertised gig at CBGB's on September 1. In homage to this legendary punk venue their set that night included a countrified pisstake of The Sex Pistols punk anthem 'Anarchy In The UK'. The following day, they performed 'Sister Madly' on the Letterman show – an invaluable three minutes that virtually justified the entire trip – after which, on September 3, they flew to Toronto for a low-key gig at the Siboney Club. The mere 400 tickets for the show had sold out in 10 minutes, part-testimony to the fact that they could easily have packed a venue ten times the size. On this occasion, they preferred to showcase their new material in a more intimate setting.

Next stop, LA. A gig at the Whiskey club was notable for the presence of hard rock superstar Dave Mustaine of Megadeth, who hung out backstage with Crowded House after the gig. "I like Neil's lyrics – they're really deep," he told a *Spin* reporter there. "Whenever I get depressed, I slap on their music and immediately get happy again." His praise wasn't just liquor-fuelled. In *Melody Maker* the next month, he placed Neil Finn in a list of heroes that included Frank Sinatra, Mike Tyson, James Dean and Aerosmith.

Also backstage was Maria McKee, then singer for highly-touted LA roots-rockers Lone Justice.

• CBGB New York, September 1988

Neil declined a publicity shot with her, explaining: "It's weird getting your picture taken with somebody you don't know. It's too false." Coincidentally, both Maria and Neil were later to share a certain eccentric English producer. Another notable feature of the gig was that Crowded House performed out-of-costume. Nick's colourful hand-painted outfits, featuring various band-related illustrations from lyrics to album covers, had been *de rigeur* right from the start of the band's career – an echo of Neil's days with Split Enz.

Killing time in LA that trip, Nick and Paul dropped in on a tattooist favoured by the local hip rock'n'roll/movie set. Their friend Warren Costello, Managing Director of Mushroom Records, takes up the story. "They're talking to the guy, and Nick is being a smartass, showing off his art background. He says he's thinking of getting a Picasso tattoo, and the guy says, 'Which period? The blue one?' It turns out this guy is more a body artist than a tattooist, so they get into a big discussion. The result of their encounter was that Nick Seymour now sports a reproduction of Picasso's *Weeping Woman* on his right shoulder.

"While this was going on, Paul Hester was doodling. There's one he does all the time of a Fifties television set [later to appear as artwork for his later band Ultrasound]. So he said, 'I want three of them, arranged like that' and so gets this tattoo of TV sets on his arm.

"Life goes on, Paul gets back to Australia and goes to the far north of Queensland for his holiday. He suddenly realises he's going to have to tell his mum he's got a tattoo! Apparently the first time he wore long-sleeved shirts throughout and managed to keep the secret. But the next time, he's completely forgotten about it. He's in the backyard doing some work, takes his shirt off and his mum screams, 'You've got a tattoo!'."

At the MTV Awards in LA on September 7, Crowded House presented the Best New Artist award (which they had won the year before) to Guns N' Roses. Somewhat tongue in cheek, Neil later described them as 'a very fine group of young men'. Crowded House then performed 'Better Be Home Soon' from their seats in the auditorium, with Neil dedicating it to wife Sharon

and son Liam.

By now, Neil Finn had stopped bothering to hide his fatigue and distaste for showbiz ritual. US rock monthly *Spin* published a transcript of a post-show interview with MTV VJ Randee, one that never aired because of Neil's patent lack of enthusiasm for the evening. When asked whether he was having fun there, Neil made it clear he wasn't. "Fun is going to be the next two months when we're going to be having a holiday."

"So you've been working real hard?" asks the VJ.

Neil's reply was hostile and evasive: "Yeah, we've been whining and whining about how hard we've been working. Everyone's entitled to a good whine now and again." The interview was abandoned, having descended into hopelessness.

The expectation that they should always be 'on' had become tiresome to Crowded House. "Once you do a couple of interviews where you've been really loose or managed to be witty, people tend to feed off that," explained Neil to *Spin*. "It becomes an entity of its own, despite and beyond the music. I'm getting a bit sick of it now. I've had some very radical notions the past few months."

Neil's 'radical notions' included taking a much-deserved, much-needed break; something which, on the face of it, wasn't very radical at all. However, industry ritual demanded that the group get back on the road and tour America to bolster the now-flagging album, and they were about to brazenly flout that convention. For Neil Finn and his Crowded House comrades, family and sanity took precedence. They flew home to Melbourne, postponing any major US touring.

Hinting at the disappointment and feelings of rejection he felt after the non-performance of 'Temple Of Low Men', Neil Finn told *Rolling Stone*: "The best thing I could be doing now is probably being at home writing songs instead of frantically tearing around the world trying to give the record company what they need in order to get a hit record."

Capital hadn't quite given up, though. Still chasing a US hit to salvage some chance of the album getting a belated kiss of life, the record company chose 'Into Temptation' as the next single in October 1988. With its haunting chorus and dark comments on sexual deceit, this song is unquestionably one of Neil Finn's best and was for many the stand-out track on the album, but its subdued tone didn't exactly scream 'hit single'. "Nobody perceives it to be an easy single," acknowledged Gary Stamler at the time. "But we'll kill ourselves trying, because we really believe in the quality of the song." He resisted hari-kari when it flopped mercilessly.

By late 1988, then, any hopes that 'Temple Of Low Men' might enjoy the same delayed success of the début had evaporated. The post-mortems on its failure began.

Mitchell Froom pulls no punches with his autopsy report. "I don't usually say this, but that particular record was grossly mishandled by their record company. I remember at that time that Bruce Springsteen called the President of Capitol Records and asked him what the hell was going on, why wasn't that record a hit. Bruce didn't have anything to do with the label, he just thought it was great. The label released the wrong songs, then they freaked out. As well, Neil wasn't in a very good frame of mind at that time, and he wasn't very positive in the press. A lot of things didn't work out."

Never one to beat about the bush, Neil Finn was predictably blunt in his assessment.

Interviewed in New Zealand magazine *The Listener* later, he said: "Largely speaking the record company lost that album in America through their own bungling. But because we were such a big part of the first album's success by going out and charming the Americans, when we didn't do so much for the second album, that was perceived as the reason it didn't happen. That's only ever part of it. 'Better Be Home Soon' was number one in Canada and NZ, number two in Australia. There's no way people are that different that it wasn't a hit. But when it ran into trouble they just panicked. And we weren't there to buoy their confidence. Still, there is a lot involved. The number of good songs that fail in America is staggering."

He was to be more positive about the fate of 'Temple' a couple of years later. In 1991, he told *Music Express*: "Even the second record, which didn't really have any singles on it in America, ended up selling a lot of records. It feels like people who like us are really committed, or should be committed, as the case might be. That therefore is dependable – as long as we don't put out a pure shit record, they'll stick with us. Things will come and go but we're in it for the long haul."

8

what's another finn between frienz ?

**A**fter a three-month lay off, Crowded House decided to start touring again, but only in territories that had been receptive to 'Temple Of Low Men'. A New Zealand tour in January 1989 gave Neil the chance to enjoy a family Christmas, and festivities included a musical get-together in a barn on sister Judy's farm near Cambridge, a pretty country town close to Te Awamutu and Hamilton, now home to parents Dick and Mary Finn.

For the NZ tour, Crowded House chose Schnell Fenster as their support act. This awkwardly-named pop/rock act – it's German for 'fast window' – comprised Split Enz co-founder Phil Judd, fellow Enz alumni Noel Crombie and Nigel Griggs, and Australian guitarist Michael Den Elzen, who had recently been playing with Tim Finn. Musically inventive, their impact on the Antipodean music scene was brief and fairly inconsequential, however, and the band broke up after recording two albums.

Crowded House's break from touring had served them well, and observers reported them back on fine form. Reviewing their Whangarei concert, Auckland writer Russell Brown called their live show... "uncommonly relaxed. Rather than trying to rush through gaps between songs, they take it easy, chat to the crowd and look thoroughly comfortable." With the presence of Schnell Fenster, ex-Enz and now regular Crowded House keyboard player Eddie Rayner, and occasional visits from Tim Finn on the tour, many of the show's encores became impromptu Split Enz reunions.

The final gig of the tour was at Hamilton's Founders Theatre at the end of January. Here, Tim joined Neil for 45 minutes of oldies, including 'Goodnight Irene', 'Hang Down Your Head Tom Dooley', the Split Enz classic 'Hermitt McDermitt' plus Tim's new song 'Parihaka', which appeared on the *Tim Finn* album. Phil Judd was also on hand, acting as video cameraman.

The next friendly territory begging for a House call was Canada. An extensive three week national tour in March 1989 took them from Quebec City to Vancouver. Toronto promoter Rob Bennett booked that tour, which included many smaller cities not usually on the rock'n'roll road map. "They just decided they wanted to play a lot of places," he recalls. "Sure, they made a lot of money in Toronto, but they were very fair. They said, 'Let's go to [more obscure] places like Thunder Bay and Sudbury'."

The largely sold-out tour primarily took in concert theatres of the 1500 to 3000 capacity range. The presence of Richard Thompson as opening act on most dates pleased the older section of the Crowded House audience, and he regularly joined the band to reprise his guitar work on 'Sister Madly'.

This tour also marked the Crowded House début for additional guitarist and keyboard player Mark Hart. Passing the baptism of fire unscalded, he became the band's touring extra instrumentalist of choice, prior to achieving 'official member' status with the 'Together Alone' album.

Born in Fort Scott, Kansas, the Los Angeles based musician was well-known within the city's scene as a capable, versatile player. He'd even toured with veteran British band Supertramp from 1984, and took a key role in that band's 1987 album 'Free As A Bird', playing keyboards and guitar, singing some lead vocals and co-writing one song. He has also helped on recording sessions with Aimee Mann, The Black Crowes and Michael Penn. One professional stint was touring with acclaimed female singer/songwriter Sam Phillips, a gig that saw him teamed with guitarists Rick Boston, now leader of moody rockers Low Pop Suicide, and veteran producer/musician T-Bone Burnett, who had produced and played with Elvis Costello and toured in Bob Dylan's Rolling Thunder Revue.

"We played with Mark in the electric band, which toured with Sam in America," recalls Boston. "I found Mark a very nice guy, very quiet. The kind of guy to whom you say 'Hi, how are you?', and that's about it." He pretty much stuck to playing the Chamberlin [a bizarre keyboard that runs with motor, cables, and tape loops] and electric piano in the band." Coincidentally, Mitchell Froom is an expert on the Chamberlin, and he helped Hart out in rehearsals for his work with Sam Phillips.

Crowded House manager Gary Stamler had met Mark when Hart was in LA band Combination and had recommended him for the vacancy that opened when regular touring keyboardist Eddie Rayner dropped out at the last minute, citing the illness of his father. "That jeopardised the tour because Neil was reluctant to tour without Eddie," explains Stamler. "I was lucky enough to get Mark on the phone, I sent him tapes, and he stayed up all night learning the songs."

Mark Hart first met Crowded House in Los Angeles Airport. In Nick Seymour's joke version of the encounter, "It was at the security check... Mark was operating the X-ray machine. He saw we had musical equipment, and he said, 'Gee I'm a musician'. We looked at him and thought, 'Hmm, he could make a really good sex symbol for the band!'"

According to Neil, "The real story is just as strange. Mark had his first rehearsal for the group at soundcheck for the first gig of the tour. We rehearsed half a set and the other half he played for the first time with us on stage. It was a remarkable début."

A highlight of Crowded House's Canadian tour was their March 12 special appearance at the Juno Awards in Toronto. The local equivalent of the Grammys or Brit Awards, the Junos annually celebrate the Canadian music industry. This year, Crowded House were nominated in the Best International Artist category (they lost out to U2), and the timing of the tour allowed them to join the festivities.

Nick Seymour goofed around at one Juno party that weekend, Toronto writer Mary-Lou Zeitoun recalls. "My friend [a local TV actress] and I crashed a Crowded House party in a hotel suite by shamelessly leading a couple of roadies on. As I stood there, in a leather sarong and bustier of my own creation, I felt a plop against my chest. I realised that someone was trying to toss olives down my top. It was Nick Seymour, giggling with his buddies. I guess they were placing bets on whether he'd get one in there. Incensed, I grabbed a grape, crossed the room, dropped it down his T-shirt and smashed it into his chest. He looked really mad, but his buddies laughed so he did too. However, it was not the beginning of a beautiful relationship and my girlfriend and I left after avoiding the roadies!"

In keeping with the 'black tie' nature of the Awards show, the lads sported natty suits and ties. There was nothing formal about Paul Hester's behaviour, though. Bounding onto the stage, he gave the TV camera the two-fingered victory salute, which has an obscene meaning Down Under. Clearly in a better frame of mind than at the MTV Awards six months earlier, Neil Finn led Crowded House through a couple of songs. During 'I Feel Possessed', they inserted a joking chant of 'Free James Brown', in honour of the then-incarcerated r&b superstar.

They may have lost at the Junos, but Crowded House triumphed at the Australian equivalent, the ARIAs, on March 6, 1989. 'Temple Of Low Men' won for Best Australian Album, Best Australian Contemporary Record, and Nick Seymour won Best Cover Artwork. 'Better Be Home Soon' also won Song Of The Year.

The Canadian tour was notable for the adulation of the teenage girl segment of their audience and for the quite literal Crowded House party they played in Calgary. Music video channel

MuchMusic had run a nationwide contest – make a video inviting Crowded House to play at your house. The winner was young video producer/fan Grant Harvey and his prize was having the band play a party at his house. His friend Wayne Abrams recalls that… "The band played in the basement, then jammed with us, played pool and drank with us for a couple of hours. They were totally cool!"

Grant's one regret? "I tried to tell Dad to buy a new, bigger house so I could invite more people!" As it was, dad Doug Harvey was worried about the beams on his main floor supporting the weight of the revellers! To Neil Finn, the gig was a reminder of their humble beginnings. "Lounges are our favourite places to play. It's where we started off, and as a kid I used to sing at parties like this in Te Awamutu."

Once this tour was over, Neil was able to drop down to Los Angeles and catch up with big brother Tim, who had just completed a new solo album with Mitchell Froom producing. Tim had no hesitation in using a producer so closely aligned with the sound of Crowded House. "I know some people will think it's too close for comfort," he conceded to *Music Express*."But our albums sound nothing alike, and Neil recommended

• Tim Finn onstage, Auckland, 1990.

Mitchell well before they started their first album. I responded to his dark humour and his musicality, so I have no qualms about using the same producer."

Froom was pleased Tim wasn't after any duplication of a Crowded House sound. "That'd be the last thing I'd want to do," he said later. "Whenever you try to copy something, it's always second generation, never very interesting."

A short demo session with Froom had gone so well that Capitol gave Mitchell and Tim the go-ahead to make the record. "That was an incredible three days, like two guys getting together and forming a group and getting a contract," recalls Mitchell. This experience of recording together would soon prove valuable for all parties.

Neil contributed some backing vocals to the subsequent album, 'Tim Finn', and was thrilled to be able to perform with Tim again. The April LA showcase/launch party for the album was held in a small club off Sunset Strip, and a veritable supergroup was assembled for the gig. Its members included Richard Thompson and Neil on guitars, Mitchell Froom on organ, percussionist Alex Acuna and Paul Hester on drums. As well as featuring Tim's new material, the brothers Finn delighted the Split Enz fans in the crowd with versions of Enz favourites 'I See Red' and 'Six Months In A Leaky Boat'.

Tim Finn was able to perform his new songs in Auckland the same month, playing an April 8 Greenpeace benefit concert at the Mt Smart Super Top venue. Other name acts appearing included blues-rocker Stevie Ray Vaughan and American singer/songwriter Toni Childs.

Family matters, meanwhile, were occupying most of Neil's time. Along with wife Sharon and son Liam, Neil had been sponsoring Stephen Mushame, a young boy from the war-torn southern African nation of Mozambique, through a support program run by humanitarian organisation World Vision. This wasn't something he'd publicised greatly, but when approached to help World Vision promote their upcoming 40 Hour Famine fundraising campaign, Neil willingly agreed.

"They rang me up, saying they'd seen me talking about world hunger on TV. 'Would you like to go to Mozambique for two weeks, visit some of the places we're working, and come back and tell people about it?'," Neil later explained. "It came at exactly the right time. I loved the idea and found it a fantastically uplifting experience."

In June 1989, Neil visited Southern Africa to observe the results of World Vision's work. "I was there for about 12 days, seven of those in Mozambique," Neil said later. "We visited camps where people were huddled together in secure zones, beyond the reach of the bandits who had been terrorising the place for 10 years. But because they're huddled together in large numbers, there's not enough food and a lot of disease in most of these places. It's an eye-opener."

Yet, despite the poverty and disease encountered, Neil claimed that... "Nothing I saw, no matter how tragic, made me despair. It gave me a lot of inspiration that people are so stoic, dignified and colourful. I sang a lot with them while I was there too. I came back thinking I had taken something from them, rather than giving them anything except a few kids a good time."

Neil was pleased to find his young friend Stephen, with whom he had regularly corresponded, in good shape, but the trip clearly caused him some soul-searching. Many a Hollywood star would have commandeered an *Entertainment Tonight* TV film crew and personal publicist to choreograph such a mission, got the token shots holding an emaciated baby, then flown back to Malibu. That was not the Neil Finn style.

"It was hard to come back and relate being back in Australia with what I'd seen," he explained later. "I don't know how to apply what I've seen to the rest of my life. I still have a strange uneasiness about it. I don't feel compelled to get involved in raising money for famine relief as a result of it, although I have done a bit. [Crowded House played a successful Aid For Ethiopia concert in Australia in 1988].

"In Africa, when people enjoy themselves, it's in a far more pure way than what we call pleasure," Neil analysed. "It doesn't rely on any gimmicks whatsoever. When I came back, what sickened me the most was to see advertisements for places like Sanctuary Cove in Australia, where you see couples gliding up in limousines, drink-ing champagne. What masquerades as pleasure seemed to me so soul-less and boring, with no basis in any kind of humanity. We spend so much money on things that are supposed to be enjoyable and it's just shit. Those people should go down to the local pub and have a sing-song. That's way better than going to some luxury resort!"

It's not fanciful to speculate that resonances of Neil's African trip can be seen in the lyrics of some of the songs he was to write in the months afterward, especially 'Chocolate Cake', with its vitriolic attack on American consumerism.

◆

ON APRIL 7, 1989, Crowded House were joined on stage at Pantage's Theatre, Los Angeles, by Sixties rock icon Roger McGuinn, former leader of The Byrds. They played versions of three Byrds classics, 'Mr Tambourine Man', 'So You Want To Be A Rock'n'Roll Star' and 'Eight Miles High', and the results appeared on the single release of 'I Feel Possessed' in Australia and the subsequent CD single of 'Weather With You' in Britain.

The band then went into a hiatus. It had been four years of frenetic activity since Crowded House opened for business, and that had taken its toll physically and emotionally. It was time to call a halt, reflect, and reassess just what what was happening to the band, internally and externally. But instead of 'the pause that refreshes,' this break just about killed the band. Their internal turmoil was kept well hidden, but in 1991 Neil Finn was to look back on this period as the most troublesome in the band's entire career.

"We had some severe obstacles to overcome through that period," he said. "We really went through a lot of twisting and turning, out of sight of the public. I was questioning whether I wanted a band, and the other guys were feeling remote from me. When we went out on the road in support of the second record, we weren't really appreciating how lucky we are to do this. We were just snowed under from the attention being focused on us and we retreated from it. We've since realised we are a band and do have something that is unique."

The high artistic standards Neil Finn has

always set for himself and his comrades, combined with his constant self-analysis, must make working with him a real challenge. Nick Seymour was reminded of this in the period leading up to third album.

It was never announced officially, but in 1991, the Australian edition of *Rolling Stone* carried a story to the effect that Seymour had been sacked, then reinstated by Neil Finn after a month in the wilderness. "We had to re-establish our confidence levels with each other," Nick told the magazine.

Manager Gary Stamler, however, pegs Seymour's absence as more likely four months. "We were sent on an expedition to find a replacement for Nick," he says. "I remember Mark Hart was enlisted again, and he felt strange about going to Australia to work on songs without Nick. I believe the pre-production process for what became 'Woodface' began without Nick. Mitchell Froom was very instrumental in talking Neil into letting Nick back in the band."

Stamler has a demo tape of seven songs worked on then, none of which made 'Woodface', and cites two, 'Legs Are Gone' and 'Time Immemorial', as personal favourites. One song, 'Telly's Gone Bung', was a Hester composition, likely reflecting his obsession with TV.

Referring to internal problems, Neil told *The Listener* that he... "sorted out a lot of things that were inherently problematical in the line-up of the band." He refused to be more specific, claiming: "I don't want to get into it, it's like discussing your marriage. It was just personality things that were occurring, patterns we needed to break out of, which we did."

Nick Seymour later told U.S mag *Pulse*: "We just stopped trusting each other for a while, and made the mistake of shutting each other out. Things weren't said when they should have been and we finally had a big altercation about a lot of little things." The flashpoint were problems Neil had with Nick's visual ideas for the band. "There was a real mistrust in my motivation," said Nick. "Neil thought I was trying to place a pretentious attitude on the band that he couldn't work with."

Neil's perfectionist songwriting approach also fuelled the tension. "At times I've thought we've got some killer songs and Neil has turned

around and said 'I don't want to do that song, the lyrics aren't resolved'," saaid Nick. "If there's one connecting puzzle to the lyrics, if one thing doesn't make sense or tie in with what he's trying to describe with the music, he'll throw the song away. I'll be there saying, 'How can you? We've got a great feel, a great melody and structure', but there'll be this one lyric."

The pressure on Neil Finn as the sole song-writer in Crowded House, aside from the occasional contribution from Paul Hester, was beginning to tell. In an interview with *Rolling Stone*, Paul was sympathetic towards Neil's plight. "All of us have got other things we can touch on, but Neil does *the one thing* all the time. He pours all of it into Crowded House, so the pressure is really on him to come up with 10 or 12 songs every time."

With Split Enz, Neil always had Tim Finn to count on for plenty of material, plus those trademark Eddie Rayner instrumentals. Those dreaded

• Tim and Neil performing together

of sorrow. "I spent most of 1990 wandering around in various states of intoxication, hosted quite festively by Melbourne," he told Chenery.

Scaachi was soon paired with Italian actor Vincent D'Onofrio, whom she met on the set of torrid drama *Salt On Our Skin*. When their relationship foundered, he blabbed about their love life to the tabloid press, an indescretion that Tim Finn would never commit. Tim, meanwhile, has not been publicly linked to a new partner since Greta.

Neither of Tim's later albums duplicated the commercial success of his début, 'Escapade', and his record deal with Virgin only lasted for one album, 'Big Canoe'. Capitol Records signed him in 1988, but by late 1989 it was clear the 'Tim Finn' album wasn't going to set the music world afire either. Tim had retained popularity in Australasia as something of a musical icon, but that no longer guaranteed huge record sales and sell-out tours.

Tim decided to establish his own Melbourne studio so he could record and develop musically without being at the mercy, time and money wise, of expensive, sophisticated studios on the other side of the world. Christened Periscope, his studio took over the former bedroom of his Melbourne home. This room had, in earlier days, been occupied by both Paul Hester and Nick Seymour, housesitting while Tim lived in London.

With a 24-track Dolby Sound Reduction recording system installed, this wasn't your average low-tech bedroom studio set-up. Establishing it was something of a community project. The conversion took six weeks, with Sharon Finn installing mosaic, Neil putting in a pool table, and Paul making the tea. With Periscope now up and running, it seemed a perfect time for Tim and Neil Finn to try writing songs together.

Brotherly bonds were further strengthened when Split Enz decided to reunite for four Australian gigs with Crowded House in late December, 1989. No grand design was at work here, just a bunch of mates deciding to play some summertime shows together. The timing seemed appropriate too, as they'd see out the decade with a New Year's Eve concert in Sydney.

words 'writer's block' were whispered in this pre-*Woodface* period, and Paul Hester would later explain that... "Basically, Neil was looking for a soulmate then."

His closest musical soulmate had always been brother Tim, now conveniently living in Melbourne. Post Split Enz, Tim had become quite the citizen of the world, thanks to his continuing relationship with actress Greta Scacchi. The couple spent time in Tuscany with Greta's Italian father Lucca, and, in the course of recording and promoting his second and third solo albums, 1986's 'Big Canoe' and 1989's 'Tim Finn', the nomadic troubadour based himself in London and Los Angeles, predominantly London.

Tim Finn's highly publicised relationship with Greta didn't survive the decade, however. The couple split in late 1989, reportedly devastating Tim. During their long and passionate affair, he had, as he later admitted to journalist Susan Chenery, allowed himself... "to get sucked into somedody else's vortex. It is easy to do with a woman who is beautiful and highly successful and has a very fascinating family and an extremely broad and rich variety of contacts. I almost gave up responsibility for my own life for a while and just kind of moved into her world and lost myself in the process."

The split with Greta and the commercial failure of 1989's 'Tim Finn' album reportedly triggered a bout of depression, and related drowning

This Enz lineup comprised Tim and Neil Finn, keyboardist Eddie Rayner, bassist Nigel Griggs and drummer Noel Crombie, though Paul Hester sat in for a few songs. The fact that they headlined over Crowded House proved the name Split Enz still packed a hefty punch in Australia. The December 27 opening date in small New South Wales town Mudgee went well, but then tragedy struck.

The next night's show was scheduled for Newcastle, New South Wales. Because the Mudgee gig ran late, the tour's crew postponed their load-in time at the Newcastle Workingmens Club from 10 to 11 am. That proved fortuitous, for at 10.28 am a powerful earthquake struck, demolishing the building. Tour truck driver John O'Shannassy was killed inside, and a roadie was rescued from the rubble after six hours. If the quake had hit an hour later, the death toll would have been much higher.

This tragedy cast a shadow over the rest of the tour, but both bands returned to Newcastle in February 1990 as part of an Earthquake Relief Concert. Featuring a Who's Who of Oz rock, including Midnight Oil, Noiseworks, The Angels and Jimmy Barnes, this was a huge success, musically and financially. Crowded House co-manager Grant Thomas predicted a million dollar take, and proudly declared: "This is the biggest audience ever to pay for a day of Australasian acts." At the show, Neil told the crowd of 40,000: "We were bound up in this event when a bit of paper was slipped under our door saying 'gig cancelled because of earthquake'. We lost a truck driver in it, and that's reason enough to be involved."

In January 1990, Tim and Neil Finn began their great songwriting experiment. Back in the Split Enz era, they had been highly supportive of each other's work, but only felt comfortable writing songs individually. Reflecting on this later, Neil admitted: "It surprises us too, that we didn't write together then. But we just weren't relaxed enough with each other. It was too much a younger brother/older brother thing."

Now, however, Neil was open to the idea of working together. "I'd been alone with my songwriting for five years, and that can be a very anxious task. Having somebody to bounce off was very rewarding." Their radically different career trajectories since the demise of Split Enz had injected a new dynamic into the Finns' relationship. "I felt more confident because I'd formed Crowded House and was now more on an equal footing with Tim," explains Neil. "We were very excited about collaborating."

The initial vision was of a Finn brothers album if the writing relationship proved fertile, and that was the understanding when Tim and Neil began writing songs in the summer of 1990. The experiment worked better than either could have dreamed. "When we actually established a basis for working together again, a lot of that [rivalry] disappeared overnight," says Neil. "I was aware that Tim was probably feeling a little strange because his younger brother had come along, had a hit in America and all that stuff, but as soon as we began working together, we put all that aside."

With typical candour, Tim admits to these emotions. "I found it odd to deal with. I had wanted success for so long with Split Enz, but then I had to go through the process of watching it happen to Neil, not me!"

The brothers threw themselves enthusiastically into a short but intense period of joint songwriting that has few equals in terms of calibre and quantity. Forget writers block, this was writers deluge, as great songs just kept on coming. "It was such an uplifting experience... I can't state that too heavily," stressed Neil. "You don't expect, after ten years, to find a new way of writing. You think you've defined your parameters and then all of a sudden you're able to write about different things. It was like we'd been visited by the muse and she'd been persuaded to stay for a couple of weeks. As Tim said in our press bio, 'We were visited by the voluptuous muse and we ravaged her'. He always did have a pretentious side to him!," Neil laughs.

Tim Finn confirms the ease of this session. "It really did flow. I guess it had been building up for years, but the melodies and lyrics just poured out." Of the 14 songs bequeathed by the muse, 11 have appeared, spread over three different albums: eight on 'Woodface', two on Tim's 'Before & After' album and one on 'Together Alone'.

THE CREATIVE LIFT Neil gained by writing with Tim sagged when it came to coming up with songs for the new Crowded House record. The band began recording with Mitchell Froom in Los Angeles at A&M Studios, Sunset Sound Factory and Ocean Way Studios, as well as in Melbourne, but internal tensions remained.

"There was some strain between Mitchell and Neil then," recalls Stamler. "Neil was upset that they couldn't record the whole thing in Australia, and there was Mark not knowing whether he was really in or out of the band. It was a time of upheaval."

No more so than when Capitol Records rejected the finished album! The shock waves from that verdict reverberated within Neil Finn the way the San Andreas Fault can shake up the Californian coast. Gary Stamler remembers this decision was the first difficult job new Capitol President Hale Milgrim faced. "He'd been a big fan of the band from his days at Elektra and now he had to call Neil and tell him this album shouldn't be released."

Capitol Records were understandably anxious to release a strong album after the comparative commercial disappointment of 'Temple Of Low Men', and didn't feel this one had the goods. Stamler's copy of this original third record bears a delivery date of June 23, 1990. Songs on it never released include 'Dr Livingstone', (eventually used as an extra track on a 'Four Seasons In One Day' CD single), 'Anyone Can Tell', 'Left Hand', 'Sacred Cow' and 'Fields Are Full Of Your Kind'.

"[Neil] was very emotional and profoundly negative," says Stamler. "He was not a willing listener for a couple of days, and I bore the brunt of some of that conversation. Neil didn't quite understand how he was supposed to write singles. I believe for about a month he tried to write songs to finish the record but ultimately couldn't or didn't do it."

Neil confesses that he was in a state of turmoil then. "We had said we were going to do a Finn brothers record, so it was like, 'Well, when the hell are we going to finish that and when the hell is it going to come out?' It was a schizophrenic thing in my mind and I got very anxious about it. I was trying to think of two things at once, but I could only concentrate on one thing. It was really causing problems. I had this feeling of why couldn't it be just one thing. It's like having two mistresses. You run from one house to another and you can't satisfy either."

To solve this problem before facing a nervous breakdown, Neil devised a radically daring plan. Why not combine the best from both projects and bring Tim into Crowded House as a fourth member?

The more Neil considered it, the more sense the plan made, and he seized the potential solution like a drowning man gasping for air. Once convinced, and with Tim on side, he presented Nick Seymour and Paul Hester with a fait accompli – this is how the new Crowded House will look.

This was not a decision up for negotiation. It dramatically confirmed that Crowded House, more than ever, was Neil Finn's band. The image of fun-loving camaraderie was skilfully projected in their videos, but Crowded House has never functioned as a true democracy. Neil would later claim... "There was no real resistance from Nick and Paul. When Tim and I went to them and said 'We think Tim should be in the band and we should do these songs as Crowded House,' they went 'Mm, well, OK, what do I think about that?' I guess none of us had really expected it. It was the end of an era. The three of us had done a lot together, shared a lot, and they probably thought Tim would have a strong influence on the band. He does have a strong personality. Their main worry was that they'd face some kind of Finn power bloc and suddenly that'd make the band less of a shared experience."

• Tim Finn at the piano, 1991

Manager Stamler also found it difficult to accept Tim's entry. "[It was] a bombshell," he says. "I got this abrupt call from Neil and Tim, and I remember having a funny reaction to it. Neil picked up on my lack of excitement, but that was my natural reaction. I defended it by saying, 'It could be great, but it'll be different. It throws the balance of the band off'."

One outward sign of the friction that occurred at this time is that three of the original Finn brothers songs that appeared on 'Woodface' – 'All I Ask', 'There Goes God' and 'Weather With You' – feature Ricky Fataar, a friend of the Finns since late Split Enz days, on drums, not Paul Hester. Neil told British magazine Q: "Paul has trouble accepting sudden change and always has. Unfortunately with this band it happens all the time because we're hopelessly untogether. Paul had one of his panic attacks, but when he heard the songs he agreed there was a really strong album there." Tim

Finn then facetiously interjected: "He saw dollar signs basically." It was a hint of further problems that would occur in the future.

The fact that Tim was no stranger helped ease the transition. Paul, of course, had worked with Tim in the final stage of Split Enz, and all their various paths had intersected over the years. Neil cites Tim and Nick as having much in common. "They get on very well, for a variety of reasons," he laughs, presumably referring to their partying tendencies. "There's a lot of good dynamic happening we didn't really anticipate."

For his part, Tim Finn was prepared to rein in his ego for the good of the band. In 1991, Neil explained, "I don't think that Paul and Nick really anticipated that once in, Tim would get a real feeling for the dynamics of the group and be content, in a realistic sense, to contribute, rather than coming and imposing a whole lot of his personal aspirations on the band."

Tim faced inevitable accusations that he joined Crowded House because his solo career had stalled. "If people think I did this because my own career wasn't successful, it wouldn't threaten me. Yes, there was disappointment and confusion all along. The fact that it didn't really work in the marketplace didn't diminish the experience for me, but it allowed me to join this rather wonderful band."

The announcement of an illustrious new tenant in Crowded House certainly attracted plenty of attention in Australasia. Capitol in Los Angeles were also likely to be pleased at the new arrangement, for if nothing else it meant the by now very expensive third album – Australian *Rolling Stone* had estimated a recording cost of $750,000 Aust – could finally be completed.

In retrospect, of course, Neil realised how much less of a drain on time and money 'Woodface' would have been if Tim had joined the fray earlier. Neil told *The Toronto Sun,* "We'd have chucked all the songs into the pot and had, at the most, 14 songs to work on. As it was, we worked on about 25, so just the sheer hours we spent in the studio became very wearying. It was a convoluted approach, but I think the extra time we spent worked."

Tim's entry into the band gave angle-seeking music journalists plenty of fresh copy. While Split Enz had never really broken big outside Australasia (except Canada), they remained a group that had found a place in the hearts of many rock critics, musicians, and industry types. This residual goodwill was definitely to benefit Crowded House.

With the line-up set, the key decision left was the song selection for the new album. Just six songs from the Crowded House LA sessions were to make it on to Woodface: 'Fall At Your Feet', 'Four Seasons In One Day', 'Fame Is', 'Whispers And Moans', 'As Sure As I Am' and 'She Goes On'.

By a happy coincidence, Tim had been around for these sessions and had added some backing vocals to most of those songs. The Finn brothers had been singing together for as long as they could remember, and knew there was no substitute for that kind of experience and empathy. "We cut our teeth on some pretty good harmony

songs when we were kids, and those things leave a residue," Neil explained. "Singing together again feels fantastic. There's such a familiarity to rely on. You can look around for other notes and know Tim will be there on the note he's supposed to be on. It's really *simpatico*, it's a joy."

Many of the vocal tracks for 'Woodface' were recorded in just one day at Periscope, out on what used to be the house's sunporch. "We were strangely out of whack that particular day," says Tim. "We just felt like singing!"

Their vocal approach to the 'Woodface' songs differed significantly from that employed with Split Enz. "People see Tim and I together and think, 'This is Split Enz again,' but there's more to it than that. We never really exploited two-part harmonies with Split Enz, except maybe on 'Six Months In A Leaky Boat', but on this record there are a half-dozen songs with very strong two part harmonies. That's a major difference."

The remaining eight tracks chosen for 'Woodface' included one Paul Hester composition, the eccentric love song 'Italian Plastic'. In all, eight songs were co-credited to Tim and Neil Finn, and five as solo Neil compositions. Some notable guests contributing to 'Woodface' include Los Lobos' David Hidalgo on accordion, Ricky Fataar on drums, Mitchell Froom and Mark Hart on keyboards, ace Melbourne blues singer Chris Wilson on harmonica, and Neil's wife Sharon singing backing vocals on 'All I Ask'.

Significantly, for the first time Neil Finn was given a co-production credit with Mitchell Froom. Reportedly a half-dozen songs on 'Woodface' were produced by Neil alone, reflecting his increased confidence in the studio. "We feel fairly confident we can build up a song from a jam rather than very strict arrangement," Nick Seymour explained. "Mitchell, on the other hand, is very good at a very formalised strict arrangement. He's an incredibly good arranger and that's what we go to him for – those real great pop songs."

Master mixer Bob Clearmountain was brought into the picture again in June 1990, working out of A&M Studios and The Record Plant in Los Angeles, and when he'd finished the much-troubled third Crowded House album was finally ready to fly. There were differing explanations for the album's title, but the most common was that it derived from a French term for hangover.

Although almost three years had elapsed since 'Temple Of Low Men', it was nevertheless decided that the newlook Crowded House should be given an opportunity to settle in before facing the public with 'Woodface'. A release date of early July 1991 was set, and during their 'down time' in 1990, Tim and Neil took the opportunity to work with some of their Melbourne musical peers.

In April they both sang backing vocals on 'Down City Streets', a song on highly-regarded Aboriginal singer/songwriter Archie Roach's album 'Charcoal Road'. Tim also added har-monies to 'Took The Children Away' on the same album, while Neil contributed backing vocals to 'Way You Live', a track on 'Ghost Nation' from Hunters & Collectors, the popular Australian rock band headed by Mark Seymour, Nick's brother.

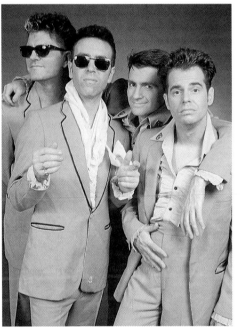

Paul Hester also kept his drumming hands busy by playing with Rose Amongst Thorns, a new Melbourne band fronted by old musical friend, singer Deborah Conway. Paul had worked with her back in 1982, on a session with her earlier band Do Re Mi, and they'd reunite after Paul left Crowded House. Hester also played in former Big Pig singer Sherine's new band. Ironically, once Paul resumed work with Crowded House, the new drummer for both Conway and Sherine was Peter Jones.

Paul and Nick Seymour also reunited as the rhythm section of the Chris Bailey Combo for some 1990 gigs. As leader of punk pioneers The Saints, Bailey is a legendary figure in Oz rock, and his short-lived Combo would mix his newer songs with Saints classics.

Neil Finn also took advantage of this extended period off the road to get acquainted with his brand new son, Elroy Timothy Finn. He joined the Finn family in early 1990, and, inter-estingly, the six year age difference between Liam and brother Elroy approximates that between Tim and Neil Finn.

The première of the Tim-era Crowded House came in Sydney, mid-November 1990, when the band played as part of the AUSMUSIC concert series, designed to promote Australian music. The US début came three months later with a rather gimmicky appearance on Valentine's Day, February 14, 1991. Crowded House performed on an early morning *Love Boat* style cruise for broadcast on Los Angeles' popular radio station KROQ, with their set squeezed between onboard wed-dings of some of their fans and contest winners.

The show confirmed the band could still handle unconventional situations with charm and humour. Neil Finn report-edly told the crowd, "I believe there are couples here today who decided to get married just because we were playing. That's a frighten-ing notion!"

With plans for the release of 'Woodface' and subsequent touring being firmed up, Crowded House began, in Neil's words, "gathering our energy for another descent into hell." He ignored the near-fatal friction the band had faced when he wrote in the record label press notes for 'Woodface' that, "We had a wonderful time preparing for this new record. Another child was born. A house built. I went to Africa. Tim and I discovered we could write together."

A new album, a new lineup, a new sound. These radical changes were to give Crowded House a fresh lease on life.

9

woodface

With 'Woodface' ready to roll, Crowded House could utter a satisfied sigh. Making it had nearly destroyed the band, but Neil Finn, Nick Seymour, Paul Hester and new member Tim Finn were confident that they had made the record of their career.

They were also aware of how much was at stake. Capitol Records had spent a massive amount on the making of the album, and had committed much more – a reported $100,000 (US) for the first video, 'Chocolate Cake', and a rumoured further $500,000 general promotions budget: impressive figures for a band whose last album had performed below expectations and who had been largely AWOL for the past two years.

On the plus side, the inclusion of Tim Finn had created a real sense of curiosity and anticipation among the music press and fans of both Crowded House and Split Enz. As well, the musical climate seemed to have warmed towards the type of classic melodic pop Crowded House peddled, and their reputation had risen in their absence. "It's very reassuring to see that you can be away and have things actually improve in that time," Neil told *Music Express* in June 1991. "You always think you might leave town and people will forget about you."

In the gap between Crowded House's second and third albums, such artists as singer/songwriter Michael Penn, Los Angeles duo The Rembrandts and Bay Area popsters Jellyfish had all achieved some success with a sound not too far removed from the House style. "I've been told often in America lately that those bands are really big fans of ours and people think they sound like us," said Neil. "If that's true in any way, great, but I think anybody doing this is influenced by a number of people. Maybe there's an aesthetic within Crowded House that people are returning to in some degree – the idea of a band being limited by its members and the way they play, and that becoming the sound. By deliberately not using the full gamut of technology, you can put personality across. Pop is a healthy word again – music designed for people to whistle along to rather than stamp their feet to."

Whistlers and their mothers found plenty to enjoy in 'Woodface'. Released on July 2, 1991, it is, quite simply, a classic pop album, crammed with melodies other artists would sacrifice their first-born to have written. It still stands as Crowded House's crowning achievement, and may ultimately prove to be one of the best pop records of the Nineties.

Tim Finn's inclusion had a galvanising effect on Crowded House's still-evolving sound. He added humour and satire to the songwriting, qualities only rarely apparent in Neil's earlier songs. Most of all, he added a distinctive voice, one that merged delightfully with his brother's.

Compared to the mood of 'Temple Of Low Men', 'Woodface' is positively bubbly. Heavy topics like religion ('There Goes God') and consumerism ('Chocolate Cake') are tackled with wit and irony, while even the seemingly obligatory song about death, 'She Goes On', has an uplifting feel. Then there are the simply gorgeous love songs ('It's Only Natural', 'Fall At Your Feet' and Paul Hester's 'Italian Plastic') and meteorological metaphors wrapped up in two unforgettable melodies: 'Four Seasons In One Day' and 'Weather With You'.

In such a diverse collection of 14 songs, even the most devoted Crowded House fan will spot at least one flaw – the rather too strident feel of 'There Goes God', perhaps, but a batting average of 12 or 13 hits in 14 will get you in the Baseball Hall Of Fame. 'Woodface' is a musical equivalent.

Also in the group's favour was the major enthusiasm within their record label, always an essential part of the jigsaw puzzle of success. Even in territories where Crowded House had never really broken, their previous hard work and attractive personalities had built up a valuable reservoir of goodwill. The band had not been happy with Capitol's support for 'Temple Of Low Men' in the US, but Neil Finn had confidently told New Zealand magazine *The Listener*, "We're their number one priority internationally for 1991."

"Back then, I never met anybody in the company who wasn't a fan," says Carrie Spacey-Foote who is now International Marketing Manager, US Repertoire, EMI Music Continental Europe. She was then Promotions Manager within Europe, and clearly recalls the 'Woodface' situation. "They have always been our company's favourite band. The problem was they hadn't really sold anything [in Britain and Europe] since the first album. There was a lot of anticipation with 'Woodface'. When we first heard it, we just thought, 'This is fantastic. All these great songs!'"

Critical support could almost be taken for granted. Aside from the likes of the *Village Voice*'s cranky Robert Christgau and some cynical British scribes, music writers were favourably predisposed to Crowded House. Give them the goods, and the raves would flow.

All the ingredients, then, were on hand for a breakthrough third album.

Typically for Crowded House, however, nothing came easily. A major mistake would seem to have been the selection of 'Chocolate Cake' as the first single. Released on May 20, 1991, people either loved or hated this sharply satirical song, with a majority falling into the latter group. It was a good album track to show-case the edge Tim Finn had brought the band, but

• **Neil and Tim Finn at the Powerstation, Auckland, 1992**

as a single from an album stuffed with gorgeous pop songs, it was a major miscalculation.

The single did attract some airplay on modern rock and college radio stations in North America, but sales-wise it flopped both there and in Britain, where it peaked at a miserable No. 69. The costly video shot by top Australian director John Hillcoat gave Paul Hester a chance to cross-dress and ham it up, but was hardly a cost-efficient exercise.

This choice of first single caused some disagreement between the US and British labels. Malcolm Hill, Head of Promotions at Parlophone Records, recalls: "We didn't want it as a single, to be honest. We were pushed into it because the Americans had spent a fortune on the video. 'Chocolate Cake' got us off to a bad start and proved it [selling 'Woodface'] was going to be difficult."

The fact that 'Chocolate Cake's lyrics could be interpreted as anti-American was also a problem. In an otherwise favourable review, *Rolling Stone* critic Kristine McKenna called the song... "objectionable. Lambasting America as a spoiled culture of overfed vulgarians seems hypocritical given that Crowded House relocated to Los Angeles in order to kick its career into high gear." However, no rock critic objected to the put down of Andrew Lloyd Webber – a far safer target than American consumerism.

Capitol in Los Angeles weren't taking media support for Crowded House for granted. In April '91 they sent out advance tapes of 'Woodface' to

• **Crowded House backstage at the Borderline, London, 1991**

select music publications and planned an expensive publicity campaign. This included flying some North American scribes, the author amongst them, to Paris to catch a showcase performance of the new-look lineup.

The June 6 gig at trendy disco Les Bains – oft inhabited by supermodels and showbiz celebs – was designed to enlist the support of media and music industry types in breaking the band out of its limited cult following in France. Such gigs also served as an acid test for Tim Finn. It was a question of whether or not he would be able to rein in his strong ego and intensely personal performance style and, instead, slip into Crowded House's loosely relaxed manner with a minimum of disruption.

In these early days of the experiment, Tim attempted this valiantly, and with some success. He added keyboard fills and harmonies to much of the material and seized the spotlight on 'All I Ask' with gusto. The vocal harmonies on the new Finn brothers material delighted the crowd, but some of the earlier Crowded House songs gained little from Tim's presence.

This show was a sweaty triumph for Crowded House. Towel draped around his neck like a victorious boxer after a title bout, Neil Finn exited in an arc of triumph. He knew this gig confirmed that Paris, and the rest of Europe, was ripe for the taking.

The following day, in palatial surroundings at the George Cinq hotel, Neil reflected on the gig and Tim's new role. "Having Tim in the band just feels like it was always meant to be," he said. "Onstage, it's feeling very strong. The one thing we were nervous about was how to incorporate Tim without him being like a Stevie Nicks character with her tambourine on the side of the stage. He has a fully-fledged function as keyboardist, so he can't slack off – have an off night and sulk on the side of the stage!"

Neil realised in advance that Tim's presence would add an edge to Crowded House's performance style. "He does add a certain animal intensity to proceedings. He can get a bit primal. If things aren't going right, he's been known to smash microphones and push cameramen over!"

The Paris scenario was repeated with other showcase European dates. Two sold-out nights at

The Borderline, a small club in London's West End, on June 12 and 13, helped serve notice that the band meant business. Malcolm Hill at Parlophone sees those gigs as crucial. "Ultimately, the sight of a few hundred people queuing for a gig they can't get into and everybody in town wanting to get into does whip up some excitement!" Having Roxy Music guitarist/Split Enz producer Phil Manzanera guest the first night, and Richard Thompson the second, helped the buzz, as did a Radio One broadcast of live highlights.

'Woodface' reached No. 25 in Britain on the July 20 chart, but soon dropped. Any signs of an imminent international breakthrough were well and truly disguised. In Canada, still the group's best market outside Australasia, the album peaked at No. 17 at the end of July (it would go gold there), while the US *Billboard* album charts saw it debut at No. 83, but exit the Top 100 after just two weeks. 'Woodface' was to perch on the lower level of the Top 200 US charts until November 1991, but this scarcely qualifies as hit status.

Crowded House's popularity in Australia and New Zealand remained firm, without exploding to a higher level, and the album reached the Top 10 in both countries, débuting at No. 3 in New Zealand. Home success may have been gratifying, but, given the huge expense of making and promoting 'Woodface', anxiety was spreading in record label boardrooms.

Some encouragement was to be had from the almost unanimous strong critical response to 'Woodface'. As hoped, Tim's entry into the band helped grab more press. In their July '91 issue, respected American monthly *Musician* chimed in with a major feature, but it contained some glaring factual errors – it referred to drummer *Nick* Hester and bassist *Paul* Seymour, and claimed Tim founded Split Enz in Australia in 1974!

Influential British monthly *Q* ran a large piece in its July '91 issue, which also contained a four star rave of the album, declaring..." the Finns' gifts for tunesmithery seem as seamlessly compatible as their creamy vocal harmonies." As was now apparently mandatory in 'Woodface' reviews, this also drew comparisons to the Lennon & McCartney songs of the late Sixties. National newspaper*The Australian*, for instance,

claimed that, "If Lennon and McCartney had been brothers, maybe they'd have continued to work together, and maybe they'd have sounded this good... If Tim is high, Neil is low. If Neil is sweet, Tim will be slightly sour."

Crowded House followed up their exploratory European gigs with a July promotional trip to North America. As had become their pattern, they mixed up rounds of interviews with private acoustic performances for music industry types.

Despite Neil's initial optimism, integrating Tim into the group's performance style began to prove troublesome during the Australian tour that followed. Gary Stamler's original scepticism was confirmed. "One thing [co-manager] Grant Thomas and I said to each other was that we'd be asked to find Mark Hart again before the band toured America. Sure enough, an Australian tour with Tim playing keyboards wasn't entirely satisfactory, and the call went out for Mark. Tim became the acoustic guitarist, Mark the keyboard and electric guitar player."

• **Nick and Neil at the Borderline**

Hart's patience must have been tried at this point. He'd been about to join Crowded House as a full member before Tim's arrival squeezed him out, and then was asked to tour again.

North American dates through August and September 1991 grabbed the usual critical praise, but confirmed their stock was falling commercially. Canadian promoter Rob Bennett recalls that attendance in the biggest markets held firm,

• **Tim Finn at Massey Hall, Toronto, 1991**

but slipped elsewhere. "In London, Ontario, they went from 2,000 people the previous tour to 900. I thought, 'They're too good a band for this', but it was also at the extreme height of the recession." A soldout Massey Hall show on September 24 saw the Toronto audience sing 'Happy Birthday' to Neil's now eight year-old son Liam.

The 'Woodface' songs pushed to American radio after 'Chocolate Cake' weren't getting the warmest of responses, so Crowded House's position was becoming shaky. It was, of course, over four years since the hits from the début album – an eternity in the pop world. Neil Finn had said in that first flush of success that... "We flirted with the Americans. We tried to charm them, and I guess it worked!" The love affair had now cooled.

FOLLOWING THIS TOUR, it was time to take a proper shot at Britain and Europe with a full tour in support of 'Woodface'. The fact that their October 10 Hammersmith Odeon show sold out was encouraging, as was the response to the second single, the gentle ballad 'Fall At Your Feet'. The song's impending chart success was helped by the coincidental hit English crooner Paul Young was having with his version of the 1987 Crowded House smash, 'Don't Dream It's Over'. "We bounced in off the back of that," admits Malcolm Hill. "We put the original of 'Don't Dream' on the 'Fall At Your Feet' single, and that helped us get higher up the charts. Paul Young's record was sacrificed [it peaked at No. 20], but we got a hit!"

Entering the UK charts on November 9, 1991, 'Fall At Your Feet' peaked at No. 13; not a mega-smash but a sign that fortunes were improving rapidly. As seems to have occurred throughout the careers of both Split Enz and Crowded House, it was all too often a case of one step forwards followed by one step back or, in this case, one

• **Tim and Nick at The Powerstation, Auckland**

step outside for Tim Finn. On November 1, in the middle of a British tour, he left Crowded House in Glasgow. His valiant effort of trying to mould his strong personality into the group dynamic had failed. Analysed Neil later: "Trying to marry Tim's performance style with ours was quite awkward, both for him and us. There was a slight unease to the whole thing on stage. We decided it'd be better to continue as we had and for Tim to go his own way."

Tim agrees with the assessment. "I tended to take a more passive role. I consciously didn't want to shake the chemistry too much, and that cost me in the sense of becoming increasingly frustrated. It was push and pull. How much do I give? Do I stand back? On stage, I prefer to be in the moment, to completely lose myself, so I got a bit frustrated with that feeling of being a square peg in a round hole."

The fact the change was made mid-tour would suggest real tension and a sudden explosion, but Tim denies this. "It was a relief for everybody, and there were certainly no bad feelings. People are asking if there was punch-up, but it was a very civilised departure. We just had a meeting in a Glasgow hotel room and it was pretty much a mutual decision."

The surprise at Tim's departure was far less than at his joining Crowded House in the first place. Though brief, the marriage had suited both parties. It had given the band a superb record that was about to become the hit they needed (in Britain and Europe at least), and it had boosted Tim Finn's own sagging reputation as a singer/songwriter. He had by now landed a solo deal with Capitol in the US, whose then President Hale Milgrim was a major fan, so he could again focus on his own career.

"It was a minor glitch that sounded worse as things led up to it than when it actually happened," said EMI's Carrie Spacey-Foote termed the change. "We had a great news story, the tour carried on and it was excellent!"

Crowded House resumed their British tour with a minimum of disruption, quickly flying Mark Hart in to renew his former role as touring keyboardist/ guitarist. The live line-up now comprised Neil Finn, Nick Seymour, Paul Hester and Mark Hart, a grouping dating back to the

• **Crowded House at the Hammersmith Odeon, London, 1991**

'Temple Of Low Men' era.

A live session on Radio One with Johnny Walker on November 7 gave valuable exposure. The next two night of shows at London's Town & Country Club sold out, and everything was finally coming together for the band in Britain. The Town & Country Club show on November 9 was recorded live and a promotional only live double CD was mailed out to the band's friends in the press the following January. Only 2,000 were pressed worldwide, 500 of them in the UK.

This all too rare artefact is actually a splendid showcase, featuring some amusing ad-libs between the band as well as superb versions of 'When You Come', 'Italian Plastic' – complete with now obligatory segue into Tommy Roe's 'Dizzy' – and 'Chocolate Cake'. Nevertheless, the band weren't entirely happy with the release. "We didn't know that the record company was going to do it at all," said Neil Finn later. "We had sent them a DAT of the shows so they could take a couple of songs off for a single, but they ended up doing this CD thing. It indicated that because we are fairly loose about what we do and not precious about letting things go out warts and all, people will start to take advantage and assume we'll be okay about everything that comes out."

Inevitably, some of these promo CDs found their way on to the collectors' market, and it has become the most expensive piece of Crowded House memorabilia around, with prices now exceeding £50.

All that was now needed to push Crowded House over the edge was a bona fide Top Ten single and Britain and Europe would surely fall at Crowded House's feet. That came in February 1992, with the release of 'Weather With You', a slightly surreal song with such an irresistable hook line that it's a wonder this wasn't chosen as the first single way back when 'Woodface' was first released. It quickly became the band's first ever British Top Ten hit, reaching No. 7, and brought 'Woodface' into the Top Ten with it.

Helping the single's acceptance on radio was a newly edited version done by the UK label without the group's prior knowledge. "It was done surreptitiously, but the band reluctantly agreed later," explains Gary Stamler. "This new version brought the chorus up quicker."

"Everything seems to have come together because we finally got the timing right," Neil told *Record Collector* magazine in the UK. " In England it seems if you're not there in the right two weeks you might as well not be there at all; everything goes up and down the charts so fast."

To Parlophone's Head Of Promotions Malcolm Hill, Crowded House's willingness to tour was a key. "It's about the right single being picked, being available at the right time for the right TV shows, and touring at the right time." The band's strength as performers proved their strongest weapon. "It's always a happy experience seeing their shows, and people buy things that make them happy, like memories," says Hill. "There's always something memorable at their shows, and their forte is they make lots of people feel part of what they're doing."

This British, and subsequent European, breakthrough nearly didn't happen. Gary Stamler credits the commitment, financial and moral, of Capitol President Hale Milgrim and the enthusiasm of the British label. "It was a very dark fork in the road that we reached after 'Fall At Your Feet' had run its course. If Hale had decided against coming up with another 200 grand or so of his money to break the band in England... That was a very difficult financial call. His superiors were clearly not in favour of spending any more money in support of an album that had already proved very expensive."

Major budget decisions regarding Crowded House were still made out of Los Angeles, so Milgrim's support was crucial. He now recalls that... "All I could really do at that time was say, 'We'll spend as many dollars as makes sense and have Crowded House spend all their time over in

Europe to try and build a strong base there, for the future as well'. I kept having an optimistic attitude that [the success] would spread, but it never did."

For their part, the UK company contributed, in Stamler's words, "... a very organised and successful marketing campaign to take the band from sales of 12,000 for 'Temple Of Low Men and a gig at the Borderline to the platinum record they ultimately achieved with 'Woodface' and gigs at Wembley Arena."

Sensing that Britain and Europe were, by early 1992, the best remaining hopes for the success of 'Woodface', Crowded House intensified their efforts in those markets. An eight-date British tour in late February sold out, and plans were made for major summer performances, including their début at London's Wembley Arena. Yet another joint Finn composition with meteorological overtones, 'Four Seasons In One Day', was selected as the new single to coincide with that tour.

Between these assaults on Europe, Crowded House kept their Australasian fans happy with March and April dates there, under the tag Then There Were Three. The band interrupted their regular tour to play in front of the largest crowd of their career on Saturday March 28 at Centennial Park, Sydney. Billed as The Concert For Life, it was a fundraiser for AIDS and heart transplant wards at the local St Vincent's Hospital. About 90,000 concertgoers paid $21 (Aust.) each to hear an Oz rock bill headed by INXS – still the major band Down Under – and Crowded House, plus Yothu Yindi, Deborah Conway, Diesel, Ratcat and Kiwi star Jenny Morris. Crowded House scored best with the audience and press, the *Sydney Morning Herald* declaring, "They pretty much saved the day with a fine performance which reached out and forged a real link with the crowd."

Across the Tasman, 'Woodface' had done well in New Zealand, selling platinum, reaching No. 1 in April, and achieving saturation airplay with its singles. At the 1992 New Zealand Music Awards in April, Neil Finn won as Best Songwriter for 'Fall At Your Feet', and Crowded House were Top International Performers, but in the botched live telecast of the show, Neil's thank you's to family

• Crowded House with Platinum awards for Woodface

and management were cut off, much to his annoyance.

Neil showed his commitment to the New Zealand music scene by giving a free Crowded House concert in Auckland's Aotea Square in aid of Moana and the Moahunters, a cash-strapped local band invited to the New Orleans Jazz & Blues Heritage Festival. The event raised $3,000 for their trip.

Also getting a career boost from this tour was young Christchurch pop-rock band, The Holy Toledos. They were chosen as support act for this tour and also the Split Enz reunion tour a year later, and a good rapport with Paul Hester saw him produce five tracks on their 1993 album, 'Blood' and help them get a record deal with Sony. Singer/songwriter Brendan Gregg enjoyed Paul's production style. "He said, 'It's just a record. This is about having fun and playing the best you can'," said Gregg.

In Australia, other awards rolled in. The local edition of *Rolling Stone* held Readers Picks that saw Neil Finn placed second as Best Male Singer (behind Jimmy Barnes) and Best Songwriter (behind Paul Kelly), but 'Woodface' won as Best Album and Best Cover Art. The band placed fourth as Artist Of The Year (INXS won). Confirming they remained the critics fave, the magazine's writers cited them as Artist Of The Year, Best Band and Best Album.

Accolades at home are nice enough, but all concerned were quite aware that Europe was now their key market. News from the 'Weather With You' front was increasingly bright, for the British Top 10 success of that single was now being duplicated on the European continent. Germany, the biggest, most influential market in Europe, finally succumbed to Crowded House's charms with 'Weather'. "It was the biggest hit single on German radio in 1992," recalls EMI's Carrie Spacey-Foote. "The only rival was MC Hammer's 'You Can't Touch This'. It stayed on airplay charts there for five months, and that has so much influence on the rest of Europe. One exception is Holland, per capita the biggest market for Crowded House in Europe. They sold over 100,000 copies of 'Woodface' there!"

Saturation play on MTV Europe for the 'Weather With You' video was a major asset, and the result was a formidable sales figure of 250,000 for the single in Europe. Further helping the cause was the band's willingness to devise or go along with attention-grabbing promotional stunts. In Holland, they painted canvases onstage, then auctioned them off for charity. Spacey-Foote recalls one full day in the MTV studios. "Nick was painting a backdrop that they'd perform in front of that night, Neil was out on the street followed by a roving camera, auditioning for a musician to join them in a one-off performance, and Paul was lying on a bed in the studio co-ordinating the whole thing. It culminated with them playing live on TV with a guy they found outside a tube station playing sax. That was phenomenal stuff, never seen before there!"

Neil Finn was, by now, shrewdly aware of the importance of record company goodwill. Addressing the 1992 New Zealand Music Convention, he said: "Part of the reason now that 'Woodface' is becoming successful again in England after six months of waiting around is because those people [label allies] have made it a personal mission to not let our record go. Personal relationships with the people you deal with and recognising the real people amongst them, those who are actually into your music, is

probably the single most important thing I've discovered."

This realisation has been crucial to Crowded House's very survival. When their career has hit major roadblocks, it has often been personal goodwill that has seen them through. As former ally at Capitol Heinz Henn put it, "Those who endear themselves to those around them are the ones who last. Make people want to work for you as opposed to having to."

The phenomenal success of 'Weather With You' in Britain and Europe led to a renewed effort by Capitol to break the song in North America, but radio simply shut the door. "We were going to do a campaign to Top 40 radio in which we'd send a map with flags in – another Top 10 hit here," explains Stamler. "Programmers would say, 'When my transmitter reaches London, I'll play the record'." He theorises that the time simply wasn't right for the song. "America was into a dance, funk, rhythm thing, or else big ballads by

• Neil and Paul, Frankfurt, 1991

superstars. They didn't have a slot for what they saw as a light airy pop thing."

The failure of 'Woodface' in America still distreses former Capitol President Hale Milgrim. "That was extraordinarily frustrating to me, as a fan and friend of the band and somebody I felt they were open to listen to. I can tell you as a fact we worked very hard to make it a success. When you sense you have a lot of the right elements together and for whatever reason they don't coalesce, that's always frustrating."

Milgrim was encouraged that huge British and European success confirmed his faith in the band, and takes solace in his belief that there is no formula for success in the rock'n'roll business. "If there was we would have patented it," he says. "You can have the right group, the right tour, but yet the timing may not be quite right in other areas."

Hale does heartily praise Crowded House and Gary Stamler for living up to their end. "They delivered me a record with hit after hit on it and bent over backwards to work with the record company, radio, retailers, everything."

If America was clearly a lost cause by mid-1992, Crowded House's ascension to the arena ranks was confirmed with a Wembley Arena triumph in June and subsequent British dates at other large venues. Their impact on the British concert-going public was vividly demonstrated in November 1992, when readers of top music mag *Q* voted them Best Live Act of the Year, beating out such superstars as U2 and Guns 'N Roses. Subsequent singles off 'Woodface', 'Four Seasons In One Day' and 'It's Only Natural,' also enjoyed British chart success, confirming their breakthrough into pop's first division there.

◆

AS THE LIFE of the album stretched on past the one year mark, the band's stamina began to lag.

Hinting at future strife, Paul Hester was beginning to resent the long grind, as Malcolm Hill recalls. "I believe with 'It's Only Natural' the band committed to returning... coming back here to appear on *Top Of The Pops*. They agreed on the Thursday, then Paul refused. I spent the whole weekend talking to [co-manager] Grant Thomas

in Australia trying to persuade them. In the end, they did it because we bought first class air tickets on Qantas. They arrived Tuesday, did the show Wednesday, flew back Thursday. Yes, it's a murderous schedule, but if you commit..."

Ironically, the single's chart position dropped the following week! "I doubt if flying them in was cost-effective," concedes Hill. "But it's all profile, keeping them in the public's mind." The strategy certainly worked in the long run, as 'Woodface' continued to sell steadily, even re-entering the British Top 40 charts in July 1994!

That unusual phenomenon confused the band a little, according to Gary Stamler. "When they toured Britain in 1994, 'Woodface' sales outpaced 'Together Alone' dramatically. They were touring 'Together Alone' and selling 'Woodface'."

Obviously, Crowded House couldn't keep traversing the globe in support of 'Woodface'. As with the début, it had taken an unduly long time to run its course, and Neil Finn was anxious to get back to writing and recording new material. Some relaxed family time back in Melbourne was definitely high on the agenda too.

Any autopsies on 'Woodface' would have brought mixed conclusions. As Gary Stamler noted, "Our position in the US, Canada and Australia retreated a step with the album. What had been the band's strongholds of the big sales markets had been going backwards." Britain and Europe, however, had finally warmed to Crowded House, and that marked a huge step forward. "It was yet another oddity in a 10 year collection of oddities," added Stamler.

Some fingers were pointed at Capitol in the US for the disappointing result there. "It is one of the great albums of all time, and it failed in America. That tells you something," is the scathing assessment of Finn's friend Mike Chunn. "Neil told me there has been a different President at Capitol for every Crowded House album. That's crazy! I've been inside major labels, and they're very fickle creatures. They don't like inheriting rosters, and the band has always had to face that."

There was no time for post-mortems, though. Preparations were about to begin for the making of the fourth Crowded House album, and it would prove to be their wildest recording experience ever.

10

karekare

With the gruelling world tour for 'Woodface' behind them, it was time for Crowded House to take stock and give some thought to their fourth album. Typically, they resisted any temptation to quickly capitalise on its breakthrough success (in Europe, at least) by pumping out a 'Son Of Woodface'. Instead of the tried and true path, they opted for the tightrope.

In the words of an early Split Enz classic, the band realised it was Time For A Change, creatively speaking. In a 1994 radio promo interview, Neil Finn analysed their predicament. "We'd worked with Mitchell Froom for three albums and we'd fallen into rather a standard way of working. We needed to break out of that, and since then he has too. We just thought it was time for a change. We then thought we'd find somebody totally different to Mitchell, someone with a completely different aesthetic and who is a bit wild, who'd add a random element to our work. I think we wanted to draw something out of ourselves we hadn't found before. Of all the people we met, Youth was by far the strangest."

Indeed. 'Youth' Martin's first claim to infamy was as bassist in the original incarnation of Killing Joke, the now legendary early Eighties post-punk band whose brutally apocalyptic sound is seen as a forerunner of industrial rock. On hand for the group's first three albums, he quit in 1982 "to pursue different vibes of production".

"I went to New York and did some rap, but under a different name," he explained later. "I just wanted to get some new challenges going, to

prove I was more than just a bass player."

A highly varied production career since then included work with artists as varied as The Orb, American songstress Maria McKee, Kate Bush and even Paul McCartney (1994's The Fireman collaboration). "It's great to be able to touch so many people in so many areas of life through the single vehicle of music, yet be so diverse within that one vibe. It freaks me out!"

This "wild and woolly bloke from Brixton", as Neil described him, once listed his occupation as "vagrant" on his passport, and he was definitely not the most obvious choice for Crowded House. Nor was he the first potential producer they auditioned. The mileage meter of David Field's car can testify to that.

Field is an English musician turned record label A&R executive with a growing reputation within the industry. A stint with Elektra Records in New York and London turned sour when he became embroiled in a feud with the president's son, so he jumped ship for Capitol. "[Capitol President] Hale [Milgrim] had been a fan of my work," he says, "and he welcomed me with open arms there. I was based in both London and America, with responsibilities in both territories." This new position would see him play a pivotal role in Crowded House's career.

By the time Field joined Capitol, 'Woodface' had been out for 18 months and had become a British smash. "They'd only ever worked with Mitchell Froom as a producer, and they'd made all their records in America," analyses Field. "They were thinking of doing something a little different, of spreading their wings a little. Hale said they should speak to me, so Neil called me up, we met, and he asked if I had any ideas."

The pair came up with a list of top British producers, including Steve Lillywhite, John Leckie, Gil Norton, Stephen Hague and Dave Bascombe. Crowded House were on their June 1992 British tour so Field escorted potential producers to the shows. "They did about 10 shows, so I put about 2,500 miles on the clock of my car, driving producers every other night or so to a Crowded House show – Liverpool, Sheffield, Cardiff, Norwich, Brighton, Scotland. I remember taking Gil Norton to Brighton. This was so the band could meet them and just discuss ideas."

None of the required sparks were struck, however. "At the end, Neil was very pleased to have met everybody and was excited such lofty people wanted to work with them. But he was still clearly looking for something else. The last day the band was in the country, I said 'Well, you should meet this guy Youth'. They said, 'Why, what's he done?' I read his list of credits and they said, 'What the fuck has he got to do with us? Blue Pearl, The Orb, Bananarama?'" Field's persistence paid off, however, and the unusual pairing came to be.

So why Youth? "At the very least, I felt something unusual would happen," reflects Field. "It's not as if Neil Finn needs that much production. He's a marvellous songwriter and musician, both lyrically and musically. With the band's input, you know the songs are going to get made. It's not as if you're relying on a producer to build things from scratch. From conversations with them, I sensed they wanted a more spontaneous approach. They've crafted in a more laborious way on their records before, and they wanted something a bit edgier, less laborious."

Neil picks up the story. "When we met Youth, we talked about music, and his enthusiasm was infectious. His record collection also found favour. We discovered we liked a lot of the same music. Even though he's more known for his trance/techno kind of remixes probably than anything else, he's done a lot of work in different fields. At the end, it was a risk, and we wanted to take a risk, not the safe choice. And we recorded in New Zealand for the same reason. It felt like more of an adventure. We wanted to create a

unique experience for ourselves, so we came to the ends of the earth... Karekare!"

Finn soon hit it off with Youth. "There's actually a lot more to him than you might think when you first see him. He's an ex-punk turned hippie, so he's a streetwise, eccentric character." Youth bristles a mite when this description is relayed to him. "He can call me what he likes, but I never called myself a punk or a hippie!"

Neil and Crowded House instinctively felt Youth would shake up their normal working methods. "And he did!," says Neil. "It's sometimes a stressful way of working because you don't know what you've got until the end. Nevertheless, I feel it's worth it. Like a good live show, it's worth it for the transcendental moments. It's worth enduring the embarrassment or the deflation of the mess that sometimes occurs."

Youth's reputation and unconventional working methods created some consternation at the band's American label and management. "I had a fair amount of criticism then," confides David Field. "The band's American manager, Gary Stamler, was appalled by the idea of Youth producing the album. Because the band had done so well in Europe with 'Woodface', he felt this was a crucial record for them.

"He couldn't see for one minute the idea of getting someone as eccentric as Youth to do the record. He wanted someone safer. He was totally opposed, and he was constantly going into the label in America saying 'this is a stupid idea, we shouldn't be doing this.' He was giving the Americans a lot of doubt about the whole idea, so I was consequently under a great deal of pressure."

Gary Stamler confirms his reservations at the time. "Neil felt I wasn't particularly supportive of his decision to use Youth, and that was accurate. I wasn't but that didn't mean we couldn't have got a result."

Such doubts were expressed at a subsequent A & R meeting in California, and Field admits to some nerves by this point. "So much negativity does get through. I was still confident about my idea, but it affects you."

David's colleagues were keen for him to supervise things personally, in the Field, so to speak, so flew down to New Zealand in late 1992 with no little trepidation. He was on the road to paradise...

KAREKARE is a small seaside community on the west coast of New Zealand's North Island, approximately 45 minutes drive west of Auckland. Getting there is half the fun, for the only road winds its way through the picturesque Waitakere Ranges, which have been left appealingly wild as part of a scenic reserve.

Most travellers take this road through to the more popular beach resort of Piha, just a few miles up the coast, but a turnoff down either the evocatively named Lone Kauri Road or Karekare Road will do the trick. It is a steep and narrow road, lined with ferns, and the buzzing of cicadas and chirping of a wild birds offers a soundtrack to the journey. The narrow valley broadens as the Tasman Sea approaches, and ahead lies a vista guaranteed to inspire awe in the most hardened of hearts. "You get a lump in the throat from the landscape," says Nick Seymour.

• The surf-club building at KareKare

On a calm day, the glistening surf rolls onto the sandy beach in deceptively leisurely fashion, but there's no mistaking the wild grandeur of the scene. Over the millenia, this surf has eroded away the jutting cliffs in dramatically violent fashion, while the windswept look of the vegetation further confirms this is no oasis of tranquillity.

It's surprising to learn, then, that Karekare

was a thriving beach resort from the early 1900s. First settled by Europeans in the 1870s, it also was home for, at different times, a flax mill, a wood-turning factory and sawmills for the local supply of kauri, a much-coveted timber. The place was originally named Waikarekare, which in Maori means 'ripple on the crest of the waves'. Maori were the first inhabitants here, settling on the valley floor, where they could grow kumara (sweet potato) and taro (breadfruit). The rocky headlands became pa (fortified villages) sites, and the area witnessed skirmishes between rival Maori tribes.

In 1940, the beachfront area was designated a Memorial Park to help commemorate the centenary of Auckland. And, yes, this is the very beach captured in cinematic splendour by Jane Campion in her Oscar-decorated historical drama, *The Piano*. That shot of Holly Hunter's beloved piano stranded in the desolate sand, its dark colour reflecting its natural iron oxide base, has already become part of film-making history. Indeed, Karekare has now gripped the imagination of New Zealand's two most celebrated contemporary artists – film director Jane Campion and singer/songwriter Neil Finn.

Neil sensed the time was right to record in New Zealand, and he decided Karekare would be the perfect antidote to the soulless urban record-making experience. "I'd never recorded in New Zealand before, which is amazing considering I'm a New Zealander," he said. "We got the vibe to do it there when we were touring New Zealand last year and it felt that things were much more positive, the mood was good. I just looked longingly at the country and thought, 'This is a really inspiring place. Why don't we record here?' I found a house, luckily, that we could do it in."

The breathtaking scenery of this area was the main selling point. "It's just very inspiring but oppressive at times. The weather is relentless, the wind whistles in from the south, off the Antarctic at times. It's a very emotional landscape. It really draws it out of you, it's harrowing and elemental. I heard a statistic that 70% of marriages in that community break up. It's a hard place to live."

Indeed, by a strange coincidence, the recording took its toll on the personal lives of Nick

Seymour, Mark Hart and even co-manager Grant Thomas. "Nick's marriage fell apart during the recording process," says Gary Stamler. "Both Mark and Grant ended up getting divorced then, Paul left during the tour and Neil went through his usual ups and downs. It was a record that was obviously very hard on a lot of people."

Neil and his comrades have sometimes been prone to a little exaggeration in describing the Karekare environment. Once there, it does indeed feel remote, cut off from civilisation. In

• The famous beach at Karekare, where *The Piano* was filmed.

practical 1990s terms, however, you're less than an hour's drive from a city of a million people. There are no shops here, but Neil's description of the experience as "Mosquito Coast with guitars" is a mite fanciful. Similarly, it's closer to being sub-tropical than near-polar, geographically. When a cold southerly does blow in, you're unlikely to hear most locals curse the Antarctic.

The comparative isolation of the place was a decided plus. "We were attracted to Karekare because it's about as far away from the music industry as you can get," stresses Neil. "We wanted to isolate ourselves so we were only thinking about music – no other considerations. It wasn't so much the idea of getting beachy and relaxed. More a matter of getting caught up in the elements." Youth confirms that… "It wasn't like, 'let's go to the beach'. I think we only went to the beach twice in the whole three months there."

The publicity surrounding the recording of

Together Alone will only add to the slowly increasing tourist traffic now descending on Karekare. The popularity of *The Piano* led to travel stories in international newspapers, and its likely that Crowded House's own rising success will cause some zealous fans to come and see for themselves.

Initially, at least, the area residents welcomed this bizarre invasion with open arms, and homes. Nigel Horrocks, owner of the house cum studio used as centre of operations, explains that "I went around the locals here to ask about it, and they were incredibly positive about it." Just a few months earlier, Horrocks' house had played host to another star. American actor Harvey Keitel had rented it while on location here filming *The Piano*.

Elderly neighbour Gilbert Haslam reminisces fondly about the Crowded House experience. "I just remember a lot of happy people running around. I like to see the young people around. It's good they like the out of doors!" Apparently not everyone agreed. When Crowded House played a free show in the valley to say thanks to the locals at the conclusion of recording, someone called the local noise pollution police!

Just a few hundred yards from Karekare beach, a narrow track branches off the road and leads up to Nigel Horrocks' hillside home. The grey concrete house is, at first sight, formidably austere. "It looks like a bunker, a James Bond sort of place," says Neil. It commands an impressive view of the valley and sea, and in the antipodean summer of 92/93, it underwent a radical transformation.

In the making of what is generally agreed to have been the most expensive album ever recorded in New Zealand, a 64-track studio was installed in the house, the equipment coming from Auckland's largest recording studio, Revolver. Says Horrocks: "I couldn't believe it was my own home. The dimensions seemed changed with all that equipment and all those people packed in there, but I felt very happy about it."

The original plan was to separate the players into different rooms, but that was modified to create a better atmosphere. "We eventually decided it was better to move outside," recalls Neil. "Mark and I found ourselves on the lawn, and Nick found himself in one of the spare bedroom with his bass amp."

As a break from the mayhem at the studio HQ, the lads rented other houses in the valley. "We basically had the whole valley," says Paul. "Everybody was offering their houses to us. By the end of the time, we were renting them all! It was like, 'I got to get my own place'."

"It'd be great going down the track for dinner at a neighbouring house. Sometimes it'd be in the pitch black, and quite adrenalising," adds Neil.

When David Field arrived in Karekare, he observed, euphemistically, that Crowded House and Youth... "were all in a fairly experimental state of mind, shall we say. It was still early in the proceedings, so it was just a lot of backing tracks and roughs down. I heard some really dramatic rhythm tracks and percussion ideas. There was the plan then to get the Cook Island log drummers in and the Maori choir. It was just very exciting, brilliant really."

The primal nature of the recording locale of Karekare and Youth's own eccentricities were beginning to leave their mark. "There was one song they were having problems with," recalls Field, referring to 'Private Universe'. "They were thinking about it too hard. Youth thought if there was this distraction of everybody taking their clothes off, including he and the engineer, they'd be so preoccupied with the fact they were all naked that it'd take their minds off thinking about the track too much. It'd also be a way they could get in touch with the earth! But, no, I'm not supposed to say which track that was for."

Seems getting naked was a bit of a theme here. "On the first day there, we took off our clothes and had a swim in the waterfall," reported Paul. "Then we sat on the beach and thought, 'What an odd way to start a record!'"

Youth came prepared for his role as musical shaman for the recording of 'Together Alone'. "He travels around with various artefacts I believe he feels can help create a certain atmosphere," says Field. "All sorts of strange things. He's fond of enhancing the atmosphere with various herbs and plants."

The experience clearly left a mark on Youth. A year later, while out promoting the new Killing Joke album, he reminisced fondly: "That album

was intense and hard work, but I fell in love with [recording locale] New Zealand. The weather, man! Scary but beautiful too. *The Piano* is really about the weather there, isn't it? The dark oppressiveness of it sometimes. When you're there, you can't get away from the weather. It brings out emotion. With Crowded House, it brought a lot of stuff to the surface. It was quite difficult for them emotionally at times."

Youth's partner in Killing Joke, Jaz Coleman, has made his home in New Zealand and is active in the recording industry there between his work with the revitalised Killing Joke, whom Youth has rejoined. "I want to move there too, set up a butterfly wing, like the studio we've got in London," says Youth. "It's a fantastic location and a great opportunity. The people there are really strong. Politically, I like the vibe, the extreme green. It's got a real good-looking future, New Zealand. Maybe that'll be a good place to observe the end of the world as we know it."

Neil later described the 'Together Alone' experience as... "almost like a two-month retreat, but that was the idea – to create a unique experience for ourselves that would be an end in itself. It took it away from just being a job of work. It became more an all-round sensory experience. Those two months are etched into our souls now. It was a very intense period. We talked, and we had some amazing conversations because we weren't going home at night. We were hanging with each other, and we had some peak experiences, just amongst the enormity of the landscape."

Neil credits Youth's influence on imparting pyschedelic overtones to some of the new songs arrangements. "We were attracted to that. In our own way, we've been interested in that atmosphere anyway, but I think he encouraged us to go for it."

As well as his 'endless entertainment value', Youth is praised by Neil for... "some very good suggestions at vital times. He's also very unorganised – a chaotic and random sort of person. He had flashes of brilliance and a good handle, a good aesthetic on it. Sometimes, though, when he was lying in a near comatose state on a cushion, you'd be forgiven for thinking the album wasn't making much progress! But in fact it was moving forward even then, in mysterious ways."

Others closely involved didn't necessarily share Neil's faith. Gary Stamler, conspicuously absent from the Karekare sessions, reports that Mark Hart told him: "Neil would sometimes ask how the vocal was and it turns out Youth was asleep." Such tales only increased Stamler's initial forebodings.

Paul Hester enjoyed Youth's production style. "He'd say, 'Keep playing, don't stop'. Which is great. In the past, we've made records in America where people like to be able to have an ending, a middle, a beginning, and they like to know where it fits. All that stuff. Youth couldn't really care about all that. If it felt good, he'd be dancing, conducting, saying 'go on and on'. He'd come over and give directions like, 'Paul, at the end of that song, just freak out, freak out'. I'd go, 'OK, freak out, gotcha'. It was lovely to be given something like that."

While Hester adopted a positive stance in interviews after the record was released, Gary Stamler has reason to believe he was unhappy during the actual recording sessions. "I think the band was beginning to unravel a bit then," he says, "with the most pronounced problem being Paul's performance and dark attitude."

Aside from Youth's laidback experimentalism, 'Together Alone' was deeply influenced by the landscape in which it was recorded. Neil singles out 'Fingers Of Love' as an example. "We did that on a very sultry, windy, melancholy day in Karekare, and that song really captures the atmosphere of the day we recorded. And one keyboard sound I found had a real resonance, this low low sound that seemed to reflect the way the clouds were passing over the hills outside.

"It was amazing to have a landscape dominating the atmosphere. Normally in a studio you have four walls and you've got your eyes closed most of the time dealing with just music. Having a context for the music makes it come alive again. It was like that every day in Karekare."

"We had to change songs mid-day sometimes because the weather would change so dramatically, and you'd have to get into it," says Neil. "Every song on 'Together Alone' goes on a bit of a journey from how it was written. 'Black & White Boy' began as a rather sensitive ballad and ended

up rather as our tribute to glam!" Nick Seymour agrees: "It directly affected the music. There'd be this mist rolling off the sea, and it'd change the valley from sunny to misty and dark.'

Both 'Karekare' and 'Together Alone' were written in the valley. The latter song emerged from Neil's desire to stir some indigenous musical ingredients into a novel sonic stew. "We wanted to get a Maori choir, Polynesian log drummers and a brass band together. We had the notion that they'd possibly never played together before. It was all just down the road in Auckland, sitting there. I thought we had to write a song that could feature all these things. Whack them together and have a great day doing it. It was like a happening. If you weren't there, you were square!"

Adding authenticity to the song 'Together Alone' were some lyrics written in Maori by Bub Wehi, leader of the Te Waka Huia Cultural Group Choir featured on the track.

Almost farcically, a potential disaster for Crowded House was averted on the eve of recording that song. "In the middle of the night at the studio, some inebriated person mistook the Polynesian log drums for firewood," recalls Neil. "Nick snatched them from the jaws of the inferno."

"There'd have been a curse on us that'd have followed us for years," adds Nick. "They're blessed by a Cook Island elder."

"The final day of recording was incredibly emotional," says Paul. "The Maori choir cut loose and sang songs especially for the occasion. They brought their children, and there must have been 2-300 people around the studio and the big barbecue on the lawn."

One observer of that cultural and musical crossover experience was Auckland music journalist Russell Baillie. "I was there the afternoon they recorded the song. A slightly weird day, as you can imagine. The Maori choir was by the fireplace, the brass band was in the kitchen, and the log drummers out on the porch. Youth was mainly stuck in the control room, trying to co-ordinate it all. There'd be one band member with each part of this weird New Zealand orchestra, with Youth then wandering around after each take going, 'Yeah, man, great. Let's do another one.' That was about the extent of his presence that day. He seemed to spend a lot of time sitting on a

• Crowded House with Mark Hart, far right.

cushion, suitably beatific. It did sound great, them all playing together."

The experiment of 'Together Alone', the song, was to become a focal point of much of the press on the album. Neil Finn's sincerity deflects possible accusations of cultural appropriation or musical dilettantism. "It wasn't a deliberate attempt to become a world music band or anything like that," he emphasises. "It's just that, recording in New Zealand, we felt it'd be a shame not to employ some local colour. Maori singing and Pacific Island log drumming is incredibly inspiring to listen to, so we combined them in one song, with a brass band thrown in as a nod to our past."

Neil admits the five piece brass band... "were a little wonky, so we had to have them mixed back a bit. It's a nice sound, but if we had them featured, it might have alarmed a few brass band purists up there in the north of England!" Mark Hart's diligent work in scoring the arrangement for the brass section earned him great respect from Neil.

Nostalgia figured in Neil's desire to feature a brass band. "Every Christmas in Te Awamutu one would go round the town on the back of a truck doing Christmas carols. It'd drift over the back fence – a very mournful, melancholy sound."

To Russell Baillie, this musical experiment, and the whole decision to record in Karekare, was... "a bit like The Beatles wandering to India. It's a stage they were at. But at least Neil is doing it in a culture that is somehow familiar to him. The whole Maori issue had been present when he was growing up. If you're going to capture some part of New Zealand on a pop record, the sound of 'Together Alone' is as good as any."

Baillie is more cynical about the work of some other expatriate New Zealand musos, singling out Jenny Morris and ex-Dragon singer Marc Hunter as examples. "You'll get Australian-based NZ musicians that'll do some horrible token little song and call it 'Aotearoa'. They do it totally patronisingly, treating the place as a kindergarten they once went to."

One dissenting voice on the validity of the 'New Zealand orchestra' experiment of 'Together Alone' comes from local *enfant terrible* Chris Knox. He's been one of the most colourful and influential figures in New Zealand music since the late Seventies, from Kiwi punk pioneers The Enemy and Toy Love through to his long-time Tall Dwarves project and countless solo endeavours. Although firmly tied to his Auckland base, his music has found a devoted, if small, audience in North America and Europe.

Knox always shoots from the lip. "This Pacific log drum thing did annoy me," he says. "I've always had the fantasy of having log drummers for a few gigs, along with a cellist. So I was quite interested when Neil did that. But when I heard it, I just thought it was a very token thing. It didn't seem to have anything intrinsically to do with the song, and I thought that was disappointing."

The extravagance involved in the recording of 'Together Alone' in Karekare was later criticised. Murray Cammick operates Auckland indie label Wildside and is used to working to a tight budget. "There were amazing tales of wasted resources," he says. "You heard of them purchasing extra bits of equipment that were so unnecessary they were just given to people working on the project or visiting. Hundreds of thousands of dollars were thrown around. And this in a local industry that sees a big budget for an album being $20,000 NZ, with most being done for less. So you don't really see that [the recording] as being a relevant part of the New Zealand music industry."

That expenditure was boosted by the use of a helicopter to bring the larger pieces of recording gear into the valley. And, in what has now become part of recording industry lore, this budget covered building a bridge to transport equipment to the house. "I was told it was the only A&R budget ever that had 'bridge building' on it!"

laughs EMI's Carrie Spacey-Foote.

Gary Stamler confirms that 'Together Alone' was a big-budget album, even by Los Angeles standards. "The recording costs were as high, if not more than, the traditional manner of recording an album," he says.

Once these intense Karekare recording sessions were over, the band called in mixmeister Bob Clearmountain again. Neil Finn has described Clearmountain as the safety net – 'our insurance policy' – underneath their risky high-wire recording act. "We needed someone to organise us. We had all these ideas down, but it was pretty loose," Neil admitted. "Bob is the most focused, concentrated person I've ever encountered. And he's very quick. Most of the mixes were done in six or seven hours. He went through all the tapes of the wild sounds we'd collected, and left most of them off!"

In a case of the (Clear)mountain coming to Mohammed, Bob flew down to Melbourne for this process, coming up with 15 mixes in an intensive 14 day session. The result shows off his trademark sonic clarity, although some observers and fans would have preferred to hear the untamed musical beast.

That category includes Gary Stamler. "Bob and Neil, at the time, thought they should take a conservative position and, in my opinion, they lost some of the electricity and dynamism they might have got out of the tracks," he says. "In its original form they had some very interesting, cool, edgy moments."

Relieved the recording was now wrapped, Neil and Paul could now relax. They did this by returning to their musical roots – Split Enz.

11

together alone

In March 1993, a month after the 'Together Alone' sessions, Split Enz reunited to tour New Zealand. Interest in the band had been re-ignited by Mike Chunn's biography of the band, *Stranger Than Fiction*, and the group had reconvened in December 1992 for a book launch party at Auckland's Wynyard Tavern, exactly 20 years after their first-ever gig there. Prior to that, they had played one mid-1992 gig, entertaining travel agents in Sydney on behalf of the New Zealand Tourist Board, while Tim and Neil performed together at a Christmas 1992 party for Stratford Productions, the Auckland company responsible for the 'Four Seasons In One Day' video.

Unlike most dinosaur rockers' desperate 'one for the mortgage and alimony payments' reunion tours, a real sense of celebration surrounded Split Enz's return to the road. Some 55,000 Split Enz fans, new and old, attended the week of dates, with 13,000 fans showing up for their Mt Smart Supertop show in Auckland, described by *Rip It Up*'s Alister Cain as 'a triumph'. "It was good to see consummate frontman Tim Finn settle back into his rightful position with ease," he wrote. "He appeared to enjoy the show more than anyone else." Indeed. "I'll never do a better show in my life," he later told *Music Express*. "Half the crowd were kids who'd never seen Split Enz, but they knew every song. That was a great feeling!"

One notable absentee was Enz co-founder Phil Judd. "He was originally going to do it, but then we decided we didn't want him around," explained Tim. "Much as I love him, he can be so negative and poisonous. He hasn't been able to get over a feeling that we somehow shafted him. That's absolutely terrible, but it's also very funny. He sees himself as someone who's bitter and twisted. But he's a brilliant talent and he's organically attached to us." Reports on the reclusive Judd now have him house painting in Australia.

A live album, 'Anniversary', was culled from the tour, and major Australian press coverage proved the Split Enz legend still thrived there. Sensing this, Mushroom Records re-released all Split Enz' CDs in two boxed sets. History can repeat.

Post-tour, Neil, Sharon and their two sons remained in Auckland for a few weeks, scouting out houses. They'd decided to make the big move back to New Zealand, some 16 years after Neil's departure with Split Enz. Almost simultaneously, former comrade Eddie Rayner moved his family from Melbourne to Auckland.

This wasn't an easy decision for Neil. Like so many compatriots who chose to live abroad, including brother Tim, he'd long had an ambivalent relationship to his home country. Despite his long residence there, he'd never become 'Australian', but hadn't felt the time was right for a return to New Zealand.

In the past Neil had felt emboldened enough to be quite critical of certain prevailing attitudes there. "I crave New Zealand sometimes, but I don't have any real immediate desire to live there now," he said in Paris in 1991. "I get the feeling that if you live there, it's easy to become a bit closeted. You're not encouraged to be unselfconscious about your work there. People are quite happy for

• Split Enz Reunion, Auckland, 1993

you to make music or art there as long as you think small with it. If it tries to be anything grand, people tend to sneer. You're equated with pretension. It's a desire to justify the fact they're not really fulfilling their ambitions there. I feel that sometimes."

Two years later, he'd softened his stance. "I missed certain things about New Zealand," he told *The Sydney Morning Herald*. "The landscape, and that very familiar feeling of being in your place of birth. Before, it never felt like the right time; it felt like New Zealand was stuck in a rut. Recently, it feels to me like the country has gone through a bit of an attitude change. The Maori and Polynesian cultures feel stronger to me now."

But it was family that clinched it. "My parents are here and getting older. I wanted to be around them more, and have my kids grow up with them a bit... a sense of family is important. Also, Liam can go to school in bare feet, just as I did. It's a very New Zealand thing."

In May, 1993, Neil, Sharon, Liam and Elroy made the move from St Kilda, Melbourne, to Parnell, Auckland. This is one of the most desirable districts in central Auckland, an area full of chic cafés. The Finn home, described as "airy and white", is reportedly far from ostentatious, and is decorated with traditional Maori and Polynesian wall-hangings.

There was some speculation that Tim Finn would return home now too.

"I talked about it a little bit," he conceded later in the year. "They always ask 'When are you coming back?' as if they need legitimacy for their own being there. That doesn't just come from insecurity now, but from a different pride that is there now and that's good. I sense a hybrid culture emerging. Overall, it's more celebratory now than when we were there."

Tim was in good spirits through 1993. Post-eviction from Crowded House in November 1992, he had got right down to work on his fourth solo album. He cited a 10-day meditational retreat in January in the Blue Mountains, outside of Sydney, as revitalising, and from there the nomadic soul made forays to Dublin, London and Los Angeles, writing and recording en route. His Melbourne home studio was also put to good use in this period.

Songwriting collaborators included Richard Thompson ('Persuasion') and, on 'Many's The Time In Dublin', Hothouse Flowers singer Liam O'Maonlai and Belfast singer/songwriter Andy White, the other two-thirds of what would become the ill-fated ALT. Two other songs, 'Strangeness & Charm' and 'In Love With It All', had been held over from that fertile 'Woodface' writing spurt with Neil. Mark Hart produced a couple of tracks in LA, and other producers involved included Clive Langer and Alan Winstanley, David Leonard and the ubiquitous Ricky Fataar. In April 1993, tapes of the new album, 'Before & After', were sent to the media, well in advance of the July 13 release date.

Mid-May, Tim visited Los Angeles and New York for a press promotional trip, then did the same in England and Europe. In London working on the sequencing of 'Together Alone', brother Neil made a guest appearance at Tim's London Borderline showcase on June 16 and their English visit coincided with the announcement that both brothers had been awarded OBEs (Order Of The British Empire) for their contributions to New Zealand music. The honour elicited some teasing from Nick Seymour and Paul Hester, given their republican leanings, and brought forth yet more Beatles comparisons.

Tim returned to New Zealand for dates in July and August, including a hometown gig in Te Awamutu, then toured the album in Britain and

North America. He mixed in some Enz classics and joint Finn songs in with his solo work, joking about Crowded House – "a little band you might want to watch out for". Despite some positive reviews and successful concerts, including a sell out at The Forum in London, 'Before & After' didn't live up to commercial expectations, and he was later dropped by Capitol.

MEANWHILE, Capitol were planning to release 'Together Alone' in Britain and Europe in October 1993, while holding off on a North American release until January 1994, so avoiding the Christmas rush of superstar product there. Crowded House were eager to begin playing their new material, though, so some touring was planned in advance of 'Together Alone'.

First came their début tour of South Africa in August 1993. In those heady days of Nelson Mandela's remarkable triumph, it had become politically acceptable to venture there, and the band found it a fascinating experience. The African National Congress had encouraged the visit, a highlight of which was a visit to Soweto.

Appropriately, this was followed by North American dates as part of a WOMAD (World Of Music, Art and Dance) package. Prior to the musical exploration of 'Together Alone', they'd scarcely have seemed a logical choice for a world music extravaganza. WOMAD driving force Peter Gabriel topped the bill, supported by Crowded House, British popsters James, and dance hit-makers P.M. Dawn and Stereo MC's.

Toronto had long been the only North American city to host an annual WOMAD music festival, and it was to be the opening date on this September tour. Ticket sales for the arena version proved slow, however, and this date was cancelled. Obviously disappointed at not being able to play one of their favourite cities, Crowded House typically made the most of the extra time on their hands.

In trademark fashion, the band refused to allow a bland press release speak on their behalf about the no-show. *Speakers Corner*, a virtual public soapbox at Toronto's CITY-TV facility, was commandeered by Nick and Paul for a televised direct explanation/apology to their fans, deliv-

ered with their usual wit and flair.

The group did get to play a local gig – an unannounced appearance at a charity fund-raiser. Toronto clothing boutique/chain Roots hosted the evening at the Palais Royale, an historic dance hall on Lake Ontario. The social schmoozers were treated to a handful of Crowded House songs, including a killer version of their most-performed cover song, Hunters and Collectors' 'Throw Your Arms Around Me'.

• **Nick Seymour at WOMAD, 1993**

Media interviews in advance of the release of 'Together Alone' were conducted, and the already-scheduled video shoot for its first single, 'Distant Sun', went ahead. Local director Curtis Wehrfritz has established himself as Canada's best via acclaimed clips for such artists as Leonard Cohen, jazz chanteuse Holly Cole and rockers 54-40, and his show reel had reached Capitol in LA.

"They responded to my work and asked for a

• **Neil Finn at WOMAD, 1993**

the shoot witnessed a fun party for cast, crew and friends. "Friends of mine at La Hacienda [on the trendy Queen Street strip] opened up the restaurant at about midnight," he says. "The band were about to drive down to New York, so we had a Mexican dinner with the gang. Nick and Neil got out their acoustic guitars and did some tunes for us.

"The band loaded up the bus for a seven hour drive, then the cops came and fined the bar for staying open! I explained it was essentially a private party, and that we were just trying to thank the band. That didn't work, but I told the cops the best thing was that they hadn't come a half-hour earlier. Neil and the gang had already left, so the good impression was intact. They weren't able to screw up the deal!"

Wehrfritz was impressed with Crowded House's video smarts. "They're very astute visually; they know a lot about film. It's part of Nick's background. He had a camera here, and we developed some footage from South Africa he had shot there. If you look at their past work, you'll see they have always taken an interest, much more so than certain other bands. There's some great work there."

Across the Atlantic, Crowded House's UK label, Parlophone, were chomping at the bit to hit the marketplace with a new album. 'Woodface' was still selling strongly, so they had every reason for confidence, without taking anything for granted. "Again, we didn't think it was going to be easy," admitted Head of Promotions Malcolm Hill. "As a fan, though, I just thought it was fantastic, and I wanted to see them live again."

The early going was easier than for any previous Crowded House album there. "People were more prepared to give it a chance," explains Hill. "Like [all-important] Radio One. They knew how big the band was and were supportive, even if it wasn't easy for them at times."

David Field, the A&R man who played such a major role in the making of 'Together Alone', confirms the label's enthusiasm. "They were very enamoured with it. It's a strong, spiritual record, one that showed different sides of the band and was a necessary progression. It was viewed as such by the Americans too, but then out goes the label, in comes a new label, and I was fired!"

treatment," Curtis recalls. "I then had a conversation with the band in Cape Town. Talked about some ideas and they seemed interested." The result was a seeming dream shoot. "The thing went down quickly, we got along great, and they were happy with it. It took two days of main shooting here, plus another day of pickups. They were very pleasant and congenial, and gave me the freedom to do what I do."

The resulting clip is high on visual metaphor. "One thing Neil showed was an interest in nature – its patterns and rhythms, the fact that certain things have a psychedelic feel," recalls Wehrfritz. The director's mix of compelling imagery and band portraits worked well, and the result was another in Crowded House's collection of superior music videos.

Curtis recalls the band roller-blading through Toronto in the middle of the night, and the end of

In yet another major shake-up at Capitol in LA, Hale Milgrim was replaced by Gary Gersh, and the A&R department was also drastically revised. Field remembers his day of departure clearly and bitterly. "Neil Finn was in LA having a meeting with Gary Gersh about the record, 10 minutes before I got fired. I wasn't exactly fired, but Gary asked me to go and work for the UK company, actually a downwards move. Neil was hanging around the office, waiting to see what my fate would be, and it was a dastardly one. It was very emotional for me, and Neil offered his shoulder."

This latest Capitol purge meant the exit of a key Crowded House supporter in Milgrim. Gersh, in his late thirties, became the youngest CEO of any American major label, his reputation based on signing such hit makers as Nirvana and Counting Crows to his previous label, Geffen. Quite how committed he was to a band he had inherited, rather than developed, was open to question.

Certainly, the new regime was a little concerned upon hearing 'Together Alone'. Bruce Kirkland, a New Zealander appointed by Gersh as General Manager/Senior Vice President of Capitol, later told *Rip It Up*: "We couldn't hear an out and out hit single. We gave Neil the option of going back in and adding a hit single to sell a multi-million dollar album." Always opposed to that 'just go write a hit' mentality, Neil Finn refused.

These were turbulent times for Crowded House, according to Gary Stamler who paints a picture of an extremely unhappy band. "There was a very tense, combative atmosphere, "he says. "The band was very much four separate individuals. Paul and Nick were not getting along, and I think the band was dejected and demoralised about the success of the record, based on the record company environment. There was support there for the band, but the tour was somewhat dysfunctional in a lot of ways."

Neil told Auckland magazine *Metro*: "I had a meeting with the new president who said 'Great record, love your music', the usual spiel, 'but... could you go back and do a couple of real straight love songs for the radio?' Of course we said no, and they said 'Don't be disappointed when it sells 200,000', which is exactly what it did."

The British label had a more laissez-faire attitude to Neil's songwriting. "We leave them alone and hope they'll deliver two or three radio-friendly singles," explains Mitch Clark, London-based Director of International Promotion for EMI Music. "This isn't a band where you go and say 'We need a good backbeat and catchy chorus, dudes'. Because he's such a classy, intelligent songwriter, it'd be awful to say 'You have to deliver us a radio-friendly track'. You'd probably get a big 'fuck-off'."

Its integrity intact, 'Together Alone' was released in Australasia, Britain and Europe on October 11, 1993, preceded by first single 'Distant Sun'. A dispute over production credits, however, almost put the album in limbo, as EMI's Malcolm Hill recalls. "The band felt Youth didn't have 100% of the ideas, and felt their contribution deserved a co-production credit. That did get a little nasty towards the end, right to the point where the album was almost stopped from coming out."

The disagreement escalated to the degree that lawyers were involved, but, in the end, 'Together Alone' did come out as "Produced by Youth" rather than "Youth and Crowded House".

On 'Together Alone', Crowded House stepped away from the often bright, sunny pop of 'Woodface'. It is closer in tone to 'Temple Of Low Men', and the influence of the recording location can be detected in its emotional intensity. The experimental nature of Youth's production method, or lack of method, helped encourage the band to explore some rockier terrain, but the results, as on 'Skin Feeling' and 'Locked Out',

• **Neil on stage with Suzanne Vega, 1993**

occasionally sound forced. The brave attempt at coming up with a multi-cultural anthem, 'Together Alone', falls just shy of the mark. Nevertheless, it remains a rich and rewarding work, and such gorgeous melodies as those of 'Distant Sun', 'Kare Kare' and 'Fingers Of Love' rank with Neil Finn's best.

With Crowded House's reputation as darlings of the music press intact, it was no surprise that the album and single were greeted with near-unanimous praise. Even the hitherto scathing *Melody Maker* recanted, making 'Distant Sun' Single Of The Week and declaring 'Neil Finn pisses genius'. By now, Neil was almost smug about British press support. "We've got some people on those papers who are almost semi-fanatical about us now," he told New Zealand journalist Stephen Dowling then. "*NME* and *Melody Maker* are reactionary and we have suffered some vicious slagging. Now the total irony is they like us."

Leading the press applause was *Q* magazine, now generally recognised as the most important British music publication. On its release, they chimed in with their maximum five star rating for 'Together Alone'. In a full page review, critic David

Hepworth evoked comparison with pop greats Lennon & McCartney, Brian Wilson and R.E.M.. "This is emotional music, as intimate as Neil Finn has yet got," he wrote. Down Under, the album received Australian *Rolling Stone*'s maximum five star rating, the only album of 1993 to achieve that feat. *The Times* chimed in with "It abounds with rich and colourful dynamics sufficient to win over all but the most sceptical of listeners."

Previous producer Mitchell Froom was also pleased. "I really liked a lot of the songs, but I didn't feel Youth served their needs very well. If Neil had done it himself, it'd have been better. The idea was to have it be really loose and rough around the edges, but in my opinion it ended up being a bit overdone. Neil and I disagree on this," he laughs.

Given immediate press and radio support, 'Together Alone' quickly streaked to the upper reaches of the charts. 'Distant Sun' had only lasted three weeks in the Top 30, peaking at No. 19, but the album debuted at No. 3 in October, behind Take That and Pearl Jam's 'Vs.'. From there it dropped to No. 7, then took a 10-12-18-22-30 slide. It did, however re-enter the album charts in January, climbing back into the Top 20, and

encountering a resurgent 'Woodface'. The March 5, 1994, UK chart in *Billboard* placed 'Together Alone' at No. 14 and 'Woodface' at 38! Follow-up singles 'Nails In My Feet' and 'Locked Out' reached numbers 22 and 12 in the UK singles respectively. Later, in the summer of 1994, Capitol released 'Fingers Of Love' (No 25) and 'Pineapple Head' (27).

Wisely, Crowded House decided to strike in Britain and Europe before any initial excitement over the new record faded. On November 9, 1993, they kicked off an extensive 25 city European tour – with 10 UK concerts – in Glasgow, the site of Tim Finn's exit almost exactly a year earlier. Three sold-out nights at London's Hammersmith Apollo capped off the triumphant British dates. Another highlight of the month was a repeat victory at the *Q* Awards, this time to Neil for Best Songwriter. In attendance was Elton John, who decreed Neil one of his personal favourites – a proud moment for someone who devoured Elton's music as a Te Awamutu teenager.

Crowded House then criss-crossed the globe with wearying regularity. Christmas with the family back in Auckland was a top priority for Neil Finn, and he found time to perform at another Christmas party at Stratford Productions, the company responsible for many of Crowded House's videos. This time Neil played with Dave Dobbyn, a top Kiwi singer/songwriter with whom he would spend a lot of time over the next year.

After a month's break, Neil and comrades were back on the road. A video for planned single 'Locked Out' was shot in Wales, in uncomfortable circumstances. "Spending two days running down a Welsh road in the freezing cold with a pair of really flimsy plimsolls on was a total nightmare," Neil moaned. "It was a great idea when we were sitting on the bus, but on the second take of running behind a car, we're all, going 'Whose stupid idea was this?'"

With 'Together Alone' released in North America on January 25,1994, it was time to visit there for promotion. Tellingly, Paul Hester decided to head home, leaving Neil, Nick and Mark Hart to handle the interviews and 'unplugged' performances as a trio. "He has a pregnancy to deal with in Melbourne, but he sends his apologies," Neil told his Canadian TV audience then, but he point-

edly dedicated their live MuchMusic rendition of 'Black And White Boy' to Paul. "It's about people who are so extreme they'll take you on a roller coaster ride every day," he added. Clearly the tension caused by the volatile drummer's mood swings was escalating.

As with 'Woodface', the new album received the now standard rave reviews, but didn't exactly scorch its way up the charts. In Canada, still a proportionately happier home for Crowded House than the US, 'Together Alone' peaked at No. 18 on the charts in February 1994, later going gold (sales over 50,000). Hindering its chart ascent, however, was the fact that die-hard CH fans had snapped up British import copies prior to its local release. In the US, it entered *Billboard*'s Top 200 on January 29 at No. 73, which earned it the tag of Hot Shot Début, a poor choice, as it plummeted to 107 the next week. Six weeks later it was out of the Top 200, an abysmal performance. Capitol US were pushing 'Locked Out' as a single to modern rock radio, but making the Top 10 in that chart did little to boost the album.

Much of February was taken up with an Australian tour, which meant Crowded House missed the annual Brit Awards on Feb. 12. They emerged triumphant as Best International Group, beating out such heavyweight contenders as U2, R.E.M., Nirvana and Pearl Jam. Neil relished the irony of the situation. "We'd just beaten bands who sell five times as much as us and we were playing some little shit-hole in the outback the same night," he told London's *Time Out*.

Their victory should have been front page news back home, but as Neil's friend Mike Chunn noted disgustedly, "It just got a 30 word mention on Page 5 of the Auckland paper, whereas some golfer got half the front page for being New Zealand Sportsman Of The Year! But what an achievement that was, to be regarded by the music industry in Britain as the best band in the world."

Select New Zealand gigs included a February 25 fund-raiser for Amnesty International. "That's an organisation central to stopping most of the things going wrong around the world, and it's one we've supported privately," explained Neil. Similarly altruistic was their free show at the Manukau City Square in Auckland two days later,

• Crowded House free concert, Manukau City, Auckland, February 1994

designed to spotlight young Polynesian musical talent there.

On March 16, 1994, Crowded House launched their North American tour at Los Angeles' Wiltern Theatre. An extensive series of gigs in theatre venues (mostly a 1,500-3,000 capacity range) proved they had a loyal core of fans who'd continue to buy their albums and attend their shows, but hopes for a new US commercial breakthrough with 'Together Alone' were looking forlorn. Some music scribes expecting the more extroverted band of old were disappointed this time out. Reviewing the Wiltern show, *Music Connection*'s Oskar Scotti claimed: "Whether it was fatigue, ennui or a tapped creative gland, Crowded House seemed to be merely going through the motions."

This tour witnessed the end of an era. On April 14, 1994, founding member and resident jester Paul Hester walked out of Crowded House, just two hours before a gig at The Roxy in Atlanta. In courageous 'the show must go on' fashion, the band played the concert, reportedly an emotional two and a half hour show that ended with Neil dedicating 'Better Be Home Soon' to... 'A man I love very much, Paul Hester'. Amazingly, *Rolling Stone* later ran a lukewarm review of the show that failed to mention the unfolding drama.

To those close to the band, Hester's departure wasn't a total bombshell. Gary Stamler says he hinted at quitting just two days before the tour began. "He said something like 'It wouldn't be the dumbest thing in the world to look for another drummer'," recalls Stamler. Paul's intense unhappiness at the time had been vividly demonstrated just a week earlier during a live *Intimate & Interactive* performance on music video channel MuchMusic. Usually a witty and warm presence in such a situation, Paul's dark mood and sarcastic response to fans' questions soured the whole event. "He took a lot of heat for that from the band and record company," says Stamler. "He got surly and mean about innocuous things, and there were more than a few of those moments, believe me."

Although later expressing relief at his departure, Neil Finn and Nick Seymour were understandably infuriated at its timing. "Yes, there's bad feeling," fumed Nick. "I had two

hours notice. I'd never do that to anybody. But when he left the band I felt this incredible burden, this huge cloud, just leave us."

Both Nick and Neil used terms like "dark cloud" and "virus" to describe the effect Hester's

• **After the show at Manukau City**

moods had on the band over the past year. "There were nights he wouldn't even sing. He was down about the band for 12 months and had been threatening to quit all that time. We didn't push Paul, but there were times I wanted to," says Seymour.

Neil Finn had been in bands with Paul Hester ever since the drummer joined Split Enz in 1983, and he held nothing back when discussing Paul's exit with *NME* in May 1994. "He's always been a bad-tempered little bastard," he said. "As much as he's incredibly funny when he's up – totally funny and an incredibly gifted sense of humour – the other side of that is very black. We'd wake up on any given day and not know whether we'd find him up or down. He was casting a shadow over the whole organisation."

Speculation over the root cause of his unhappiness ran rife. Road-weariness and the advanced pregnancy of his Melbourne girlfriend Mardi Sommerfeld were the reasons most commonly aired. The official Capitol release said: "Hester cites the pressures of touring and declining motivation as the main reason for his decision to quit. He also feels that over the last few months he has drifted apart from the rest of the band."

"As a person and musician, he was very frustrated at the clown prince tag he was getting," suggests Nick Seymour. "He'd get so infuriated, we'd hide reviews that called him that."

"There were quite a few domestic problems with Hessie [Paul], and obviously his commitment to the band was getting less," says Parlophone Head Of Promotions Malcolm Hill. "Paul could be a pain in the arse. The only reason we didn't end up pummelling the guy to death was that he was really funny and we really liked him!"

While most rockers lustily chase the holy grail of fame, Hester viewed the band's rising international success with concern. In his first public explanation for quitting, he wrote in a Sydney newspaper: "I was thinking if things pick up, then we are on a course for world domination. The idea of being the most popular band in the world didn't appeal at all." Such status would, of course, put a serious dent in his TV watching, a personal addiction.

On a TV talk show a few weeks after his return, he again fielded queries. Wrote *Sydney Morning Herald* critic Tony Squires: "Hester couldn't really answer the question in words any of us understood, but he was emotionally coherent. Basically, the bloke was jack of the whole business." That translates as 'sick of the showbiz grind'.

A band of lesser mettle would have cancelled or postponed their tour to audition new drummers. Crowded House soldiered on, with Wally Ingram, drummer for opening act Sheryl Crow, acting as replacement for many of the remaining North American shows.

Catching the first post-Paul show, in Nashville, was Barry Coburn, Split Enz's first manager. "It was a consummate display of professionalism and showmanship they way they just went on with a fill-in drummer," he says. "He knew the songs because he was a fan and ran over them at sound check. I noticed they weren't as tight as I expected, but most people didn't even notice." Also filling the drum stool on some gigs was former The The drummer Andy Kubiszewki, usually referred to from the stage as 'Andy from Cleveland'. Before the others learnt to pronounce his name properly, he was gone, and the search for a more lasting replacement began.

Most of the remaining North American dates were on friendly Canadian soil, and both audiences and press were generally tolerant of the undeniable gaps in these post-Paul performances. "The first couple of nights were pretty hairy, skin-of-your-teeth, seat-of-the pants shows. Typical for us really," Nick Seymour explained to *NME*.

During this gruelling tour – 52 dates in 60

days – Crowded House bonded with opening act Sheryl Crow. "I came out of that tour extremely inspired because of the emotionality of it," Sheryl explained later. Neil would occasionally guest during her set, and a few tears were reportedly shed at their final date together in Vancouver. By the end of 1994, ironically, Sheryl Crow had sold more records in North America than Crowded House ever did!

The group's traditional addiction to adventure and spontaneity in performance definitely helped them weather the post-Paul storm, a setback that'd have blown a less resilient band right off the rails. Replacing everything Hester had brought to the band could not be done with a quick call to Dial A Drummer though. His vocal harmonies, occasional composition ('Italian Plastic', the new 'Skin Feeling'), and, of course, his usually exuberant presence on and offstage, had been central to the appealing persona of Crowded House .

More than a year later, the impact of Paul's departure is still one of the hottest topics between the band's fans on the Internet. Some even argue the group should disband or change their name because of it.

Crowded House's Down Under manager Grant

Thomas put a brave face on the news. "I don't think the band has any desire to become deep or introspective or moody or to escape from the lightness that Paul brought. I just think we're going into a different phase."

The end of that troubled North American tour also saw the end of original manager Gary Stamler's relationship with Crowded House. A year after the firing Stamler was still clearly upset at the way it occurred. "To this day I can't tell you why it happened," he says. "After the Seattle show Neil had a breakfast meeting with me for about 15 minutes. He basically told me they were firing me but didn't go into detail. To this day we really haven't covered it. The one tangible thing of any substance Neil said then, before running for the bus, was 'Oh, there's no vibe in America'."

Stamler appears to have been the scapegoat for Crowded House's ongoing commercial disappointments in the US, even though he played a crucial role in their original success there. "Given the previous ten years, this is still something I feel bitter about," he says. "I'll forever be confused and dissatisfied with the way this was handled."

Gary feels this decision was not unanimous on the band's part. In July 1995 he maintained that, "As recently as a couple of weeks ago, one member told me he thought it never should have happened." Reflecting on the situation, Stamler states: "Crowded House is a band I'll always feel a close attachment to and a large amount of affection for, in spite of what happened. I feel very proud of what we all achieved together. Even through the bitterness I wish Neil Finn the best."

One of Stamler's observations is particularly telling. "I wish someday that Neil Finn can find some sort of spiritual peace with himself, that his success and talent should allow him to have."

His split from Crowded House hasn't affected Stamler's standing as a prominent member of the LA music community. He continues to work with Richard Thompson, whom he's managed since 1982, Van Halen, and producers Mitchell Froom and Van Dyke Parks.

BACK IN THE Crowded House camp, preparations were in hand for a major British tour in late May, and a call was put out to Melbourne drummer Peter Jones. Born in Liverpool, he'd been prominent on the Melbourne music scene since the mid Eighties via stints with blues-rockers Harem Scarem and Crown Of Thorns, jazz trumpeter Vince Jones and singer Kate Ceberano. He'd actually drummed for Deborah Conway and Sherine, two local singers with whom Paul Hester had also played.

Jones was in tow when Crowded House began their British tour in Glasgow on May 27, 1994. Two dates at London's Wembley Arena on May 31 and June 1 reaffirmed the band's mass appeal, and they returned to London later in June for a memorable headline appearance at major Irish music festival The Fleadh. This choice ruffled a few feathers and provoked some mirth. *Vox* ran a facetiously funny photo caption – "Neil Finn discovers his cousin had an Irish milkman". "The Fleadh's cultural schizophrenia reached a climax as a choir in traditional Pacific dress marched onstage [for 'Together Alone']," wrote their reviewer. Fans weren't worried about nationalistic nit-picking, and the band received a very warm welcome. Besides, Neil Finn qualifies for an Irish passport, and he drew cheers when he told the

crowd his Limerick-born mother became tearfully emotional when she heard about the gig.

New Zealand journalist Mike Houlahan interviewed Neil backstage. "That day was a good insight into how truly international Crowded House are now," he later said. "It's at an Irish festival, and they had other interviews to do with South African TV and Radio Chile!" Press reports were glowing, none more so than Jennifer Nine's in *Melody Maker* – "Crowded House are simply the most beautiful noise in the world."

In Europe, 'Together Alone' had proved a harder sell. "It was almost as if *Woodface* was their first album in Europe, so this was almost a second album syndrome," recalls EMI's Carrie Spacey-Foote. "You have to hope the first single will go all the way, and it didn't hit the heights we hoped. I think 'Distant Sun' and 'Nails In My Feet' were two incredible songs, but neither of them had massive impact in Europe."

Lacking the big pop single that 'Weather With You' became in Europe, 'Together Alone' sold, in Carrie's estimate, about half that of 'Woodface', which clocked in at a half-million. "The critics and fans loved it, but it passed by the new people that bought 'Woodface' on the strength of the pop single."

In Britain, EMI Head Of Promotion Malcolm Hill says the company was very happy with what 'Together Alone' has done. "Within the UK company, Crowded House are in our top three to five acts. They're massively important for us in terms of sales and acceptance." The success of the last two albums has dramatically increased sales of the first two, Hill citing the début as at 106,000 with 'Temple Of Low Men' closing in on the 100,000 mark.

In Australia, 'Together Alone' represented something of a holding pattern for Crowded House. "It's not as though we're dealing with a failure here," explains Ian James of Mushroom Publishing, the music publisher for all Neil and Tim Finn's work. "As Grant Thomas and I keep reminding people, it's not a problem, it's just that when you follow an album like 'Woodface'..."

Given the history of delayed success for both the 'Crowded House' and 'Woodface' albums, and the need for taxing extended tours to promote them, Neil, Nick and Mark could be forgiven for

● ABOVE: Neil on stage at London's Wembley Arena, 1994, with the Maori choir and drummers
BELOW: With Mark Hart at the Fleadh, London

feeling relieved 'Together Alone' didn't repeat that pattern. As activity around the album slowed, the trio returned to their various bases – Mark to Los Angeles, Nick to his new haunt of Dublin, and Neil back to Auckland.

Once on home turf, Neil could indulge in such fun ventures as yet more informal Split Enz reunions, one of them at his alma mater, Sacred Heart College. The school needed funds for new music rooms, and a concert by such illustrious ex-pupils seemed an appropriate money-raising method. Organiser Mike Chunn recalls his feelings of deja vu. "The old stage of the Assembly Hall looked the same as when Tim Finn and I were last on it, in 1970!," he said.

Among the old boys performing were Tim and Neil, Eddie Rayner, Dave Dobbyn, Enz alumni Wally Wilkinson, Geoff and Mike Chunn and Kiwi rockers Rikki Morris and Peter Urlich. The three hour plus show featured material by Split Enz, Crowded House and Dobbyn and Th' Dudes. " About $33,000 was raised, 700 old boys went completely crazy, and at the night's end, we screamed at each other 'We came back and we conquered!'" says Chunn exuberantly.

Split Enz reunions aside Neil's new musical preoccupation was producing other artists, something he'd never tackled before. "Now that we've finished touring for the foreseeable future, I'm just wanting to make records really - my own or others," he said on his return to NZ. "I just want to stay in the studio for a long time."

Much of August and September 1994 were spent in Auckland studio Revolver, where Neil produced and played on 'Twist', the new album from long-time friend Dave Dobbyn, a much-respected New Zealand singer/songwriter via earlier bands Th' Dudes and D.D. Smash and later solo work. "I was flattered to be asked to produce. I'd never done that before," Neil explained to *The New Zealand Herald*'s Russell Baillie. "I really liked Dave's songs and his voice. This [job] still feels like a holiday. It's low pressure because I haven't got the added burden of the songs, the lyrics, the rest of the band."

To Dobbyn, Neil's presence was invaluable. "I've now found my niche, just being a babbling artist! Musically, there's been a lot of slashing and burning but something new came out of it." Indeed. 'Twist' is a superb work, the finest of Dobbyn's long career. Musically varied and adventurous, it sometimes evokes a similar atmosphere to 'Together Alone'. Like Neil, Dobbyn is a recently returned expatriate rediscovering the beauty of his homeland. Neil's guitar work is dazzling (he also adds keyboards and backing vocals) and his production skilled, but it's the strength of Dobbyn's voice and songs that carry the day. Tim Finn adds backing vocals and drums on one track while Neil's sons Liam and Elroy get to shout on the chorus of 'P.C.'. Engineering and mixing was Tchad Blake, long time engineer for Mitchell Froom. The rhythm section comprised Ross Burge on drums and Alan Gregg on bass, from The Mutton Birds, one of New Zealand's most popular bands. Gregg also sings Neil's praises. "He has a lot of good instincts about what works and what doesn't in a song. Neil experimented most of the time, trying ideas for other things I guess."

The 'Twist' band celebrated the record's wrap with a show at a local youth club. "Tim added backing vocals and percussion, [Mutton Birds singer] Don [McGlashan] played too, along with Ross, Dave and Neil," recalls Alan. "Neil played some fantastic things on guitar that night."

Similar musical revelry was held at the official opening party of Revolver Studios, a lavish facility used for 'Twist'. This bash is still being talked about in Auckland, for it featured sets by The Mutton Birds, Dave Dobbyn, and yet another Split Enz reunion. Tim Finn, Mike Chunn and Eddie Rayner, who works a lot at Revolver, joined in and Ross Burge was recruited as drummer. "They only did the old hits, thank God," says Ross. "I made a major fuck-up on the first song, 'Shark Attack', but it was all great fun."

"I just got up and sweated like a dog," adds Mike Chunn. "I don't give a damn about the fact I wasn't in the band when they got really popular."

Released at the end of 1994, Dave Dobbyn's 'Twist' began a long run on the NZ charts, selling platinum. Neil's other 1994 production project, 'Greenstone' by highly-rated local Maori singer/songwriter Emma Paki, hit the Top 10 in January 1995, but Neil's production here didn't receive the same praise as his work on 'Twist'.

One harsh critic was Murray Cammick. "That song has about the whitest-sounding drum sound I've ever heard. If that's the rhythm of the Pacific, we should forget it." he said.

Paki enjoyed the experience, telling *The Listener*: "He's very considerate, very creative, he applies himself and he's humble. I went in with only a vocal sound in my head, and he and the musicians arranged the music." As well as lead guitar, Neil played mellotron, the same one on those early Split Enz records.

Interestingly, Emma Paki's previous hit single, 'System Virtue', had been produced by Killing Joke's Jaz Coleman. Further expanding the circle of coincidence, in mid 1995, Paki began recording her début CD in Karekare with Mark Hart as producer.

From late 1994 on, Neil Finn was all over the local charts. Young Auckland group Purest Form scored a major hit with a remake of Neil's tender ballad 'Message To My Girl', the song he'd written in Split Enz in 1983. By popular vote, this became Single Of The Year at the 1995 New Zealand Music awards. Split Enz/Crowded House keyboardist Eddie Rayner produced this version, which singer Mark Tuati described as "our way of paying tribute to Split Enz".

Neil's songwriting was further recognised by his peers on two occasions in November. At the Auckland APRA (Australasian Performing Rights Association) Awards for New Zealand songwriters on November 7, Neil and Tim were on hand to receive the trophy for Most Performed Work In

New Zealand And Overseas, for 'Weather With You'. Two weeks later, at the Australian APRA Awards Neil was named Songwriter Of The Year and 'Distant Sun' was Song Of The Year. In 1993, Tim and Neil Finn won this award for 'Four Seasons In One Day'. Both brothers shared in another 1994 award, the Most Performed Australasian Song Overseas, for 'Weather With You'. Such awards may lack the glitz of the Brits or Grammys, but they mean a great deal to crafts-men like the Finns.

Down Under, though, Crowded House certainly aren't just an industry favourite. In Australian *Rolling Stone*'s 1995 Reader's Picks award, they won as Best Band, Neil as Best Singer, 'Private Universe' for Best Video and Nick Seymour and Paul Hester as Best Bassist and Drummer.

Around this time, Neil and Dave Dobbyn took their families to Rarotonga in the Cook Islands for a much-needed two week holiday. Tim Finn and friend Tracy Magan went along too, and the break spawned a song for the new Finn Brothers album Neil and Tim had begun planning. Recalls Magan, "Tim fell off a motorbike and grazed his hand, so he wrote this song called 'Hit The Road In Rarotonga'. We feel the song belongs to us, so they asked Dave to play bass on that track."

As 1994 drew to a close and Neil Finn settled into his New Zealand family Christmas, he reflected on the year gone by and life inside and outside Crowded House. Beating the New Year's rush, he began making some resolutions. "I feel in the last year I've changed a lot," he told Auckland magazine *Metro*. "What's important to me has changed. I've cast off all the bullshit I thought was important and focused on the stuff that really was." One example of the "bullshit"

he pledged to never repeat was the crazed three day trip to London to play *Top Of The Pops* back in 'Woodface' days.

To *The Sydney Morning Herald*, Neil confided: "First and foremost, surviving quite a troubled tour was a great achievement for 1994. I felt more satisfaction about our abilities than I had for a long time, given that we were able to triumph over adversity. Also I finally think I've won a mental battle with myself to get things in my life the way I really want them without feeling the pressure of other people's expectations. I've turned a corner."

Neil's determination to avoid lengthy touring with Crowded House, the outside recording projects, and talk of writing for an orchestra inevitably fuelled speculation he was about to close down the House. Such rumours would pick up early in 1995, but he paid them no heed.

With or without Crowded House, Neil Finn vowed to have a productive yet more relaxed 1995.

12

together or alone ?

Given the rigorous, sometimes traumatic events of 1994, Neil Finn could have been excused for packing up his guitar, kicking back, and settling into the Kiwi holiday spirit. Mid-December through January is serious holiday time in New Zealand. Schools are closed throughout and most folk schedule their annual time off for this period. The beaches are jammed, and the weather and the state of the national cricket team are the hot topics of conversation.

"I went to New Zealand, and it was closed." In earlier eras, this was a common refrain from tourists who happened to arrive on a Sunday or during the holiday period. It no longer holds as true, but New Zealanders still relish their holiday time, arguably more than any other nation. With physical surroundings such as theirs, who can blame them?

Christmas festivities with the family were clearly a top priority for Neil Finn but his musical work rate through January and February would certainly disqualify him from slackerdom. There were Crowded House concerts in Australia and New Zealand, further recording with Tim on the Brothers album, benefit concerts, school reunions and fund-raisers, and guest performances with rock superstars. Some vacation!

It had been well over a year since 'Together Alone' appeared in the Antipodes, so the Crowded House shows weren't designed to plug a new album, more to prove to local fans that, yes, there was life after Paul. Besides, these were comparatively stress-free gigs. They were back on home turf and often alongside bands with an equal or higher-profile who were guaranteed to bring in their own, generally compatible crowd.

January's Australian dates with Midnight Oil were billed as the Breaking Of The Dry tour, in celebration of the end of a punishing drought. On January 24 they pulled into Sydney's Enter-tainment Centre, the city's premier venue for big-name artists. Advertised as 'Four Bands, Four Full Sets', the concert also featured Electric Hippies and Hunters & Collectors, so the brothers Seymour shared a stage again.

Surprisingly, the show didn't sell-out, perhaps because the three shows R.E.M. had played there a week earlier had drained the pockets of local music-lovers. Those attending were treated to three now-legendary Australasian bands, each with a distinctive sound and vision. That they could share a bill with nary a hint of ego-driven strife again testifies to a general level of camaraderie within the local music scene. Exceptions exist, of course, but it remains a refreshing situation.

Not that their audiences always possess the same tolerance. Midnight Oil fans are a notoriously dedicated bunch, and include the kind of noisy macho Aussies all too often viewed as typical. Young New Zealand opera singer/Crowded House fan Christian Lamdin was at this show and reports that this contingent began their cry of worship –"Oiiii-llls" – during Crowded House's set. It was defused with some vintage Finn ingenuity. "When it began, Neil started this song I hadn't heard before. I think he just improvised it on the spot, and he used that cry of 'Oiiillls' as its chorus," he reports.

Sydney Morning Herald reviewer Jon Casimir was underwhelmed. "For a band regularly capable of producing magic onstage, Crowded House's performance was a day at the office. They were helped out on a couple of songs by Tim Finn, but it was never really anything more than a support slot, a chance to play a few songs and wave at some Sydney friends."

Crowded House crossed the Tasman a few days later to hook up with R.E.M.. The killer triple bill at Auckland's Western Springs comprised fast-rising Americans Grant Lee Buffalo, local heroes Crowded House, and rock gods R.E.M., finally out on the most-anticipated world tour of the Nineties. A crowd of 30,000 in the natural amphitheatre were treated to a gimmick-free night of fine music. Crowded House scored good notices here. Describing them as "The local(ish) meat in the overseas sandwich," *Rip It Up*'s Martin Bell reported: "Neil Finn and co. were in relaxed mood as the band swung through a song selection that concentrated on lesser known (but not lesser) album tracks." Grant Lee Buffalo manager Peter Leak recalls that Crowded House... "seemed very relaxed, and went down really well."

All these bands hung out together offstage. "Neil invited us out to the beach at Karekare while we were there, but none of us got up in time to do it," laments Leak. Seems Nick Seymour got to relax one Auckland night by going night clubbing. "We went to a club called Squid for their so-called Cheap Sex Night," reminisces Leak. "It was full of drag queens and transvestites – really a scene! I left about two or three, but I gather after that, Joey from Grant Lee Buffalo and Nick ended up dancing on the bar topless.

"It was pretty wild. I'd left to go around the corner and have a drink with Grant Phillips and Michael Stipe. We then went to Michael's room for pizza and Grant and I ended up walking to our hotel at five am, knowing we had to get up for a flight at 7.30! This guy crossed our path in leather shorts, suspenders, nothing else on but a pair of boots – handcuffs dangling from his belt and a rubber chicken under his arm. Just hilarious!" So much for New Zealand's reputation as a bastion of Puritanism.

After the R.E.M. gig, Crowded House headed south for a motley assortment of New Zealand shows. At the end of January, they faced a disappointing turnout in Nelson, a popular beach resort in the north of the South Island. Only 800 showed at the Trafalgar Centre, and that poor response became a news story in itself. *The Evening Post* in Wellington quoted an obviously disappointed Tracy Magan, the New Zealand tour promoter: "This is an international act. They sell out stadiums around the world, from Stockholm to South Africa, and when they can't sell more than 800 tickets in their own home country then it's a bit sad really." It should be pointed out that, even during the summer holiday, Nelson is a very small city. Taken on a per capita basis, that figure isn't as atrociously low as it first seems.

Another off-the-beaten-track tour stop was the South Island winter resort of Queenstown where ticket sales were healthier. Spirits really soared next with a show on February 4 before 80,000 fans, the largest audience Crowded House have ever faced as headliners in Australasia. (Their biggest ever audience was a German festival in July 1994 that reportedly drew 120,000.) Organised by The Christchurch City Council, it was a free concert in beautiful Hagley Park.

National hero Dave Dobbyn roused the crowd with tracks from his current, Neil Finn-produced triumph, 'Twist', Neil joining him for a gutsy version of 'Rain On Fire', and Dave's closing anthem, 'Whaling'. Unfortunately, Crowded House suffered sound problems, and as the group attempted to keep the crowd occupied, including three joining in on percussion, one wag commented it was like watching Marcel Marceau. Sound problems aside, the band was in a jovial mood. At one point, Neil teased the crowd that the Cricket Council was snooping around looking for pot smokers, a reference to a recent scandal involving Kiwi cricketers and drugs.

From this Christchurch triumph, Neil Finn's itinerary took a hectic detour, one that showed his emotional ties to his hometown and alma mater remained strong. A reunion of his classmates at Te Awamutu College had been organised by Dean Taylor, now a reporter on local paper, *The Te Awamutu Courier*. After initially declining the invitation to attend because of Crowded House's touring schedule, Neil made the effort.

Not an easy one, as it turned out. To catch the Sunday February 5 reunion function at local pub the Rose & Thorn, Neil had to fly from his Christchurch concert to Rotorua, drive to Te Awamutu, then head south for the band's Palmerston North Waitangi Day (a national holiday) show on February 6. Judging from the photographic evidence in the *Courier*, the reunion was a roaring success. It marked 20 years since most of these classmates/friends had left school, and was their first full reunion since then. "Atmosphere prevailing at the weekend proved that this spirit of friendship and camaraderie had not been diminished by the years," ran the local paper's feature.

The good times continued a couple of days later when Neil invited his old classmates to a Crowded House concert at Auckland's Powerstation club. Present at that gig was Mike Chunn. "The first three rows were filled with a busload of people who had come up from the Te Awamutu school reunion. I think the crowd was beyond excitement!"

Gestures such as this have definitely endeared Neil Finn to his old town. "He has made people here really proud, and he's still so nice," beams May Rhodes, Co-Ordinator of the Te Awamutu Information Centre. Now quite aware of his status as an international pop star, she has begun a Neil Finn file at the centre for the use of visiting fans.

Another Te Awamutu resident who retains a special fondness for Neil is Felicity Saxby, Neil's musical mentor in his teenage years. They re-established contact a few years back, under sad circumstances. "He and Sharon came to my daughter's funeral, as he arrived in the country that day. We picked up the guitars and played all the old songs. It was wonderful," she reminisces. "Fame hasn't gone to Neil's head at all. I think he's slightly uncomfortable with it – the plastic-ness of the accolades from people he hardly knows. He values his friends, he's honest and he doesn't like all the adulation, although I think he's very aware he's very good at what he does.'

The legendary spontaneous Crowded House antics continued on these NZ shows. In Palmerston North, Nick Seymour did a ballet dance up in the rigging and Mark Hart demolished 'Smoke On The Water'. To *Evening Post* reviewer Mike Houlahan, the gig was... "Just yer old mate Neil and his cobbers back in town to play you some songs. There's a total absence of stadium 'glitz'. They're a stadium act who behave as if they were a pub band playing their first gig." Halfway through their set the band stopped the show to organise a running race in the audience, a Kiwi holiday tradition. "How many bands would do that?" observed Houlahan.

Performing hijinks over, Crowded House again dispersed to various corners of the globe – Peter Jones back to Australia, Mark Hart back to the US, Nick Seymour to Ireland, with Neil Finn staying put in Auckland.

——◥◣——

IN MELBOURNE, meanwhile, Paul Hester was again venturing out into the musical world he had fled so hastily in Atlanta, April 1994. Post-retreat, he settled into the role of fatherhood, with girlfriend Mardi Sommerfeld giving birth to a baby girl in July 1994. His return to music came in the comfortable company of some long-time Melbourne friends. His new group Ultrasound is led by singer/songwriter Deborah Conway, long one of Australian rock's most popular performers, and includes Bill McDonald and Wally Zygier as well as Paul.

They recorded their self-titled début CD in Tim Finn's studio, Periscope, in January 1995. A pleasant and eclectic confection, it had scant local chart success. Warren Costello of Mushroom Records, Ultrasound's label, reports that Paul was involved himself only superficially in the songwriting, but was prominent with the artwork. Inevitably this featured doodles of his favourite appliance, the TV set, while Mardi contributed the group photograph.

Other reports had Paul doing some radio work – he'd be a perfect talk show host – and co-owning a Melbourne restaurant, not the most stress-free of occupations.

Across the Tasman, Neil Finn could reflect on a job well done. As Crowded House took a break, he was reminded that his songwriting prowess continues to be recognised by American radio,

albeit for songs written a decade earlier. At a special ceremony on February 18, he was presented with a special award to mark the fact that his hit single 'Something So Strong' had received a million airplays on American radio. This was presented by Rick Riccobono, vice-president of American performing rights association BMI, who quoted a mind-boggling statistic.

"One million performances on radio means that a song of an average length of three minutes has been on the air at least 50,000 hours – that's 5.7 years of continuous play." This marked Neil's second such award – the first, for 'Don't Dream It's Over', came in 1991 – and it placed him in the commercial elite of Australasian songwriters enjoying success in the US.

Along with the prestige, the resulting royalty cheques are nothing to be sniffed at. The award did, in fact, spark a rather snide piece in one Auckland newspaper, speculating on the extent of Neil's wealth.

Alongside Dave Dobbyn and Emma Paki on the New Zealand charts in the summer of 1995 was Tim Finn's single, 'Runs In The Family'. Not exactly his shining moment artistically, this was a song Tim wrote on commission to celebrate the centenary of New Zealand cricket. Aided by a cute video of family cricket on the beach, it made the Top 10.

By this time Tim and Neil Finn had more important things to do than chart watch. They were in York Street studios in Auckland putting the finishing touches to the new Finn brothers album, and the select few who had been privy to those sessions were buzzing with excitement. Co-owner of York Street, Martin Williams was clearly thrilled at his illustrious clients. "Everything went really smoothly. The fact that Neil lives just a couple of minutes down the road and that Tim stays with him when he's over from Australia makes us convenient, and this is a comfortable studio to work in."

This was a stress-free recording situation for Tim and Neil. They had no set schedule and no record label pressure. Williams reports they worked for eight to ten hours a day, continuing until midnight if they were on a roll. They pretty much pleased themselves, which is evident from the sound of the record.

Unlike the highly polished and expensive 'Woodface', this "brothers' album" has a more spontaneous feel. Tim and Neil co-produced it with long-time Crowded House engineer, Tchad Blake, who added various incidental sounds to the album. The Finns played all the instruments on the album, save for Dave Dobbyn on bass on 'Kiss The Road Of Rarotonga'. Tim returned to an early love, the drums. The primal nature of drumming appealed to his temperament. "Playing the drums was it for me. I've never felt so needed before. You are the engine, the motor, instead of this fey creature, waiting to apply his tune." According to Neil, "Tim alternated between terror and jubilation before and after takes on the drums. The tea-chest bass, made by our Tongan friend Sita, was the find of the album, ending up on five tracks."

Neil also felt a sense of accomplishment from repairing their antiquated Chamberlain keyboard. "Tapes were tangled through it, and Tchad said it was unfixable. Prior to that, my greatest practical achievement was changing a tyre. It's legendary that the Finns are useless at those things!" Neil describes the album as "pretty indulgent and kind of quirky. There are a few harmony songs, but it's not The Everly Brothers. Some songs have more unusual textures than either of us have used before. We were quick and didn't double-guess ourselves, so it's got a nice sense of immediacy."

The ease of the recording mirrored the smooth joint-songwriting process. "It was a very easy, joyful time," Tim told Australian journalist Kathy McCabe. "There was sweat but no real angst. Who did what varies a bit from song to song. One of us would have a musical idea, the other would bring a lyric, and then we'd both finish it. We swap roles all the time."

On both 'Together Alone' and 'Twist', Neil Finn had stretched himself musically, and the same sense of adventure permeated 'Finn'. Mitchell Froom goes so far as to say that 'Finn' may be the best thing Neil has ever done. "Towards the end, our relationship was sometimes a little touchy, and I think that's basically because Neil wasn't happy with the idea of someone else having control over his music. So I was really happy to be able to tell him I thought that the record was good!"

Froom's view of 'Finn' as Neil's best-ever work is definitely a minority opinion. The melodic gifts of both brothers are clearly in evidence, but the tunes demand patient, multiple listenings before totally ingratiating themselves. That's no chore for the committed fan, but the lack of instantly hummable songs here would pose problems commercially. There are also a couple of duds. 'Kiss The Road Of Rarotonga' is musically and lyrically lightweight – a holiday snap that should never have left the island. 'Bullets In My Hairdo' sports nonsensical lyrics and a lame melody. If the musical results were mixed in terms of quality, this renewed collaboration clearly showed things were smooth on the sibling front for Neil and Tim.

When 'Woodface' was released, Tim had speculated on future joint projects. "There is that desire to work together, but that's not enough. It has to come from mutual need." Tim has become quite used to ongoing questions about their relationship. "The reason everyone asks in a particularly probing way, looking for dirt, is that everybody has their own dirt, and they project it onto us, because ours is a high-profile sibling relationship. The sibling relationship is fundamental. That's just being explored in psychology. Unfortunately, there's precious little dirt with us. It'd be a more glamorous story if there was!"

With all the attention surrounding this much-anticipated Finn Brothers' record, speculation about the very future of Crowded House heated up again. With these new outlets for Neil's creative energies, his desire to spend more time with his family, and his now guaranteed financial security, what better time to put up the shutters?

Anxious Crowdies fans on the Internet discussed their concerns, while those close to the band had differing views. Neil's own ambiguous comments just fuelled the fire.

In the Auckland magazine *Metro*, in early 1995, he stated: "We're in a sort of rethinking phase and I don't know exactly what will emerge from this. If we get some new songs together and it's feeling good we'll go in and do another album pretty soon. If we haven't found a motivation to do anything in the short term I'm sure we're not going to break up, but we might put everything on hold. Being in a band is a kind of regime which I'm keen to break away from for now. It's like being married to four people and I'd like to be married to just one person for a while."

The Finns' long-time friend Mike Chunn thought matters were still very undecided. "If they asked me, I'd probably tell Neil and Tim to stick together," he said. "I just thought 'Woodface' was so significant. The two of them write stuff together that is different from what they're capable of individually."

Former manager Gary Stamler believed Neil Finn was still confused about the role of the band in his life. "At one point in late 1994, he clearly didn't want it to be the case, but he's someone who's inclined to change his mind on more than one occasion, so it's very hard to know where it'll all end up," he said.

Mitchell Froom also viewed the situation as being up in the air. "I think Neil's of the mind that he only wants to do something if it's really going to be fun to do," he said. "I don't think he cares much in terms of financial success or that kind of thing. He doesn't want to be in the biggest group in the world or any of those sorts of things. I think Crowded House will only work if that group is a viable, working entity, with its own energy.

"When they hit their straps as a trio, they really had a personality, a sound. In order to be a viable group artistically, they'd need either to come up with some new personalities or new sounds or something. You don't want to do a pale version of what you did better before."

Clearly, the decision on whether there'd still be a Crowded House rested squarely on Neil Finn's slight shoulders. His hesitancy must have been tough on the other members, but Nick

Seymour, at least, was used to his comrade's periods of doubt and introspection by this stage. After all, he had been sacked briefly by Neil a few years earlier, and, as the only other remaining original member, had witnessed Finn's internal conflicts for a long time.

While Neil appeared to be weighing his options, Tim Finn threw himself into his new project, ALT, which reunited him with Irish buddies Liam O'Maonlai from Hothouse Flowers and Andy White. They had worked together on Tim's 'Before And After' solo album in 1993, but, both critically and commercially, the ALT record was a virtual dud. As with 'Together Alone', British Parlophone A&R man David Field was closely involved. He arranged their first meeting, and when Tim was dropped by Capitol, Field had a plan. "I gave him some money and told the three of them to go into Tim's Melbourne studio and make a spontaneous album... jam, indulge yourselves, make a record and we'll see what we've got. I think it's very interesting, a kind of bootleggy, anti-industry kind of record. There are moments of genius and beauty and moments of pure indulgence."

Unfortunately, it's the indulgence that dominates, and the memorable melodies that have characterised so much of Tim Finn's work are conspicuous by their absence here. Critics judged the album harshly when it was released in Australasia in March and the UK in June. Undeterred, ALT played selected gigs including WOMAD events in Australia and the Fleadh in London, but the 'ALT' album made few ripples commercially.

• **Tim Finn at the Fleadh, London, 1995**

Neil and Tim Finn found themselves back in local headlines together at the end of March 1995, via a memorable Pearl Jam visit to Auckland. A year earlier Neil had sharply slagged PJ mainman Eddie Vedder in the press. "I find it kind of sickening the way he's complaining all the time," said Neil. "He's suddenly developed all this angst now he's massively successful. It just doesn't seem right somehow."

Amazingly (if he knew anything about this outburst), Vedder bore no grudge, and was keen to meet up with Neil and Tim, based on his love of Split Enz. "Talking to him here, I found out he has every single Split Enz album, on vinyl and CD," said Auckland artist manager/Crowded House tour promoter Tracy Magan. "He knew all the songs."

Eddie contacted Neil in advance, asking if the Finns would join Pearl Jam on stage at both Auckland shows. They agreed, choosing Enz classics 'History Never Repeats' and 'I Got You' and drawing huge cheers. Pearl Jam actually began the show with their own version of 'Throw Your Arms Around Me', the Hunters & Collectors ballad often played by Crowded House.

On March 25, between shows, Tim Finn took Vedder out to Karekare for a swim. There, the surf almost entered the rock'n'roll history books, for Vedder found himself in difficulty and the adjacent Karekare Surf Club was called to bring him to safety. The incident made the front pages of New Zealand newspapers the next day. "Rock Star Rescued From Surf," *The New Zealand Herald* headline blared. "Rocker In A Jam At Beach," went *The Sunday Star-Times*. One of the senior lifeguards involved, Eric Davis, admitted to the *Herald* he had no idea of Vedder's identity. "Tim Finn said, 'Do you realise what you have just done? You have rescued the lead singer of Pearl Jam. He's got to play in four hours and it would have been utter chaos if he hadn't turned out for the concert."

According to Tracy Magan: "Tim and Eddie were swimming together. A bit of a current caught Eddie and took him away from Tim, and Eddie couldn't be bothered swimming against it. There was no panic. The lifesaver guys got on the boat to check it out and asked how they were doing. Eddie said OK, but decided to go with them. Tim swam in on his own, not as the story said. It was exaggerated like hell!"

The Finns' appearance onstage with Pearl Jam did have some fallout – an extraordinary outburst from Neil Finn over a review in *The New Zealand Herald* that suggested ending the show with two Split Enz songs had deflated its momentum. A fax from Neil to reviewer Russell Baillie began: "You patronising prick!" and continued: "From where I stood, the audience seemed really energised for it and their obvious enthusiasm gives lie to your description of it as a whimper. Tim & I really enjoyed hearing Pearl Jam play Split Enz, one of life's surprising little twists, and take great exception to the suggestion that we somehow spoiled an otherwise triumphant show. Go fuck yourself. (signed) Neil Finn."

Baillie admitted he was rather shaken by this tirade. "I'm a huge fan of the band [Crowded House], and to have this come out of your fax machine is like having all your party balloons burst at once."

He did respond by fax to Neil. "Aww... there there. Had Pearl Jam come back on after your guest spot – as they really should have – then it wouldn't have seemed like an anti-climax of an ending. Take exception all you want, I certainly canvassed enough opinion to that effect from people at the show to consider it wasn't just me thinking it. Though as you say, 'the audience were really energised for it.' Of course they were – wow, Eddie Vedder says Split Enz were OK. Wahoo. Now that's patronising. No, you didn't spoil an otherwise triumphant show and I didn't say so. Just helped turn it from gutsy to cosy. But that's usually what you get from rock star mutual back slapping sessions, eh? Nice to hear from you. Yours prickedly, patronisingly and self-fuckingly, Russell."

Baillie later reflected upon this incident. "I guess for someone that has been 90% totally supportive and adoring, to actually say something not totally adoring and getting knocked around for that was pretty amusing really. I don't know how well he takes criticism."

This wasn't an unprecedented reaction from Neil Finn. In 1994 he took exception to a *Rip It Up* review of a Toronto show Crowded House played shortly after Paul Hester's departure. The writer pointed out some flaws in the show, and Neil's wrath was subsequently vented on the magazine's publisher Murray Cammick at an Auckland music industry function. "The Finns might cry 'tall poppy syndrome' [the Antipodean habit of cutting down those who rise above the flock] at this criticism," said Cammick, "but I'm prepared to cry 'sacred cow syndrome'. I think some of these artists think they're above criticism. In this country's perception, there's a certain angelic quality hovering over the Finns that they didn't ask for."

For a musician of Neil Finn's international stature to respond so fiercely to criticism from a couple of journalists previously highly supportive of his work has to be considered surprising. It certainly indicates that the intensity of his passion about his work hadn't weakened. Nick Seymour later observed that "lead singers are always trying to hone a method for their own madness and can be overly sensitive to criticism. If you throw a curveball into that, they tend to doubt everything they've done."

In March 1995, Neil played another benefit concert, one with an unhappy aftermath. Bruno Lawrence was a New Zealand musician/actor who had become a national cultural icon. A big-hearted free spirit, he had gone from jazz drummer to leader of a travelling multi-media (music, film, theatre) extravaganza BLERTA that shook up the country in the Seventies to one of the most popular actors in Australasia. He seemingly appeared in every New Zealand film produced from the mid-Seventies on, including the internationally acclaimed *Smash Palace*, *Goodbye Pork Pie* and *The Quiet Earth*. When diagnosed with cancer, he decided to fight it with experimental treatment in Mexico, and his many musical friends, including Neil Finn, rallied around with a concert to help cover his expenses. Sadly, Lawrence lost his battle a couple of months later.

While Neil Finn may have alienated some local music writers, his return to New Zealand has energised the Auckland scene. Even Chris Knox, NZ's most controversial musician, was pleased at Neil's return. "It's really positive people like Neil and [fellow singer/songwriter] Dave Dobbyn have moved back," he said. "They're now using New Zealand studios and engineers and it helps the so-called industry a lot."

Knox's first real encounter with Neil came in 1994 via mutual friend Martin Phillipps of The Chills, Chris's houseguest. Family men Chris and Neil spent most of their time talking about kids and schools. "We did talk about our different methods of recording and budgeting," says Chris. "My method is hi-fi but lo-tech [meaning tiny budget home recording]. I sensed he'd like to do that at some stage. It'd be nice to talk more about methods and madness. He's an intelligent guy with a real gift, but I think I could teach him a thing or two."

"It's good to have the top echelon in town," says Mike Chunn. "Their presence rubs off. People see them and know it's the level to work towards." For Chunn, it also means the odd fun foray down memory lane. In March 1995, for instance, Neil, Mike and two other Auckland musician dads played a fund-raising afternoon concert at the primary school their kids attend. "Neil played stuff he hasn't done for ages, like 'I Walk Away'. The parents went nuts as they'd smuggled beer and wine in and were as pissed as newts! He's a joy to play with, I must say, and he really put effort into it."

With Neil now integrating himself smoothly into the NZ music community, his potential as a talent scout will be valued by David Field, with whom he has remained on good terms. "We're talking about working on projects together," he said. "I'm going through the process of setting up my own label, and he may find New Zealand artists to put on it. I'm confident we'll work together again."

Mike Chunn observes that the New Zealand temperament suits Neil's desire for privacy. "People don't hassle you here as much as they might elsewhere. Neil can walk down the street taking the kids to school and no-one says anything. They might think he's the greatest thing since sliced bread, but they're too shy to do anything about it."

In between these bursts of recording activity and spontaneous live appearances, Neil enjoys surfing the Internet, a new passion for his young son Liam. Neil found himself unable to resist checking out a Crowded House site, Tongue In

The Mail, but the preoccupations of some of his devoted fans were sometimes annoying. "I'm tempted to get off the Internet," he told *Metro*. "It's been amusing to read what they're expecting from the brothers' album. They're really worried that Tim's drumming on it. But then people spend their time talking about your hairstyle. People are obsessed with it. That amazes me."

The Tongue list now boasts over 500 international subscribers, and scanning it confirms the unadulterated enthusiasm of hardcore Crowded House fans.

As a songwriter, however, Neil Finn is concerned that such technological innovations as the Internet pose a potential threat to the intellectual property of writers and performers. On April 27 1995, he joined other notable Australasian artists in a Who Took The Music protest event in front of Parliament Buildings in Canberra. Along with the likes of Midnight Oil's Rob Hirst and INXS's Kirk Pengilly, Neil played a concert broadcast live over the Internet as a way of lobbying for a transmission right in the copyright act. He performed 'Be My Guest', a song written especially for the occasion.

In late July 1995, it was reported that Crowded House would soon reconvene to begin work on the band's fifth album, temporarily stifling rumours of their impending demise. Such a timetable tallied with their UK record label's expectation of a new album to market in the northern spring of 1996.

In mid-1995, Crowded House's record label situation was in a state of flux. Prior to his dismissal, Gary Stamler had been working on getting Crowded House released from its commitment to Capitol US. The continuing commercial disappointments in the US and the band's ongoing dissatisfaction with the label's efforts on its behalf made such a divorce seemingly inevitable.

The success Capitol/EMI enjoyed with the band in other territories meant that this relationship was still seen as desirable. In July 1995, Stamler assessed the position. "The band, and/or Neil Finn, as Crowded House or as Neil Finn, will record the next several albums for release on Capitol affiliates throughout the rest of the world except North America," he said. "That's the most accurate thing I can say. Whether the Finn Brothers' record is part of this is unresolved and undefined."

It was expected then that Capitol US would initiate a 'Greatest Hits/Best Of' collection. Considering they had only had a few charting singles in the US, 'Best Of' may be the most appropriate term. "This would be a worldwide release on Capitol Records at a date to be determined," said Stamler. Such an album would include two or three new songs, and its commercial prospects were considered bright. Before returning to Crowded House activities, Neil readied himself for the release of 'Finn'.

13

recurring dream

Before returning to Crowded House activities, Neil readied himself for the release of 'Finn'. In September 1995, he and Tim sat down with music journalists in Australia and New Zealand to prime the promotional pump.

Rip It Up's John Russell reported them in good form. "Neil was in a quite jubilant and very confident mood then. He told me Crowded House would be back in the studio, and there was no inkling of a split then. I didn't leave the interview thinking, 'He's just told me to read between the lines and the end of the band is coming up'."

Neil and Tim visited the UK in late September, dropping in on an FMI sales conference (where they encountered the champagne-swigging members of Blur) and promoting the upcoming album's release there. One interview was with *Mojo*'s David Hepworth. He praised 'Finn' as "admirably organic... warm and loose," but correctly predicted it'd have trouble winning over the general public. The most interesting new information to surface in his article was Neil's admission of first experimenting with LSD as an 18-year-old in London, shortly after joining Split Enz. While staying with the pharmaceutically more experienced Noel Crombie (Enz spoons player), Neil took acid under Noel's direction. "I'm very grateful to Noel, as he taught me you had to treat it with respect," said Neil. "You had to make sure the house was tidy, you put on a clean suit of clothes, you shaved. Then you'd go for a walk and come back and everything would be nice clean lines." Neil was concerned such an admission in

print might upset his parents. Given the drug culture that flourished in New Zealand in the early psychedelic era of Split Enz, however, they must surely have had prior suspicions.

'Finn' was preceded in both Britain and Australasia by the first single 'Suffer Never', but it didn't exactly set the charts afire. The October 14 issue of *Melody Maker* recorded its first appearance at No. 29, but the following week it dropped off the British Top 30 into oblivion. A bad omen for what was to follow. A week later, the October 28 *Melody Maker* showed 'Finn' making its chart debut at No. 15, but without a popular single to sustain interest, the album also disappeared from

• **Tim and Neil performing together on the 'Finn' tour.**

the Top 30 a week later. The second single Angels Heap' was released in December, but it quickly crumpled into a heap, not even hitting the Top 30.

Clearly the British public and music press were more interested in the Gallagher brothers than the Finns at this stage. Neil Finn may have been the darling of some rock critics, but the puerile snideness of others remained. *MM*'s Everett True, in a review of 'Angels Heap', referred to the "unmistakably dreary Crowded House", before dismissing the song as "a grey slice of folky, formless AOR cack which makes The Beautiful South sound like someone very exciting indeed."

He did, however, praise Tim for having punched out daytime TV show host Richard Madeley of *Richard And Judy*. The Finns were lured to Liverpool to perform two tracks on this

show and be interviewed, but when they arrived were told the show's schedule was too tight and there was only room for an interview and one song. The Finns proposed dropping the interview and keeping the songs, but were then only able to do one number, which was rudely interrupted by the credits after only a minute. An incensed Tim reportedly called Madeley a "shoplifter", referring to a much-publicised earlier incident and court case involving the host.

'Finn' was released in Australasia on October 30, to mixed reviews and less than stellar sales as it hovered in the lower reaches of the Top 20. The brothers weren't immediately willing to tour extensively to breathe fresh life into it, but in mid-November they did play two well-received

SRO London gigs in the rustic ambience of the Union Chapel in Islington, blending material from the 'Finn' album with Crowded House favourites, material from Tim's solo albums and songs from deep within the Split Enz catalogue. For much of the evening Tim played drums while Neil chopped and changed between guitar and piano, and no-one could complain about the abundance of songs.

One of the few ways the 'Finn' project got ink in Britain came via a dispute over the name. London-based quartet Fin claimed the likeness of the brothers' name was damaging to their own career, and, in December 1995, they won the argument. All forthcoming releases from Neil and Tim had to come out under the name The Finn Brothers. Such a bland name would suggest an Irish folk duo to those not in the know.

By the end of '95, however, both brothers had better things to do than fret about that and the comparative commercial disappointment of their album. Neil had begun working on new tunes scheduled for inclusion on a future 'Best Of' collection, and Tim was preparing for his next solo record. As has happened throughout their careers, however, the legacy of Split Enz came knocking again. In December both Neil and Tim went into an Auckland studio to add vocals to tracks that had already been recorded by The

New Zealand Symphony Orchestra and the National Youth Choir. The 'ENZSO' project was the brainchild of former Split Enz and early Crowded House keyboardist Eddie Rayner. He originated the concept of symphonic treatments of Split Enz classics, then recruited some of New Zealand's best singers to guest.

• **Eddie Rayner.**

"This isn't Split Enz, the band reformed," he stressed. "This is the New Zealand Symphony Orchestra playing Split Enz songs, but with all sorts of singers. Neil and Tim started out encouraging but sceptical, but it was important for me to have them on board." Vocalists included local stars Dave Dobbyn (who sang 'Poor Boy'), Annie Crummer (on 'I Hope I Never') and poet Sam Hunt, while Enz percussionist/spoon-man Noel Crombie also joined in. Other revamped songs included 'Message To My Girl', 'I See Red' and 'I Got You'. A two hour documentary on the project was filmed for later airing on Australasian television.

• **Left to right: Dave Dobbin, Annie Crummer, Tim and Neil on the 'ENZSO' tour.**

Neil's musical juggling act now involved Split Enz, Crowded House and The Finn Brothers, and he merged them early in 1996 by touring Australia and New Zealand with Tim. Billed as 20 Years Of Song – An Evening With Neil And Tim, the tour began with an invitation-only gig in Auckland. As in the UK, it encompassed Split Enz, Crowded House, solo Tim Finn and Finn Brothers material. It helped 'Finn' up to a more respectable chart position (35 to 22, coinciding with their Melbourne visit). Returning to his long-time hometown evoked some nostalgia in Neil, and his former fellow citizens showed up in large numbers for two sellout shows in a modern Masonic hall.

The brothers were joined on the Australasian dates by bassist Dave Gent, on leave from his part-time jobs playing bass in NZ band The Exponents and as Neil's gardener! A six-city tour of New Zealand began on February 29 on which the support acts were highly-regarded NZ singer/songwriters David Kilgour (ex-The Clean) and Bic Runga. The tour of mid-size theatres (1,500 to 2,000 seats) was a major success, confirming that the Finns remained their home-land's pop heroes. Auckland music journalist John Russell reported: "They got full houses every night, and the reviews were phenomenal. Live, it seems people couldn't get enough. Commercially and critically, the tour fared far better than the 'Finn' album. People just wanted to see them together live again."

THE FIRST ORDER of business for Crowded House in 1996 was to reconvene and record some new material. It was now standard industry practice for 'Greatest Hits' or 'Best Of' collections to include some fresh or previously unreleased songs. That way, committed fans who already possess all the artist's work still have to shell out for the compilation.

Given a track record of ten years and four studio albums, a 'Best Of' collection could be justified. The driving force behind 'Recurring Dream' however, was more practical than aesthetic. Crowded House's relationship with its US label, Capitol, had reached the point of no return. Since the first record, both their profile

and record sales in the US had fallen dramatically, and the rapid turnover of Capitol executives had left Crowded House feeling alienated from the company. The band just wanted out. Capitol insisted on being given a 'Best Of' album before they'd release the group from its contract, a stipulation Neil Finn admitted publicly.

Neil and Co. took every effort to come up with an attractive package, musically and visually. They even invited fans to help choose the songs. "We took a sample by going down to the mall with clipboard and pen and polling our audience," Neil later joked to DJ Kim Hughes. "No, that's a metaphor, but we did sample our audience via our English record company. They sent out little questionnaires to the fanclub on their database, and found out what people most wanted to hear on a 'Best Of'. We took notice of that, had our own input and came up with a compromise. There'll be a couple of songs people are disappointed not to have, and there'll be some they got perhaps they didn't want."

Some of the obvious omissions show up on a bonus limited edition 15 track live album that came free with initial copies of 'Recurring Dream'. Compiling this was former Split Enz bassist Nigel Griggs, who went through 220 tapes of Crowded House shows before final selections were made. As Griggs explained in the liner notes, "It soon became apparent that each show is quite different... the songs, the music, the humour: allowing themselves to extend and develop songs, they're prepared to welcome any variation or distraction that may occur, musical or otherwise."

This characteristic is highly prized by Crowded House fans, and this live album is an essential document for them. As he told *Mojo*, Neil Finn likes these versions because "they're raw and energetic and show a different side to the band".

Of most interest, however, are 'Recurring Dream''s three new songs. Their recording marked the reunion of the original Crowded House team – Neil Finn, Nick Seymour, Paul Hester and producer Mitchell Froom. Mark Hart and engineer/co-producer Tchad Blake also contributed to the March 1996 sessions at Auckland's York St. Studios. Froom and former manager Gary Stamler were apparently the catalysts for this line-up. "The idea of Mitchell producing and getting Paul to drum was something Mitchell and I discussed long before the fact," explained Stamler. "I spoke to Neil about it when he visited LA in December 1995, and he sounded open to it. He talked to Mitchell, and obviously it happened."

Stamler's premonition that Crowded House wouldn't survive much longer was a factor here. "Part of the suspicions I had led me to feel it was important to conclude it properly. I took a shot with giving that advice, Neil took it and they went forward."

Finn confirmed this version in a later interview with Paul Myers for music magazine *MPACT*. "Mitchell was the prime motivator, but in the end we did think there was something appropriate about having a good experience to round it off. We were sentimental at the end of the day." Froom agreed the reunion "put a positive period at the end of the sentence" of Crowded House.

Neil selected three new songs he thought would suit this line-up, and they settled into York St. for a ten-day recording session. Gary Stamler reports: "They did it in somewhat the fashion of the first album, with Mitchell and Neil getting together for several days ahead of the tracking, working on the arrangements before the rest of the band came in."

Paul Hester was in good spirits, relishing the chance to make music with his mates again. Bill McDonald was bassist in Ultrasound, the Melbourne band Paul joined upon fleeing Crowded House, and he notes that, "Paul never spoke nastily about the band. He was actually very sad about what had happened."

Hester told journalist Chris Bourke during these sessions that "It's great returning like this. I'm back in the studio for 10 days, so there's no pressure. It's like I'm having a dirty weekend with my ex-wife."

The odd man out in the studio was Mark Hart. "He complained a little to me that there wasn't a lot of space for him on the record," recalls friend Stamler. "Mitchell played the keyboards and I guess Neil and Mitchell decided there was room for just one guitar."

Another Froom contribution to 'Recurring Dream' was to select its running order. "He's interested in stuff like orders," said Neil. "The good thing about CDs is you can put them on random sampling. You don't have to live with the album's order."

The first song recorded was 'Instinct', later the first single in most markets. Neil had laid down its rhythm track at his home studio (and it shows!), and the band added a Sixties British pop flavour. Although far from Finn's most memorable tune, lots of attention has been paid to the lyrics, retrospectively prophetic about Crowded House's demise. "The song fairly obviously describes that moment of being informed by your instinct that you have to take a leap into the unknown," he explained to Paul Myers.

Far stronger melodically is the blatantly Beatlesque 'Not The Girl You Think You Are'. Neil wrote it using an Optigan keyboard, which he described as "an old plunky thing from the Sixties, which reads optical discs. It's like a primitive sampler, and you get these little loops of real instruments, very low fidelity." The song took just ten minutes to pour out. "I had this little piano loop, so I put down a pattern on that and placed the vocal over the top of that." The vocal harmonies on the song bring to mind both Lennon and McCartney, and Froom later explained that "many people assume the high harmony was sung by Tim. We've never been that successful double-tracking Neil's voice before, but it's a nice rough double. You can hear the seams."

Observers are divided over whether the song is a Beatles parody or pastiche. To Stamler, "it's possibly one of the nicest recordings they've ever made. It does sound so Beatles that some people at Capitol have told me that if they could have put it on the third Beatles anthology, it'd have shot right to the top without anybody knowing the difference! It's clearly superior in their mind to The Beatles' remake songs ['Free As A Bird' and 'Real Love'].'' Finally came 'Everything Is Good For You', featuring some OK harmonies and catchy guitar and keyboard riffs, but a definite notch below the band's best work.

Taken as a whole, in fact, these three songs just don't stack up against the finest moments of Neil Finn's repertoire. One can speculate that he didn't want to waste his best post-'Together

Alone' songs on a collection that was primarily a contractual necessity. Or perhaps, aside from the 'Finn' songs, he simply hadn't come up with much new Crowded House material in this period.

With the new songs recorded, Neil, Tim, Dave Dobbyn and orchestral arranger Eddie Rayner joined in with The New Zealand Symphony Orchestra for a concert of Split Enz tunes at Auckland's Aotea Centre on April 3. The well-received concert helped send the 'ENZSO' album on its way high up the local charts.

The Finns were less successful ten days later at the inaugural New Zealand Music and Entertainment Achievement awards. They were nominated in the International Achievement and Best Group categories but were shut out by, respectively, pop-funk band Supergroove and rock veterans The Exponents and metal merchants Shihad (a tie for Best Group). The results most likely reflected a feeling that Tim and Neil had enough trophies on their mantel-pieces.

With 'Recurring Dream' completed and the Finn Brothers project on hold, awaiting a North American release, the rest of Crowded House stood by waiting for the call to begin work on the

next studio album. In March, English music journalist Paul Du Noyer tracked Nick Seymour down in London, hanging out in a hip Soho bar. Searching for an intermediary, Nick pleaded, just half-jokingly, "When you see Neil, ask him if he's writing some new songs. I'm not going to ring him up and nag him, but that's all I need to know. He should be writing. He's got everything to look forward to."

This incident is telling. Clearly, a band's inner dynamic is dysfunctional when they're reduced to communicating via a rock critic.

The distance between the members of Crowded House wasn't just physical. Neil Finn continued his internal wrestling match over the band's future, but he wasn't about to share his feelings with his bandmates, still dispersed around the globe – Peter Jones in Melbourne, Mark Hart in Los Angeles, Nick Seymour in Dublin or London. Publicly, at least, a positive face was still shown. "We'll start recording soon. There will be a Crowded House," Neil pledged to Du Noyer.

New Zealand music mag *Rip It Up* reported in their May issue that the band had booked York St. for July and August '96 to work on their fifth studio album. First would come the inevitable trek to plug 'Recurring Dream'. That was set for June, prior to its international release. In the final days of May, however, the tone of that trip took on a dramatic new dimension. It would now become Crowded House's swansong. The eternally-conflicted Neil Finn decided he had no option but to kill the band.

In their June 16 edition, New Zealand's *Sunday Star-Times* rather melodramatically set the scene. "It was a Friday night and as the melodies filled the darkened room of his Auckland home, Finn found himself unable to become enthused. 'I was listening to some new tunes in the workroom and I thought, This doesn't sound like Crowded House. I thought we needed to approach things in a new way. There was this overwhelming oppression about the band.

"As the inevitable solution to the dilemma dawned upon him, Neil claims 'I felt a lightness descend upon me. I was aware of this gnawing doubt and suddenly I felt excited about making a record again'.

"In retrospect, Finn feels the words to his recently-recorded new song 'Instinct' had been prophetic. 'Call it music imitating life. After I made the decision I re-read the lyrics and realised the words had an uncanny autobiographical note. They showed the desire to get out must have been brewing for some time.'"

Neil phoned manager Grant Thomas in Sydney, then Mark Hart and Nick Seymour. Drummer Peter Jones claimed he was told just two days before a June 4 London show that the band was over, which suggests that Neil Finn had never really viewed him as an integral member of Crowded House. According to Neil, "Neither of them [Mark or Nick] were surprised because they knew I'd been frustrated for some time. They didn't necessarily think it was a good idea and suggested I just take a break for a few months, but I knew you can't do things like that. It's always important to make a definite break."

Seymour disputed this version. He later told Toronto journalist Jane Stevenson that "I was surprised, then kind of annoyed. I still think it's unnecessary, but I'm not sure what alternative we have. I've always anticipated getting the [final] phone call. It surprised me because our manager [Grant Thomas] had told me that Neil was the most positive over Crowded House that he thought he'd ever seen him. Then, I thought, well perhaps that's a slight on the perceptiveness of our manager!"

To another North American writer, John Sakamoto, Nick explained "I didn't know whether to argue with Neil [on the phone]. I didn't know whether to state the case. I just felt really... pathetic."

Seymour's occasional lapse into bitterness is perfectly understandable, and it coincided with the international success 'Recurring Dream' was enjoying. "That's great... we're No. 1 in Britain. Too bad we had to break up to get it," he moaned to friends in New York during this period. Despite his chronic indecisiveness over the future of Crowded House, Neil Finn's decision seemed final this time. He flirted with the idea of cancelling the planned promotional trip for 'Recurring Dream', but agreed to carry on to avoid sabotaging the project. Given that he'd effectively just given his bandmates their notice, that was only fair.

First stop, London, at the beginning of June.

14

don't dream it's over

ittingly, a stage in London's West End provided the setting for what seemed at the time to be the last act in the story of Crowded House. The Hanover Grand, an intimate venue (capacity 700) near Oxford Circus, was chosen to host a June 3 invitation-only Crowded House performance. The lucky audience primarily comprised long-time members of the band's fan club, and this appeared to be the perfect occasion for Neil and comrades to bid farewell personally to old friends and loyal supporters. The only problem was that he neglected to tell them that this would be the last live performance by the band! Just prior to the London gig confusion reigned as EMI, Crowded House's UK label, sent out a press release stating that the demise of the group had been announced at the concert that night.

The first to be informed of the end, reportedly on Neil's authorisation, were actually those Crowded House fans plugged into the Internet. That was a little surprising, given Neil's ambivalence, sometimes antagonism, towards the often obsessive trainspotting-type mentality of some subscribers to the *Tongue In The Mail* Crowded House site.

An onstage announcement was the strategy agreed upon by all of Crowded House, but Neil just couldn't do it. According to one spectator, the only possible inkling of what was to come was Neil's comment along the lines of "we're all very much looking forward to the future." The crowd roared at this, thinking he was talking about more great Crowded House albums to come. This observer, a long-time Crowded House fan, did notice that "Neil didn't seem to be having that great a time. The band seemed a bit under-rehearsed, and there were some mistakes in there. It wasn't quite the uplifting night they usually produce."

Scarcely surprising, given the circumstances. An extended version of 'Don't Dream It's Over' assumed a poignant irony. Neil's procrastination meant he had to issue his own press release the following day to sort out the mess and clarify the numerous radio and press leaks that had already sprung around the music world. It read "A press release was sent out saying that Crowded House were breaking up and that it was announced on stage June 3 in London. In fact, I said nothing on stage. I couldn't bring myself to be that dramatic. I do, however, confirm that the band is indeed over, and the name too. We have had many moments of great intensity between band and audience and I will always value that, but there have been creative frustrations lately – I think we were beginning to repeat ourselves. I crave a new context to draw something fresh out of me as a songwriter. I have every desire to keep making records and find the challenge of new possibilities exhilarating.

"There has been a lot of emphasis on the past, with the 'Best Of' album. I stand by it as a document of some of our best moments and will make a few appearances to acknowledge its presence but there are no plans to tour – no farewells for us. I need to get on with it, the future that is. Thanks to all our supporters of the band for giving us heart. Thanks also to Nick, Mark, Paul and Tim for playing my songs so well. We remain good friends."

So sounded the death knell, and the inquests and obituaries echoed immediately. It was, unsurprisingly, front-page news in Australia and New Zealand, and media outlets there scrambled to cover the unfolding story. Television New Zealand (TVNZ) phoned Neil Finn at his London hotel, the luxurious Landmark, at 2 am, just after the "last" show. They had a crew ready to film any interview, but Neil chose to return to sleep.

NZ newspapers were forced to recap the band's history and repeat quotes from the press release. "It's not just a bad dream – it really is all over," declared the June 5 edition of *The New Zealand Herald*. "Over too soon," chimed in *The Wellington Evening Post*, while *The Sunday News* of June 9 went with "Bringing the House down". The official comment from EMI New Zealand was banal. "It has been a privilege to work with all the guys and I know we'll be hearing more wonderful music from Neil, albeit, maybe, under some other name," commented managing director Kerry Byrne.

Two weeks later, Neil admitted that the events of June 3 and 4 were "just a bit messy in terms of information. It [the first release] didn't force my hand particularly. I feel pretty good and

• On stage at the Hanover Grand, London, June 3 1996.

resolute about my decision."

The wording of Neil Finn's own release is significant. He thanked the others "for playing *my* [italics added] songs so well." Check your Crowded House records and you'll find shared songwriting credits on many of the songs. Tim, of course, featured prominently with eight co-writes on 'Woodface'. Surely using the phrase "our songs" would have been a more generous choice, but by now any pretence that Crowded House functioned as a democracy was stripped as bare as a nudist colony. Neil Finn started the band, Neil Finn finished it. No group consultations were held before the decision to close the door. As Gary Stamler commented, "the idea had long fallen by the wayside for Neil." Despite the official end, Crowded House soldiered on in true "the show must go on" fashion. All commitments to promote the imminent release of 'Recurring Dream' were honoured, but obviously a different mood fell over that record now. It didn't just mark the end of an era for Crowded House, a summation of past glories before moving on to new musical triumphs together. This was it.

The timing of the end panicked some English music magazines. In their July issue, *Mojo* devoted a full page to an analysis of 'Recurring

Dream' that included an interview with Neil. It ended with Finn promising a new Crowded House album by early '97. "We've rehearsed a lot and talked about it. The band may expand to accommodate a few different possibilities in terms of line-up. There'll be a new record company in the States and a different production team. We're looking to make a fairly bold step forward." No-one had interpreted the "bold step" as meaning the demise of the band.

In their news page of that issue, *Mojo* hastily announced the split, regurgitating Neil Finn's press release. The back page sported a colourful ad for the album, with the clever (and accurate) tag line, "You know more Crowded House songs than you think you do."

Also caught out was *Q* in their July issue. Stalwart Crowded House supporters, they ran a five-page feature on the band. Neil's closing line there?: "There will be a Crowded House. We just don't know what it looks like yet."

While still in London, Crowded House filmed a show for MTV Europe in their Camden Town studio, then drove to Shepherd's Bush where in the BBC studios they guested on the acclaimed TV series *Later With Jools Holland*. The star-studded bill on this show also featured Richard Thompson (an old friend/musical associate of the band), rising soul stars The Fugees, and legendary punk pioneer Patti Smith. Ironically, this was part of her triumphant resurrection, as opposed to Crowded House's swansong. They were clearly the favourite of the studio audience who demanded an encore and, off air, were treated to unscripted renditions of the new single 'Instinct' and the now anthemic 'Weather With You'. An hour-long afternoon performance at Greater London Radio (GLR) studios was Crowded House's last ever British show.

The band then set off on another hectic European promo tour, crammed with interviews, television shows and the occasional showcase gig. House calls were made to Hamburg, Amsterdam, Madrid, and Glasgow, then it was off to Toronto for one last round. Canada remained a far more successful market than the US, where the group suffered from near invisibility and a poisoned relationship with their record label. In Canada, EMI pledged a major push behind

'Recurring Dream', including television advertising. As well as the standard television, radio and print interviews, the idea of a club gig was agreed to just days before the press trip. Promoter Rob Bennett of MCA Concerts explained that "EMI phoned us at the last minute, asking if we'd put the show on. There wasn't even a signed deal."

News of the Monday June 24 show at the Horseshoe Tavern was embargoed until 7 am that day. All 350 available $25 tickets were snapped up in minutes at the club, and a charge of excitement coursed through the local music industry. Also excited was the Canadian Music Therapy Trust Fund, chosen by the band to get the night's takings. Over $6,000 was raised, and the attendant publicity was invaluable.

• On *Later With Jules Holland*.

Although billed as Crowded House's last ever Canadian show, those close to the band knew this Horseshoe gig could well have been their last public show anywhere. The audience comprised local musicians, media, record company personnel and the general public, but for once such divisions were meaningless. Virtually everyone in the room were serious Crowded House fans – very few liggers here. Even other artists on the band's Canadian label EMI paid to get in.

The choice of venue was no accident. Neil Finn played another memorable surprise gig at the Horseshoe back in 1981, at the height of Split Enz's Canadian success. Their special guest that night was guitar hero Mick Ronson (who died in 1995), and Neil reminisced about that show falling on his 23rd birthday. This one, coincidentally, was on Tim Finn's 44th birthday, noted with a brief snatch of 'Happy Birthday'.

Crowded House could have sold out a much larger theatre, but seeing them up close was a treat the audience clearly relished. They got a generous two-and-a-quarter hour show (naturally concentrating on 'Recurring Dream' selections) that was more celebratory love-in than funeral. Usually jaded local industry types wandered the club with beaming smiles, reminiscing about previous House shows they'd seen.

Having Toronto play host city to possibly the group's last hurrah was appropriate, as it could lay claim to having been Neil's Northern Hemisphere home from home over the years, dating back to the Split Enz era. On this night, it seemed Neil gave his comrades even more musical freedom than usual. Mark Hart sang Creedence Clearwater Revival classic 'Born On The Bayou' and Nick Seymour got to fool around with a disco parody and a rather silly ditty he'd just come up with, 'Ripped Off On Queen Street' (the club's location). Finn was able to tease Nick about future employment prospects – "He should do a travelling revue, half hardcore disco and half action painting onstage. He could do performance painting, backed by a beatnik combo!" This segued into a comic tale of pubic hair pinched by a guitar while recording a song on 'Together Alone' naked, and a very funny pisstake of Midnight Oil singer Peter Garrett.

Some of the more critically-inclined at the Horseshoe felt some songs were marred by ridiculously long, neo-psychedelic instrumental jams and prolonged song endings. The *Toronto Sun* suggested "a little more music, a little less banter and goofiness" would be appropriate and gave the show three out of five stars. This was a minority opinion, as the generally ecstatic crowd happily sang along to 'Weather With You' and 'Better Be Home Soon'. Things never got too sentimental, even if Neil was spied shedding a tear during 'Don't Dream It's Over'.

"It wasn't an emotional one," he laughed later. "My eyes started to sting 'cause my hair product dripped down into my eyes as I was sweating so much. I noticed these people out of the side of my eye going, 'Oh, look, he's crying'."

He did get a little emotional while thanking Crowded House's loyal entourage and fans – "We wish you all the best, Godloveya." The band then launched into the final song of the night, the jaunty offbeat 'Sister Madly', before exiting the stage to resounding cheers.

The next day they went their separate ways, musically and physically. Nick told a German magazine he intended to visit Paris for Bastille Day (July 14), to which Neil interjected, "he means he's going to get drunk from the good Cabernets."

Neil was due back in Toronto just two weeks after the last Crowded House gig, this time for a July 6 Finn Brothers show with Tim. He put the time between to fine use, reportedly taking his mother and family to Ireland for a holiday, perhaps a thank-you for providing the inspiration for a song Tim and Neil had recently contributed to a compilation of Irish music. Their warm ballad 'Mary Of The South Seas' appears on 'Common Ground', alongside such artists as Elvis Costello, Kate Bush and Sinéad O'Connor.

Producer Donal Lunny explains that "Neil and Tim were in Britain for an EMI sales convention and decided to write a song for the project. They enlisted Andy White [ALT] to write the lyrics and everybody was delighted how it came out. I think it's a great addition." Most album reviewers agreed.

One date Neil Finn didn't play during this period was the June 29 Prince's Trust extravaganza in London's Hyde Park, featuring The Who, Bob Dylan, Eric Clapton and Alanis Morissette. Neil's appearance had been the subject of highly intriguing rumours a couple of years earlier. It seems a Trust board member, pursuing the possibility the remaining three Beatles might reunite for the benefit approached Finn. "It was never a direct request, but he asked me if I'd be interested in playing with The Beatles," Neil recalled. Imagine the headlines. "Finn Forms Fab Four!" The fantasy clearly appealed to Neil. "An amazing thought. Imagine being a member of The Beatles, even for just a day. I'd be tempted, but just within four walls, in private. Not in any kind of public thing, where there's so much scrutiny," he told journalist John Sakamoto.

Although no longer a functioning unit, Crowded House had much to celebrate in the progress of 'Recurring Dream' and its singles in international territories during the summer of '96, despite some disappointments with the newer material. Its path confirmed that the band remained a hot commercial property in Britain and Australasia, were still popular in Europe and Canada, and virtually invisible in the US.

'Instinct' was chosen as the advance first single in most markets, but fared disappointingly. In mid-June it entered the British charts at No. 12, but disappeared after just two weeks. It had moderate success in New Zealand and scored some Adult Contemporary airplay in Canada. Clearly, 'Recurring Dream' would stand or fall on the demand for earlier Crowded House material.

EMI in Britain rightly sensed its potential, and launched a strong advertising campaign around its June 29 release there. Their faith was vindicated when it entered the album charts at No. 1, displacing Canadian sensation Alanis Morissette's 'Jagged Little Pill'. It stayed there for a second week before Alanis grabbed top slot again. An impressive 140,000 copies of 'Recurring Dream' sold in Britain in the first two weeks, and it was a regular visitor in the Top Ten through to late November 1996. It was certified a platinum seller (300,000) in just six weeks, by far the band's fastest-selling album ever in the UK. By comparison, the classic 'Woodface' took nearly three years to reach double-platinum status.

It also sold steadily in Europe. *Billboard*'s

Eurochart combines figures from the individual markets, and it showed 'Recurring Dream' reaching the Top Ten and enjoying a healthily long run on the chart. A surprising disappointment in August was the failure of second single, 'Not The Girl You Think You Are'. Picked by most as the best and most commercial of the new songs, it only lasted a week in the UK Top 20. In Canada, trade magazine *The Record*'s chart registered a top position of No. 29 in July. Still, the single kept selling steadily and was expected to achieve a very respectable gold status by Christmas 1996.

In Australasia, the album simply sprinted out of the record stores. EMI New Zealand reported that it shipped nearly double-platinum, the biggest shipment for a title in company history. It débuted at No. 1, and dug itself in there for a long run. Across the Tasman, same thing. It shipped over platinum, a record for a Crowded House album, and went straight to the top, outselling the second album by 300 per cent. The perverse Aussies picked 'Everything Is Good For You', arguably the weakest of the new tracks, as their first single, and it made the Top 10.

In this same period (July and August) the 'ENZSO' album was in the Top Ten in both countries (an amazing double-platinum result after peaking at No. 2 in NZ, No. 4 in Australia, with platinum sales), while the Split Enz compilation 'History Never Repeats' reappeared in the NZ Top Ten. Back in Auckland in August '96, Neil Finn spied three collections of his songs in the Top 20. Any anxiety over his future would not be financial! Tim Finn must also have appreciated this boosting of the royalty coffers, given that he hadn't scored a significant hit since 'Woodface'.

In the US, Capitol waited a full month before releasing 'Recurring Dream' on July 23. Shortly thereafter, a Capitol spokesperson admitted "there is no significant chart activity or sales to report". Such a bland utterance spoke volumes about Crowded House's presence, or non-presence, in the US.

At the time, former manager Gary Stamler admitted "it won't register a blip on the radar screen unless we go out and do something with a plan". Capitol, in fact, urged him to get involved. "I had a meeting there and was basically told that if I wasn't involved, very little would happen.

That's a lot of pressure to be put under considering the events of two years ago, to find out people are looking to me again. It is totally ironic."

Since his bitter falling-out with Neil Finn, the pair had mended fences to the point where Stamler considered working the record. "Part of me thinks it'd make a fitting bookend if we caught lightning in a bottle twice," he explained. "It wouldn't be any more of a miracle to bring 'Not The Girl You Think You Are' home as a hit than it was for 'Don't Dream' almost exactly ten years ago."

Nothing was happening with the record at radio or retail, but Crowded House still had plenty of friends in the media. The album was reviewed favourably by such major publications as *Entertainment Weekly* and *The Chicago Tribune*, and got a good plug on CNN *Entertainment News* when they ran a lengthy item on the Finns in early August. "With the release of their own album and 'Recurring Dream', the Finns may finally get the mainstream exposure that has eluded them, at least in America," summarised the item. Wishful thinking.

North American fans of Neil Finn's music, however, were gorging themselves in July '96. A month before the US release of 'Recurring Dream' came the long-awaited North American appearance of 'The Finn Brothers'. Long ago rejected by Capitol, it finally found a home on Warner offshoot label Discovery.

"Basically, we just bid for it with other companies," recalls Lisbeth Cassaday, Alternative Media Publicist at Discovery. "I believe they came with us because we felt passionate about it and would make it a priority."

Discovery doesn't quite have the promotional clout of the biggest US labels, but they did secure some good television coverage for the Finns. Despite some positive press and limited airplay for the singles, 'The Finn Brothers' had little commercial impact. The brothers did their bit with an eight-city North American tour, including television, radio and press interviews and performances. Neil Finn must have been fed up with yet more questions about the end of Crowded House, but took everything in his stride.

The Finn tour began in Toronto on July 6. The pair returned to radio station CFNY for a pre-gig chat and a few numbers, and Neil reiterated that Crowded House's Horseshoe show was likely to have been their last. "There is vague talk of doing a party in our part of the world somewhere," he said then. "It'd be for friends and family and we'd film it as our version of [The Band's farewell] *The Last Waltz*. We sort of started out playing parties, so it'd be appropriate. Apart from that, no, that'll be it. Our manager wants us to do a free concert in front of 100,000 people on the steps of the Sydney Opera House, televised around the world live, but it seems a little grand. But if you see it on TV, you'll know the manager won!" A prophetic comment.

This Finn Toronto gig was also at a venue both knew. Back in 1980 the downtown theatre, then known as The Masonic Temple, hosted Split Enz's

Toronto début. It was now called The Concert Hall, but Tim and Neil still joked about its Masonic Lodge roots during the show. Attendance here was a little disappointing (perhaps half of its 1,100 capacity), but 'The Finn Brothers' had only just been released and the strong media focus on the Crowded House visit was absent this time. Rob Bennett of promoter MCA Concerts bluntly called it "a real mistake, coming when they did. The record is flatter than a pancake. They should have done a tiny little showcase".

The duo seemed unperturbed, as they put on a spirited, thoroughly entertaining performance. Having his family in tow buoyed Neil's spirits, and he made young son Liam earn his keep by helping sell merchandise in the hall lobby. The Finns performance here covered all aspects of their careers. As Neil told CFNY, "We have a long history together, so we can dip into any period we wish. In Crowded House, we didn't do any Split Enz and vice versa, but now it's just so open." Added Tim, "Because it's just the two of us, we can branch out from the set list. We do requests, as long as they're com-prehensi-ble!" In what became a gig ritual, fans fired paper planes bearing request pleas onstage. Classic Mark Seymour song and House fave 'Throw Your Arms Around Me' got the nod for an encore choice this way.

Many Finn followers compared this show favourably to the Crowded House finale. Chris Tait had befriended Crowded House early on when his then band Chalk Circle opened a Canadian tour for them. "The Crowded House show at the Horseshoe was great, but it did feel old. It was a last hurrah, whereas the Finns show felt fresh. I preferred this." Deane Cameron, President of EMI Canada and a long-time supporter of Crowded House, declared the Finns show "better

than I'd imagined it would be. There was a real magic in the air".

Others commented that Neil looked much happier this time. Further reflection on his decision to close down Crowded House obviously hadn't elicited any regrets or second-guessing. It did seem significant he never once uttered the words "Crowded House" onstage, even though he and Tim played many of the songs they'd co-written on 'Woodface'.

With Neil playing guitar, piano and ukelele and Tim alternating between drums (including an hilarious drum solo parody), piano and acoustic guitar, the duo came up with enough instrumental variety to keep things ticking over. Stealing the show repeatedly, of course, were those familiar but still delightfully pleasing sibling vocal harmonies, put to use on a repertoire with few equals in contemporary pop. Biggest surprise of the night came when Tim sat at the piano and sang his heart out on very early ('Mental Notes') Split Enz favourite 'Time For A Change', dedicated to his comrade/mentor Phil Judd. Tim also shone on 'Dirty Creature' and 'Six Months In A Leaky Boat', dating back to his most creative period within that band. As on 'The Finn Brothers', though, Neil definitely took the most prominent role vocally. Many of that record's songs sounded better in this live setting, freed from the occasional self-indulgence of the studio versions.

The spontaneous onstage fooling around that was such a big part of Crowded House was equally in evidence on these Finn shows. Jokes about ageing crooner Engelbert Humperdinck became a long-running gag when they'd slip into his 'Please Release Me', while Neil's introduction of the humble ukelele always provoked mirth. At some shows, he destroyed it, Pete Townshend-style!

Next stop was New York. As well as playing the prestigious Supper Club, The Finns guested on network television programme *The Late Show With Conan O' Brien*, performing 'Only Talking Sense'. Other cities included Boston, Washington DC, Chicago, Boulder and San Francisco, and the tour ended on a high note with two sold-out nights at The John Anson Ford Theatre (capacity 1,100). An impressive celebrity turnout there included actors Harry Shearer, Jamie Lee Curtis

and Russell Crowe and rocker Sheryl Crow, now a good friend after her long stint opening for Crowded House in 1994. Neil, in fact, had recently guested on guitar on Crow's self-titled second album, while Sheryl called that tour motivating. "I came out of it mentally drained but extremely inspired because of its emotionality. I really felt like writing after it."

Post-tour, Tim returned to Australia, quickly reimmersing himself in the local scene. On August 4 he participated in a concert at the Sydney Domain, held to protest against government cuts to the Australian Broadcasting Corporation and the much-loved Triple J radio network. Across the Tasman, Neil joined those lobbying for a New Zealand national youth radio service.

Altruistic gestures aside, it was then time for both Finns to refocus on their individual upcoming solo records. Tim Finn was still without a major label record deal, but remained determined to keep writing for his next album. There would continue to be times, however, when Neil and Tim just fancied the idea of some low-pressure concerts together. One such scheduled date was the Marlborough Wine and Food Festival in February 1997. This is held in New Zealand's premier wine-growing region, and doubtless Tim's well-known love of the grape was a factor in choosing this gig!

Neil, meanwhile, mentioned mid-1997 as due date for delivery of his début solo record. "I'm not sure yet whether it'll be under my own name or whether I'll invent some other name," he told John Sakamoto. "There's something attractive to me about taking the personality out of the project. With solo acts, there's something about it that doesn't excite me, though in effect that's what it'll be."

Neil reiterated that "I might come up with some moniker to differentiate myself. As it is, I get called Tim Finn every day of my life. My manager suggested I should call the thing Fang, but he's got some substance problems," he joked. "I've been called Fang half my life, by those close to me anyway. It's my nickname."

Those thirsting for more Neil Finn songs and music didn't have to wait that long, however. US singer/songwriter Shawn Colvin, a long-time

an interview with *The Sydney Morning Herald*. "He is exceptional as a musician. I always like people that are playing to the edge of their ability and he is constantly doing that. There is always an element of struggle in what he does. He's really pushing his boundaries all the time and I found that very inspiring." Finn reiterated his own determination to keep experimenting. "I'd love to think that whatever happens next is more exotic than a band; different ways of generating rhythms than just guitar, bass and drums. But I may come around midway through 1997 and decide that's all there's ever been or should be."

Nick Seymour, meanwhile, wasted no time in dusting himself off and getting back in the musical saddle once he recovered from the discouraging realisation that Crowded House were no more. An interview with Australian *Rolling Stone* showed he'd also regained his playful sense of humour. He called the break-up "the cheapest, most cynical publicity stunt in the history of rock'n'roll. It's the most empowering form of publicity we've ever done. This is the most interest there's ever been in a new Crowded House record. People love it when you break up!"

Nick worked extensively on a solo record by brother Mark Seymour, of Hunters & Collectors, playing keyboards, singing and helping with the arrangements. In August he returned to his much-loved Ireland for pre-production work with New Zealand singer Bic Runga. He then played some European and Australian dates with Melbourne band Deadstar. This is a side project

• **Nick Seymour with Deadstar colleague Caroline Kennedy.**

Crowded House fan, was reported to be including a Finn tune, 'Get What I Paid For' on her upcoming record. There's also a Neil Finn co-write on 'The Seventh Wave', a 1996 solo album by popular New Zealand singer Annie Crummer. 'Here Come The Gods' was co-written by Neil and Tania Crummer, Annie's mother. Tania wrote some lyrics in Cook Islands Polynesian dialect, Neil wrote separate English lyrics, and, explained Annie, "they both seemed to be saying the same thing. Amazing". The featured Cook Island choir on the tune is actually, Neil, Tim and Annie, multi-tracked.

Another intriguing collaboration Neil entered into in late 1996 was with Midnight Oil guitarist Jim Moginie. They began writing and recording new songs, and Neil praised Moginie effusively in for Barry Palmer of Hunters & Collectors, singer/songwriter Caroline Kennedy and Crowded House drummer Peter Jones. Their self-titled 1996 CD, described as blistering pop, had won much critical acclaim in Australia and New Zealand.

In Neil Finn's mind, future work with Seymour was very possible. "I'd prefer to think that whatever good musical relationship we have has a chance of being defined in some new context. There are no plans in the short term to do anything together, but I think it'd be kind of strange if we didn't."

Mark Hart's first major post-House move was to hook up again with progressive rock veterans Supertramp, with whom he'd worked pre-House. "Mark will both record and tour with them, basically taking the Roger Hodgson role," explained friend Gary Stamler. "He also wants to do some general production work on top of that."

Clearly, the phrase "formerly of Crowded House" on the CV means excellent job prospects for all alumni of the incredibly well-respected band.

—◆—

WHETHER ATTRIBUTABLE to pressure from his manager and bandmates or just a desire to end Crowded House with a bang, not a whimper, Neil Finn finally agreed to bow out in extravagant style. Ironically, their last-ever gig also became Crowded House's biggest ever. The previously-mooted idea of a final show on the steps of Sydney's Opera House was approved, and set for Saturday November 23 1996. Fittingly, Paul Hester was invited back to join Neil, Nick and Mark for the finale, with temporary tenants Tim Finn and Peter Jones relegated to cameo roles.

As a rehearsal for the Sydney concert, Crowded House assembled a few days earlier in Melbourne for a couple of low-key gigs in a city pub, The Corner. Melbourne, after all, was the Australian city that had been home for Neil, Nick and Paul for a long, long time. The presence of family and genuine friends ensured that both two-hour shows were enjoyably intimate. Paul Hester was back in jester mode, jokingly accusing his mum of sticking pins in his condoms to ensure Mardi and Paul had another baby! Tim joined in on encores, and it was then off up the

coast to Sydney. This time Crowded House took the weather with them. Melbourne is notoriously wet compared to Sydney, so perhaps it was sniping at its rival by sending up cold, wet weather that forced the cancellation of the planned Saturday show.

A temporary setback only, as the sun broke through early on Sunday, heating up to over 30 degrees Celsius. Sydney Crowded House fans had known about the concert for a month, and a huge crowd was inevitable. Crowdies fanatics from around the world flew in just for the gig, while MTV Europe and British music mags such as *Mojo* sent representatives. The occasion was also front-page news in New Zealand, and Auckland journalists Russell Baillie (who had kissed and made up with Neil after earlier animosity) and *Rip It Up*'s John Russell crossed the Tasman to cover it. Tellingly, the event failed to register at all in the North American media.

Prior to the show, New South Wales Premier Bob Carr presented Neil Finn wih a cheque for $50,000 to go to the Children's Hospital in Sydney suburb Randwick. Crowded House had designated the hospital as beneficiary of proceeeds from the concert, estimated as potentially reaching $1 million.

Australian rock bands Powderfinger, Custard and You Am I warmed up the rapidly-swelling crowd throughout the afternoon, but some observers felt more musically-compatible support acts should have been chosen.

By mid-afternoon the area in front of the Opera House was saturated with bodies, and police had to direct thousands of concert-goers into other surrounding areas of the picturesque Sydney waterfront. These included the Overseas Passenger Terminal across the quay, where giant video screens had been set up. Local paper *The Daily Telegraph* pegged the throng at 150,000, while other estimates were in the 100,000 to 120,000 range.

It was the largest crowd in the area since the 1988 Australian Bicentenary celebrations, and some problems inevitably resulted. A St John Ambulance officer reported eight people hospitalised with broken limbs and cuts from climbing fences and broken bottles. The crush at the front of the stage was sometimes dangerous, and

Sydney Opera House farewell.
November 24, 1996.

• An appropriately crowded setting for the band's final show.

Crowded House fans on the Internet later complained about the aggressively macho behaviour of many in the crowd. The idea of people moshing to CH songs may be bizarre, but the beer-fuelled Oz rock lover can be an overly enthusiastic creature.

The concert, though, has to be scored a genuine triumph, one that fans will be talking about for years to come. Crowded House took to the stage around 8 pm, kicking off proceedings with 'Mean To Me' and 'World Where You Live'. The 24 songs in two-and-a-half hours included a couple of left-field choices in their cover of The Byrds' psychedelic hit 'Eight Miles High' and Paul Hester's solo turn, 'Italian Plastic'. Given his long absence from centre stage, the crowd-pleasing drummer could be forgiven for forgetting its opening lines. He compensated by entertaining the masses with Woodstock jokes and offers to buy everyone drinks afterwards.

Hester stepped aside to allow Peter Jones onto the drumstool for the first encore song, 'Sister Madly', but played a snare with brushes alongside Nick and Neil up front. Fitting, given that the "unplugged" charm of the core original trio was a key factor in the early success of

Crowded House. Tim joined in for 'Weather With You' and 'It's Only Natural', while the choice of the last song to ring out over Sydney's beautiful harbour was inevitable. As the final notes of 'Don't Dream It's Over' sounded, tears were shed on and off stage, fireworks illuminated the night sky and Neil Finn, Nick Seymour, Mark Hart and Paul Hester lined up in unison for their last bow. Yes, it really was over.

Unsurprisingly, this swansong was well captured on tape and video. The concert was televised on Sydney's Channel 10 on December 2 in conjunction with a telethon for the Children's Hospital, while a live CD and video may become available through the Crowded House fan club.

THEY MAY NOW no longer be an officially active group, but the sounds of Crowded House will linger for a long time to come. Such classic and accessible pop songs as their finest moments will find a welcome on many a radio station playlist as well as in the hearts and CD players of their devoted fans around the world. And you don't have to be a hopeless romantic to believe in the chance of more Crowded House concerts in the

future. It seems like Split Enz have reunited almost annually over the past decade, whether to mark some anniversary or help raise funds for some worthy cause.

Neil Finn may now be committed to solo musical exploration, but he has previously shown himself vulnerable to the siren song of nostalgia. There's no reason to believe that won't happen again. His autocratic behaviour and the circumstances surrounding the pulling the plug on Crowded House may have originally upset or angered his bandmates, but there have been no rash "when hell freezes over" declarations about never ever playing together again.

Regardless, pop history will surely look kindly upon Crowded House. Very few bands over the past decade have enjoyed as much peer respect, and that often means as much to professional musicians as platinum sales figures. Artists as diverse as Aerosmith's Steven Tyler, Megadeth's Dave Mustaine and Elton John have pronounced themselves fervent fans. Joe Jackson declared that he "loves Crowded House. 'Together Alone' is great, their best". To Damon Albarn of Blur, "they do some songs that are really clever, and they're nice blokes". Jim Kerr of Simple Minds was a fan of Split Enz, and he finds Crowded House "just awesome. They've had the sales, but I still don't think they've completely received their due". Talking Heads drummer Chris Frantz admires "their beautiful harmonies and melodies. They always remind me of The Everly Brothers, and nobody else is really doing that now".

On the Australian scene, singer/songwriter Paul Kelly has often competed with Neil Finn for Best Songwriter awards, but he says "I don't see that as a rivalry, because Neil and I are hoeing different rows. But when you hear a great song from another writer, the first thing you feel is jealousy. Neil has written songs I wish I had written." Kelly also came up with one of the best-ever descriptions of the Crowded House magic. "I think on his best songs Neil has an unearthly gift for melody – the kind of melodies that seem to come direct from heaven, as if he hasn't touched them at all."

crowded house
uk discography

SINGLES

World Where You Live/That's What I
Call Love
Capitol CL 416 (7") July 1986

World Where You Live
(extended)/Something So
Strong/Don't Dream It's Over/
That's What I Call Love
Capitol TCCL 416 (cass.) July 1986

World Where You Live
(extended)/Something So
Strong/That's What I Call Love
Capitol 12 CL (12") July 1986

World Where You Live (extended)/
Something So Strong/Don't Dream
It's Over/That's What I Call Love
Capitol TDCL 416 (CD) July 1986

Don't Dream It's Over/That's What I
Call Love
Capitol CL 438 (7") January 1987

Don't Dream It's Over
(extended)/Don't Dream It's Over/
That's What I Call Love
Capitol TCCL 438 (cass.) January 1987

Don't Dream It's Over
(extended)/Don't Dream It's
Over/That's What I Call Love
Capitol 12 CL 438 (12") January 1987

Something So Strong/I Walk away
Capitol CL 456 (7") August 1987

Something So Strong/Something So
Strong (live)/I Walk Away/Don't
Dream It's Over (live)
Capitol 12 CL 456 (12") August 1987

Better Be Home Soon/Kill Eye
Capitol CL 498 (7") June 1988

Better Be Home Soon/Don't Dream
It's Over (live)/Kill Eye
Capitol 12 CL 498 (12") June 1988

Better Be Home Soon/Don't Dream
It's Over (live)/Kill Eye
Capitol CD CL 498 (CD) June 1988

Sister Madly/Mansion In The Slums
Capitol CL 509 (7") August 1988

Sister Madly/Mansion In The
Slums/Something So Strong (live)
Capitol 12 CL 509 (12") August 1988

Sister Madly/Mansion In The
Slums/Something So Strong (live)
Capitol CD 509 (CD) August 1988

Chocolate Cake/As Sure As I Am
Capitol CL 618 (7") June 1991

Chocolate Cake/As Sure As I Am
Capitol TCCL 618 (cass.) June 1991

Chocolate Cake/As Sure As I
Am/Anyone Can Tell
Capitol 12 CL 618 (12") June 1991

Chocolate Cake/As Sure As I
Am/Anyone Can Tell
Capitol CDCL 618 (CD) June 1991

Fall At Your Feet/Don't Dream It's Over
Capitol CL 626 (7") October 1991

Fall At Your Feet/Six Months In A
Leaky Boat (live)/Now We're Getting
Somewhere (live)/Something So
Strong
Capitol CDCLX 626 (CD) October 1991

Fall At Your Feet/Don't Dream It's Over/
Sister Madly/Better Be Home Soon
Capitol CDCL 626 (CD) October 1991

Weather With You (single edit)/Into
Temptation
Capitol CL 643 (7") February 1992

Weather With You (single edit)/
Into Temptation
Capitol TCCL 643 (cass.) February
1992

Weather With You (single edit)/Mr
Tambourine Man (live)/Eight Miles
High (live)/So You Wanna Be A
Rock'n'Roll Star (live)
Capitol CDCL 643 (CD) February 1992

Weather With You (radio edit)/Fall
At Your feet (live)/When You Come
(live)/Walking On The Spot (live)
Capitol CDCLS 643 (CD) February 1992

Four Seasons In One Day/There
Goes God
Capitol CL 655 (7") June 1992

Four Seasons In One Day/There
Goes God
Capitol TCCL 655 (cass.) June 1992

Four Seasons In One Day/Dr
Livingstone/Recurring
Dream/Anyone Can Tell
Capitol CDCL 655 (CD) June 1992

Four Seasons In One Day/Weather
With You (live)/Italian Plastic
(live)/Message To My Girl (live)
Capitol CDCDLS 655 (CD) June 1992

Distant Sun/Walking On The Spot
Capitol CL 697 (7") August 1993

Distant Sun/Walking On The Spot
Capitol TCCL 697 (cass.) August 1993

Distant Sun/Walking On The
Spot/Throw Your Arms Around
Me/One Step Ahead
Capitol CDCL 697 (CD) August 1993

Distant Sun/This Is Massive/When
You Come
Capitol CDCLS 697 (CD) August 1993

Nails In My Feet/Don't Dream It's
Over (live)
Capitol CL 701 (7") October 1993

Nails In My Feet/Don't Dream It's
Over (live)
Capitol TCCL 701 (cass.) October 1993

Nails In My Feet/I Am In Love/Four
Seasons In One Day (live)
Capitol CDCL 701 (CD) October 1993

Nails In My Feet/You Can Touch/
Zen Roxy
Capitol CDCLS 701 (CD) October 1993

Locked Out (live)/Distant Sun (live)/
Fall At Your Feet (live)/Private
Universe (live)
Capitol 10CL 707 (limited edition
10") February 1994

Locked Out/Distant Sun
Capitol TCCL 707 (cass.) February 1994

Locked Out/Private Universe
(live)/Fall At Your Feet (live)/Better
Be Home Soon (live)
Capitol CDCL 707 (CD) February 1994

Locked Out/Distant Sun/Hole In
The River (live)/Sister Madly (live)
Capitol CDCLS 707 (CD) February 1994

Fingers Of Love (live)/Love You Till
The Day I Die (live)/Whispers And
Moans (live)/It's Only Natural (live)
Capitol 10CL 715 (10") June 1994

Fingers Of Love/Nails In My Feet
Capitol TCCL 715 (cass.) June 1994

Fingers Of Love/Catherine
Wheels/Pineapple Head
(live)/Something So Strong (live)
Capitol CDCL 715 (CD) June 1994

Fingers Of Love/Skin Feeling/Kare
Kare (live)/In My Command (live)
Capitol CDCLS 715 (CD) June 1994

Pineapple Head/Weather With You/
Don't Dream It's Over/Together Alone
Capitol 10CL723 (10") August 1994

Pineapple Head/Weather With You
Capitol TCCL 723 (cass.) August 1994

Pineapple Head/Weather With You/
Don't Dream It's Over/Together Alone
Capitol CDCL 723 (CD) August 1994

Instinct/Recurring Dream
Capitol TCCL 774 (cassette) June 1996

Instinct/Recurring Dream/Weather
With You (live)/Chocolate Cake (live)
Capitol CDCLS 774 (CD) June 1996

Instinct/World Where You Live/In The
Lowlands (live)/Into Temptation (live)
Capitol CDCL 774 (CD) June 1996

Not The Girl You Think You
Are/Better Be Home Soon (live)
Capitol CL 776 (7" coloured vinyl)
August 1996

Not The Girl You Think You
Are/Private Universe (live)/Fingers
Of Love (live)/Better Be Home
Soon (live)
Capitol CDCL 776 (CD) August 1996

Not The Girl You Think You
Are/Instinct (live/Distant Sun (live)/
Fall At Your Feet (live)
Capitol CDCLS 776 (double digipack)
August 1996

Don't Dream It's Over
(remix)/Weather With You (live)
Capitol CL 780 (7") October 1996

Don't Dream It's Over
(remix)/Weather With You (live)/ Into
Temptation (live)/Locked Out (live)
Capitol CDCLS 780 (CD) October 1996

Don't Dream It's Over (remix)/Four
Seasons In one Day (live)/In My
Command (live)/Pineapple Head (live)
Capitol CDCL 780 (CD digipack)
October 1996

ALBUMS

CROWDED HOUSE

Mean To Me, World Where You
Live/Now We're getting
Somewhere/Don't Dream It's
Over/Love You Till the Day I
Die/Something So Strong/Hole In
The River/Can't Carry On/I Walk
Away/Tombstone/That's What I
Call Love
Capitol EST 2016 April 1987

TEMPLE OF THE LOW MEN

I Feel Possessed/Kill Eye/Into
Temptation/Mansion In The
Slums/When You Come/Never be
The Same/Love This Life/Sister
Madly/In the Lowlands/Better be
Home Soon
Capitol EST 2064 July 1988

WOODFACE

Chocolate Cake/It's Only
Natural/Fall At Your Feet/Tall
Trees/Weather With You/Whispers
And Moans/Four Seasons In One
Day/There Goes God/Fame Is/All
I Ask/As Sure As I am/Italian
Plastic/She Goes On/How Will
You Go
Capitol EST 2144 June 1991

TOGETHER ALONE

Kare Kare/In My Command/Nails In
My Feet/Black & White Boy/Fingers
Of Love/Pineapple Head/Locked
Out/Private Universe/Walking On
The Spot/Distant Sun/Catherine
Wheels/Skin Feeling/Together
Alone
Capitol EST October 1993

RECURRING DREAM

Weather With You/World Where You
Live/Fall At Your Feet/Locked
Out/Don't Dream It's Over/Into
Temptation/Pineapple Head/When
You Come/Private Universe/Not The
Girl You Think You Are/Instinct/I
Feel Possessed/Four Seasons In
One Day/It's Only Natural/Distant
Sun/Something So Strong/Mean To
Me/Better Be Home
Soon/Everything Is Good For You

BONUS LIVE ALBUM

There Goes God/Newcastle
Jam/Love You Till The Day I
Die/Hole In The River/Private
Universe/Pineapple Head/How Will
You Go/Left Hand/Whispers And
Moans/Killeye/Fingers Of
Love/Don't Dream It's Over/When
You Come/Sister Madly/In My
Command
Capitol EST 2283 June 1996

NEIL AND TIM FINN AS THE FINN BROTHERS

SINGLES

Suffer Never/Weather With You
(demo)
Parlophone/EMI TCR 6417
(cassette) October 1995

Suffer Never/Strangeness And Charm
(demo)/In Love With It All (demo)/
Four Seasons In One Day (demo)
Parlophone/EMI CDRS 6417 (CD)
October 1995

Suffer Never/Prodigal Son
(demo)/Catherine Wheel
(demo)/Weather With You (demo)
Parlophone/EMI CDR 617 (CD)
October 1995

Angels Heap/It's Only Natural
(demo)/Chocolate Cake (demo)
Parlophone/EMI TCR 6421 (cassette)
November 1995

Angels Heap/It's Only Natural
(demo)/Chocolate Cake (demo)
Parlophone/EMI CDRS 6421 (CD)
November 1995

Angels Heap/There Goes God
(demo)/How Will You Go (demo)
Parlophone/EMI CDR 6421 (CD)
November 1995

ALBUM

FINN
Only Talking Sense/Eyes Of The
World/Mood Swinging Man/Last
Day Of June/Suffer Never/Angels
Heap/Niwhai/Where Is My
Soul/Bullets In My Hairdo/Paradise
(Wherever You Are)/Kiss The Road
Of Rarotonga
Parlophone/EMI FINN1
October 1995

COLLABORATIONS

NEIL FINN

Jenny Morris: 'Body & Soul' (WEA 25 48974)

An Australian-based New Zealand singer/songwriter who has enjoyed considerable success in Australasia. For her 1987 album 'Body & Soul', Neil contributed a song written especially for her, 'You I Know'. Released as a single, it was a top 20 hit in Australia. The same album featured a Tim Finn composition, 'Beating On The Same Drum', to which Tim added guest vocals and piano.

Yothu Yindi: 'Freedom' (Mushroom TVD 93380/Hollywood HR-61451-2)

A popular Australian Aboriginal group who scored an international hit with 'Treaty'. Their 1994 album 'Freedom' includes 'Dots On The Shell', a song co-written by Neil Finn and Yothu Yindi's Mandawuy Yunupingu. The song was recorded at York Street Studios in Auckland, and Neil contributed guest vocals. It was released as a single on Mushroom C 11692.

Hunters & Collectors

Neil Contributed backing vocals to 'Way You Live' on the band's 1990 album 'Ghost Nation'.

Emma Paki

New Zealand singer/songwriter. In 1994 Neil produced a single for her, 'Greenstone' (Virgin NZ 8770254). He also added backing vocals and played lead and acoustic guitars, mellotron and candlesticks. Mark Hart later produced Paki's début album.

Dave Dobbyn

Much respected and successful New Zealand singer/songwriter. Neil produced his 1994 album 'Twist' and co-wrote two songs with Dave, 'Gifted' and 'Ummm' (also co-written by Tim Finn). Neil played guitar, piano, optigan and other keyboards, while Tim Finn added backing vocals, percussion and drums on one track.

Archie Roach

An acclaimed Australian Aboriginal singer/songwriter. Neil (and Tim) Finn contributed backing vocals to 'Down City Streets', a song on Roach's 1990 album 'Charcoal Road'.

PAUL HESTER

Ultrasound: 'Ultrasound' (Mushroom 031360)

Ultrasound is the band Paul joined in 1995 after Crowded House.

CROWDED HOUSE

The band contributed to the Building Bridges project, which was designed to fund the National Coalition of Aboriginal Organisations, a group advocating the rights of Aboriginal people in Australia. On Paul Hester's urging, the band donated 'Mansions In The Slums' to a 1988 double album featuring major Australasian rock acts.

SOUNDTRACKS

'Hey Boys', a song written by Nick Seymour and Paul Kelly for the 1992 Australian movie *Garbo* featured Neil and Tim Finn on backing vocals.

'Locked Out' was featured in *Reality Bites*, a 1994 film whose soundtrack also included tracks by World Party, U2, Lenny Kravitz and Dinosaur Jr. (RCA 7863-663642)

Crowded House wrote and recorded the song 'Recurring Dream' for the movie *Tequila Sunrise*, which also featured tracks by tracks by Duran Duran, Ziggy Marley and The Church.

The TV mini-series *The Stand*, based on Stephen King's best seller, featured 'Don't Dream It's Over' in a pivotal scene. Heroine Franie played the song before starting out on her quest to find the vision from her dreams, Mother Abigail.

[For a detailed discography of Split Enz and Tim Finn's solo work, readers are advised to consult *Stranger Than Fiction*, Mike Chunn's biography of Split Enz.]